Questors, Jesters
and Renegades

Questors, Jesters and Renegades

The Story of Britain's Amateur Theatre

Michael Coveney

methuen | drama

LONDON • NEW YORK • OXFORD • NEW DELHI • SYDNEY

METHUEN DRAMA
Bloomsbury Publishing Plc
50 Bedford Square, London, WC1B 3DP, UK
1385 Broadway, New York, NY 10018, USA

BLOOMSBURY, METHUEN DRAMA and the Methuen Drama logo are
trademarks of Bloomsbury Publishing Plc

First published in Great Britain 2020

Cover design: Charlotte Daniels
Cover image: *Beauty and the Beast*, at the Minack Theatre, Cornwall, performed by the
Miller Centre Players (2004) Photo Minack Theatre Trust

A catalogue record for this book is available from the British Library.

Library of Congress Cataloging-in-Publication Data
Names: Coveney, Michael, 1948– author. | Branagh, Kenneth, writer of foreword.
Title: Questors, jesters and renegades : the story of Britain's amateur theatre / Michael Coveney.
Description: London ; New York : Methuen Drama, Bloomsbury Publishing Plc, 2020. | Foreword by Kenneth Branagh. |
Includes bibliographical references and index. | Summary: "This is the vital story of the amateur theatre as it developed
from the medieval guilds to the modern theatre of Ayckbourn and Pinter, with a few mishaps and missed cues along the
way. Michael Coveney – a former member of Ilford's Renegades – tells this tale with a charm and wit that will have you
shouting out for an encore. Between the two world wars, amateur theatre thrived across the UK, from Newcastle to
Norwich, from Bolton to Birmingham and Bangor, championed by the likes of George Bernard Shaw, Sybil Thorndike, and
J B Priestley. Often born out of a particular political cause or predicament, many of these theatres and companies
continue to evolve, survive and even prosper today. This is the first account of its kind, packed with anecdote and
previously unheard stories, and it shows how amateur theatre is more than a popular pastime: it has been endemic to the
birth of the National Theatre, as well as a seedbed of talent and a fascinating barometer and product of the times in which
we live. Some of the companies Coveney delves into – all taking centre stage in this entertaining and lively book – include
the Questors and Tower Theatre in London; Birmingham's Crescent Theatre; The Little Theatre in Bolton, where Ian
McKellen was a schoolboy participant; the Halifax Thespians; Lincolnshire's Broadbent Theatre, co-founded by Jim
Broadbent's father and other conscientious objectors at the end of World War II; Crayford's Geoffrey Whitworth Theatre,
where the careers of Michael Gambon and Diana Quick were launched; Anglesey's Theatr Fach, a crucible of Welsh
language theatre; and Cornwall's stunning cliff-top Minack" – Provided by publisher.
Identifiers: LCCN 2019043663 | ISBN 9781350128378 (hardback) | ISBN 9781350128361 (pdf) |
ISBN 9781350128408 (epub) | ISBN 9781350128392
Subjects: LCSH: Amateur theater—Great Britain—History—20th century. |
Amateur theater—Great Britain—History—21st century.
Classification: LCC PN3169.G8 C68 2020 | DDC 792.02/220941–dc23
LC record available at https://lccn.loc.gov/2019043663
ISBN: HB: 978-1-3501-2837-8
        ePDF: 978-1-3501-2836-1
        eBook: 978-1-3501-2840-8

Typeset by RefineCatch Limited, Bungay, Suffolk
Printed and bound in Great Britain

To find out more about our authors and books visit www.bloomsbury.com and sign up for our newsletters.

For Jimmie and Yvonne

CONTENTS

ILLUSTRATIONS

FOREWORD

Kenneth Branagh

Amateur, 'a person who takes part in an activity for pleasure, not as a job.' Derived from the Latin 'amare', to love. If the definition applies, then I continue, after a forty-year professional career, to be, in spirit, an amateur actor, continuing to love what I do.

Unquestionably, that feeling was borne by my experience of the British amateur theatre, which Michael Coveney explores here so entertainingly and with such refreshing insight.

Certainly, that other definition of amateur, suggesting incompetence, is not what I encountered when, at all of sixteen years, I arrived at The Progress Theatre in Reading, Berkshire. Here was a hive of feverish activity and organisation. Perhaps because so many people involved had 'proper' jobs, the need for a coherent approach to scheduling rehearsals and production was planned to an almost military extent.

Time was money for many in the group, who had demanding careers elsewhere, and so I was swiftly introduced to the central paradox of Amateur Theatre – success and efficiency depended on a professional approach. This certainly applied to production values – set construction, costumes, special effects, sound, lighting – all highly ambitious, and there was enormous personal pride in their expression at the very finest level.

Indeed, there was a healthy spirit of competition with our local professional theatre, The Hexagon. We were very aware that if we could produce well on stage, then we had a competitive advantage with lower ticket prices and a more intimate experience. And one also learned very quickly that undiscriminating attendance by supportive/indulgent friends and family could not be assumed if they were not ultimately compelled by what they saw in the plays.

For me, this switch to a very grown-up approach was a marked difference from the enormous fun I had enjoyed previously in school plays. In that case, discipline was supplied by a very few dedicated teachers. Here, the entire population of the group was leant-in to the endeavour and, in my experience, incompetence, or an 'amateur' attitude, was not tolerated.

I learnt this to my cost when I had my single nightmarish experience as a Stage Manager. I was in charge for the Christmas show, *The Rose and the Ring*, which its author, William Makepeace Thackeray, described as 'A Fireside Pantomime'.

Through a gargantuan ineptitude, I presided over an (unintended) onstage fire. I also caught numerous costumes in the trap door, making instant disappearances (the very purpose of the trap door) impossible to achieve. Finally, I contrived to have the great end-of-show snowfall effect land spectacularly (and far too early) in the drawing room – rather than outside, where snow tends to fall, usually – and instead tumbled it over a gentlewoman of a certain age, who was not best pleased with finishing the performance as a snow-woman.

After the performance she gave me a carpeting: 'Young man, if you choose to remain in the theatre, and if the theatre chooses to have you, never, ever, ever, again claim to know something that you so conspicuously do not know. And by the by, stick to acting. The world of stage management will lose nothing by the decision.'

She was right. Since then I have never knowingly set fire to another actor. And her call for honesty in the work – what you might describe as the bedrock of a professional approach – is something that I found in the amateur theatre and is something I've tried to carry with me ever since.

What I also carry from that day to this, and to my proudly borne patronage of the Little Theatre Guild, is the intense love for the theatre that I bore witness to then and now.

This book conveys much of that in its colourful account of the amateur theatre's life and times. It comes from a distinguished critic, whose reviews have always carried, regardless of their content, a similarly transparent love of the art form.

This book takes the amateur theatre seriously, but not solemnly, and places it in its unique and critically important historical context. Charming and informative, it is a hugely enjoyable account of a delightfully British phenomenon.

ACKNOWLEDGEMENTS

Thanks are due for their help, advice, friendship and conversations to the following: Anne Aldridge, Paul Allen, Tony Barber, Michael Barry, Michael Billington, Jackie Blackwood, Sir Kenneth Branagh, Gyles Brandreth, Simon Brett, Jim Broadbent, Charlotte Broughton, Linda Brown, Simon Callow, Jean Carr, John Chapman, David Coates, Sheila Cooper, Yvonne Cooper, Martin Coveney, Steven Day, John Dobson, William Dudley, Paul Edmondson, David Emmet, Robert Gill, Georgina Godley, Michael Godley, Vivien Goodwin, Chris Goulding, Dominique Goy-Blanquet, Janet Grant, Justine Greene, Clare Greer, Jane Hall, Bridget Hayward, Leighton Hirst, Ross Holland, Martin Hoyland, Lucy Hughes-Hallett, Michael Ievers, Celia Imrie, Phil Jackson, Paul Johnson, Richard Johnson, Audrey and Tony Jones, Toby Jones, Nick Kent, Jude Law, Sarah Ley, Andrew Lowrie, Iain Mackintosh, Charles McDonald, Sir Ian McKellen, Jo Matthews, Kevin Mears, Martin Mulgrew, Stephen Murgatroyd, Ross Noble, Jacqui O'Hanlon, Robert Pennant Jones, Peter Rankin, Eddie Redfern, Deborah Rees, Emyr Rhys-Jones, Griff Rhys Jones, Ian Ribbens, Lesley Robins, Roger Sansom, Ian Sharp, Michael Shipley, Michael Simkins, Mike Smith, Kevin Spence, Roland Stross, Noel Tovey, Maurice Tripp, Laurence Tuerk, Penny Tuerk, Irving Wardle, David Warner, Rebecca Wass, Rowena Webb, Sir Stanley Wells, Erica Whyman, Alice Wright, Manon Wyn Williams, Hugh Wynne-Griffith.

Thanks, also, and especially, to Joanna Godfrey for her encouragement, Anna Brewer at Methuen Drama for her astute editing, and to Caradoc King and Kat Aitken at United Agents for their patience and wise counsel and to Sue Hyman, my wife, as usual.

PROLOGUE

I gave up reviewing professional theatre on a regular basis in early 2016, after forty-five years at the coal-face. I wanted to reorganise the rhythm of my life without the permanent obligation to deliver a late night or early morning review. I also wanted to be more selective in my theatre going and writing, not to be constrained by having to re-review 'new' plays I'd seen at their premieres or 'old' plays about which I'd had my fill, and said too much, for so long, even though classics – Shakespeare and the Greeks especially – take on a different glint with every passing year and each new production.

As for the brand new work, that might best be left to a new generation of critics coming through, though the focusing of new authoritative critical voices is a challenge at a time when the online explosion of opinion coincides with a lurch towards the endorsement, or trolling, of celebrities, the collapse of the newsprint industry and the proliferation of social media commentary where 'everyone's a critic'. Now is a good time for real critics to stand up and be counted.

How could I best do this myself? I felt like renewing my roots, rediscovering what appealed to me about theatre in the first place and approaching the idea of popular theatre in the most obvious way: an investigation into the amateur theatre, its origins in the medieval guilds, its more refined manifestation in the private theatricals of the eighteenth and nineteenth centuries and following through to the modern pattern of 'Little Theatres' at the start of the twentieth century. These sub-divisions will be explored later, but the point of greatest interest to me in devising my own custom-made refresher course, was to examine the world of theatre as I have known it over the past decades through the prism of amateur theatre.

I quickly discovered that between the two world wars of the last century, the amateur theatre movement was endemic to the growth of the modern serious theatre. The great dramatist and polemicist George Bernard Shaw, and his colleague at the Royal Court in the early years of the last century, the actor, playwright, director and eminent Shakespearean, Harley Granville Barker, joined the campaign for a National Theatre, also an objective of the British Drama League founded in 1919 as a focus for the revival of theatre after the First World War.

The amateur theatre started to get organised after the Second World War, and the Little Theatre Guild (LTG) was founded in 1946 to promote closer cooperation between the little theatres and to further 'the highest standards in the arts of theatre as practised by the little theatres, and to assist in and encourage the establishment of other little theatres'. This happened alongside the slow recovery of the professional regional theatre, the establishment of the Arts Council, and the first Edinburgh Festival in 1947, which heralded the birth of the – at first totally unsubsidised, if not necessarily amateur – fringe theatre movement.

Thus the LTG was at the centre of this 'new dawn', and this sense of a fresh start and 'planting' for the future was confirmed in the prime condition for membership: ownership of your own venue. And so it remains. The nine founding member theatres of the LTG – including the Questors in Ealing, the Crescent in Birmingham, Highbury Little Theatre in London, the Great Hucklow Village Players in Derbyshire and the People's in Newcastle – were joined by eight more – including the Halifax Thespians, the Maddermarket in Norwich, the Stockport Garrick and the Tavistock Repertory Theatre (the Tower) – by 1951, growing to double that, thirty members, in the mid-1960s, and reaching a membership of 110 in the present.

It is one of the narratives I contemplate that, while the serious, often socialist, idealism of the early amateur theatre groups is still stamped through the movement like the lettering in a seaside rock, the wheel has also turned nearly full circle to the promulgation of popular West End comedy with the additional bonus of reviving the recent new play repertoire in fresh and often revealing ways.

The traffic between professional and amateur theatre is increasingly two-way: whereas the amateurs were the custodians of new writing between the wars, they are now recipients of a repertoire coming out of the Royal Court and other new writing venues while returning that repertoire, and indeed the repertoire of the more distant past, to the theatre culture at large. These days, you are more likely to see a play of Somerset Maugham or J. B. Priestley in the amateur theatre than you are in the West End or at the National Theatre.

And I increasingly realised that the story of amateur theatre, especially in the last century, and continuing into this, is one that runs parallel with, and complementary to, the overall story of our national theatre. Very few professional actors arrive on our stages without first participating in amateur theatre, or in student groups. In terms of actors, I endorse Ian McKellen's assertion that the amateur theatre is the rock, the foundation, upon which is built the theatre of our time.

When I realised I wanted to read more about all of this I quickly also realised that I'd have to write the book that I wanted to read, a book fusing elements of research, personal experience, critical analysis and historical investigation, above all a book synthesising the good and the bad, the beautiful and the ugly of amateur theatre. It might also emulate the anecdotal writing of thespian wits like Michael Green and Michael Simkins in charting the absurdity of achievement outstripped, you might say upstaged, by the hilarity of mishap.

That world of misplaced hubris, incompetence and disaster certainly exists, I'm glad to say, and blends into people's memories and experience of weekly rep at the lower end of the professional scale. I'm interested in how serious amateurs refer to themselves as 'non-professionals' in order to escape this unwarranted stigma of failure and how serious but low-income professionals on the fringe and even in the regional theatres bridle at any suggestion that their occupation is in any way comparable to that of an amateur.

They are trained, for a start. Well, most of them are. But many actors and directors on the amateur stage have backgrounds in training, teaching and even short-term professional employment. And in an increasingly 'work for nothing' culture – at least in the arts and in journalism – the distinction between amateur and professional is often rendered meaningless.

In an age, certainly in the subsidised sector, where heroic acting as a concept is as alien to the arts community as the idea of the Nietzschean superman or individual star, the demarcation line is blurred even further by the incorporation of amateurs into professional undertakings, whether in large community projects or even at the heart of the Royal Shakespeare Company and National Theatre, both of which heavily sponsored and subsidised monoliths are increasingly engaged in education, outreach, amateur participation and an admirably tireless evangelism about keeping theatre itself alive.

Armed with these reflections, I set about my task. I wanted to arrange the story of amateur theatre in the histories, peculiarities and struggles for survival of a number of them all around the country. In the first group – the People's in Newcastle, the Maddermarket in Norwich, and the Halifax Thespians in west Yorkshire – I trace the origins of the modern movement before, between and immediately after the two wars, leading to the formation of the Little Theatre Guild.

In the second group – the Geoffrey Whitworth in Kent, the Crescent in Birmingham, the Little Theatres in Bolton and Doncaster – I relate their formation and progress as significantly arterial to the motorways of the RSC and National Theatre and indeed the development of many strains and distinguished careers in the post-war professional theatre. In between, the repertory, calibre and indeed pioneering spirit of the two leading London amateur set-ups, the Questors in Ealing and the Tower in north London, are put under the spotlight. There is a stand-alone chapter on the extraordinary story of the open-air Minack Theatre in Cornwall, a magnetic focus and Mecca for many of the country's amateur groups who tour there.

And I end with a study of theatres remotely situated around Britain whose eccentricity and independence, born of their off-piste geographic status, bring something fresh and surprising to the amateur theatre table, especially vis-à-vis the overall shape of our national theatre story: the Broadbent, co-founded by actor Jim Broadbent's father, in Lincolnshire; the Bangor Drama Club in County Down, Northern Ireland; the Theatre Royal,

Dumfries, Scotland's oldest operating theatre, first theatrical home of Robert Burns and J. M. Barrie, which has been effectively saved by the amateurs of the town; and Theatr Fach in Anglesey, near the other Bangor in Wales.

En route, we have break-out sessions with three amateur practitioners who could well have been successful professionals but weren't, and illustrated insets of the origins of the movement in private theatricals and its colourful, often hilarious, representations in film and fiction down the ages. There is a point when amdram and community theatre do indeed blur into a sort of well-meaning, feelgood pageant theatre that belongs to the world of the annual Shakespeare birthday celebrations in Stratford-upon-Avon, Morris dancing or those great noisy religious festivals in Spain that glory in their natural setting of baroque churches, town squares, giant wooden statues of the Madonna, café life along the route and a frenzy of fireworks.

In 1953, Dame Sybil Thorndike, Bernard Shaw's first ever Saint Joan, and a life-long amateur theatre enthusiast, declared at an LTG luncheon: 'There is no longer any true distinction between professional and amateur, only between commercial and non-commercial.' With its cast list of teachers, solicitors and tradesmen, amateur theatre represents something wholly good in what John Major wrongly dubbed 'a classless society'. Ian McKellen disarmingly says that he went into the theatre to find a sex life. But he also said of amateur theatre: 'It's where we all began. There's something honourable about people giving their spare time after a day's work to put on plays.' It's not all about vanity or self-indulgence.

1

The Agony and the Ecstasy

My fascination with amateur theatre dates back to my own youth, the idea of escape, a fascination with people living double lives, their vanity and delusions as well as their fantasies and desire to engage with the cultural legacy and create outlets for talent and inspiration. I love the story, relayed to me by Griff Rhys Jones, of the old amateur actor who, on encountering a taciturn Alec Guinness on the train from London to Brighton, regaled the great man with his own tales of triumph and disaster, regardless of the passive non-reaction he elicited from Guinness for the full sixty minutes or so. As they drew into the station, Guinness jumped up smartly to leave the compartment only to be followed by the amateur thespian who, flinging his arms impertinently around him, cried out, 'Why do we do it, Alec, why endure this agony of working in the theatre?'

That assumption of 'the agony of it all' is a giveaway of a risible self-importance you sometimes find adopted by amateurs as a safety blanket, a reassurance of the value of the self-sacrifices they might be making for their art. It's nailed wonderfully in Ngaio Marsh's final theatrical crime thriller, *Light Thickens*, when the director of the Dolphin Theatre's *Macbeth*, Peregrine Jay, is feeling the heat: 'Why, why, *why*, thought Peregrine, do I direct plays? Why do I put myself into this hell? Above all, why *Macbeth*? And then: it's too soon to be feeling like this; six days too soon. Oh God, deliver us all.'

Admittedly old Perry is a pro, and the Dolphin an unlikely sounding professional company on the banks of the Thames in 1982 – that's six years after the National Theatre concrete complex opened for business – but the feel of the theatricality is pronouncedly amateur. Such was Ngaio Marsh's grounding in New Zealand. She knew very well the world of student and amateur theatre before, in effect, establishing the serious professional theatre in her home country. 'The difference between an amateur and a professional', she said, 'is that the amateur thinks it's fun'.

All the same, I've long thought that amateur theatre in our country is not only an expression of our national identity, or part of it, but also a key element in the evolution of that national identity, especially, as I've suggested, through the last two world wars and beyond. There's a kind of tension that exists between the world of amateur theatre and the 'real' world of our professional theatre, that grows more interesting and more interactive with every passing year.

Not everyone agrees with this prognosis. Many people I know would rather die than go anywhere near a production by amateurs. But then many quite reasonable, if deluded, people would rather eat their own feet than be caught dead in any theatre anywhere, anyway. And there is an element of white middle-class engagement with amateur theatre that you might find as off-putting as others find cosily attractive, a view of amdram once expressed by the great critic Kenneth Tynan as 'an exhibitionist's alternative to bridge'.

The moralising clean-up campaign in the theatre and film industries we've been going through is inevitable as a consequence of the #MeToo social media phenomenon, but the idea of cleansing the Augean stables of all inappropriate behaviour and sexual impropriety is probably a pipe dream. The theatre was never thought of as a respectable occupation. Even beyond the knighthood of Henry Irving. Restoration comedy and the modern plays of Noël Coward, Joe Orton, Sarah Kane and Mark Ravenhill have long celebrated the unorthodox and downright louche in sexual mores and behaviour.

And because of this, many budding actors, especially women in the immediately post-war years, have been propelled into the amateur theatre, I now realise, because of indirect censorious pressures from society and the particular disapproval of their own families. This may have changed over the past two or three decades, but one possible ironic outcome in the present climate of debate is that youngsters may be debarred again from the theatre as a profession not only because of the costs of going to drama school but also because of a renewed parental anxiety over the amoral cesspit into which they might fall.

The appeal of the theatre may well become, for those who participate in it, an opportunity to change the world through art, but it usually starts with the attraction of social intercourse, freedom of expression, escaping the humdrum and, yes, meeting people for friendship and social, and indeed sexual, interaction. Anyone who thinks otherwise is kidding him- or herself. And in terms of the amateur theatre, those instincts are intensified by the fact that the participation really does constitute an alternative to, bordering on a get-out from, the life one is compelled to lead – through social respectability and economic survival – in ordinary civilian life.

Apart from the social and belonging aspects of amateur theatre, which are germane, and indeed the opportunities for unconventional, or even illicit, behaviour, one popular view of amateur theatre is that it's always the play that goes wrong: the actors fluff their cues, the door knob comes away in the hand of the person entering, the scenery falls over and the third-act inspector enters with paper snow on his head.

All of that and a whole lot more actually happens in the play called *The Play That Goes Wrong*, a West End and Broadway hit originally conceived and performed by three then-recent drama school graduates, which panders shamelessly to our delight in disaster and misplaced props during a performance of the fictional 'Murder at Haversham Manor', by the equally fictional Cornley Polytechnic Drama Society.

The show is an anthology of what we now call Coarse Theatre, as famously propounded in Michael Green's perennial best-seller *The Art of Coarse Acting* (1964), revised and rewritten on its thirtieth and fiftieth anniversaries. And here's the thing: Green was – he died, aged ninety-one, in February 2018 – a long-standing member of one of the country's leading amateur companies, the Questors in Ealing. And Henry Lewis, one of the *Goes Wrong* trio, was a member of Young Questors before going on to drama school.

The Questors is one of many high-minded amateur companies, as we shall see, which figures prominently in any cursory analysis of the nation's community-based theatre as a whole. And yet, who does not relish Green's account of how, at one particularly amateurish dress rehearsal, he fell off the stage, broke a leg, dislocated an elbow and arrived in hospital dressed as an eighteenth-century pirate with a parrot sewn onto his shoulder? Or his testimony that one extra at the Questors, who had applied warts and boils to his 'diseased' visage as a plague victim, emitted, one night, a gigantic

FIGURE 1 *Original West End cast of* The Play That Goes Wrong *(2015), a spoof amdram mystery farce, Henry Lewis second left. (Photo: Alastair Muir.)*

sneeze which blew the pustular excrescences clean off? So afterwards, when the audience had dispersed, he crept back into the auditorium and went down on all fours, collecting stray warts and looking for his nose.

There's a Victoria Wood sketch, 'Giving Notes', in which Julie Walters as an amdram director giving notes after a *Hamlet* rehearsal catches some other aspects of over-exaggerated innovation and all-too-recognisable, but unscripted, hilarity: 'The Players' scene: did any of you feel it had stretched a bit too long . . .? Yes. I think we'll go back to the tumbling on the entrance rather than the extract from *Barnum*. You see, we're running at six hours twenty now, and if we're going to put those soliloquies back in . . . That's it for tonight, then; thank you. I shall expect you all to be word perfect by the next rehearsal. Have any of you realised what date we're up to? Yes, April the twenty-seventh! And when do we open? August! It's not long!'

Professionals actually make just as many unnecessary elaborations in their shows as do amateurs, probably more frequently. The heart sinks when there's a long, interpolated prologue, or extended dumb show, and three and a half hours of iambic pentameters and dodgy clowning still ahead, whether you're at Shakespeare's Globe or the MADS of Macclesfield. But it really is a defining feature of amdram that the rehearsal period is stretched over months, on two or three nights a week and often on a Sunday, before the whole enterprise implodes in a short run of a few (sometimes ten) performances. In the professional theatre, three or four weeks of intense, concentrated rehearsals (six or more at the Royal Shakespeare Company or the National) are followed by several weeks, or months, of performances and, in extreme cases, a year's run or longer in the West End, or – less often in these days of live screening to the rest of the country – a nationwide tour of the same or similar longevity.

There is still a prevalent (though false) notion of the professional theatre being a sort of club for which membership is limited, with amateurs the disgruntled, unentitled yokels at the gate who simply don't know what a life on the boards is really all about. This view was elegantly expressed in a *Daily Telegraph* magazine article in November 2017 by the suave actor Simon Williams, whose West End credentials are impeccable: educated at Harrow, like Benedict Cumberbatch, he is the younger brother of the poet, sometime drama critic and old Etonian, Hugo Williams, son of the after-dinner West End acting/playwriting star couple of the 1960s, Hugh and Margaret Williams, and husband of actress Lucy Fleming, daughter of Celia Johnson and niece of James Bond novelist, Ian Fleming.

At the time of writing his article, Williams was appearing in *The Archers*, the world's longest-running radio soap. *The Archers*, which is as important a cultural institution on BBC's Radio 4 as are the Promenade Concerts on Radio 3, or indeed sports commentary on Radio 5 Live, is set in the fictional farming community of Ambridge, somewhere in the Midlands. At the end of 2018, Williams as Justin Elliott appeared in the Christmas show produced by the local queen of amdram, Lynda Snell (Carole Boyd), an omnibus edition of Chaucer's *Canterbury Tales*, with linking dialogue and bits of the various prologues to the eight tales chosen.

This was then broadcast as a two-part stand-alone drama, in two hour-long chunks, as if the fictional amateurs had burst their countryside bounds and taken over the airwaves. Simon/Justin, scourge of amdram, played a peppery, rather good version of one of the eight pilgrim 'tellers' in *The Pardoner's Tale*, in which three fellows setting out to kill off Death, kill off each other in pursuit of a pile of unearned gold florins.

The adaptation (supposedly written by Lynda Snell but, in reality, the work of professional writer Nick Warburton) was further removed from Chaucerian medieval English than even Nevill Coghill's great translation but the performance was suitably fruity and explicit, with sly coupling, treasonous and unprincipled behaviour, fables of love, greed and devotion, all amounting, said one of the villagers, to 'the heart of England in an Ambridge barn'. The performance was anything but amateur as the professional cast rose to a challenge beyond that of merely playing their allotted characters in the daily soap.

A key prop in *The Miller's Tale* – a fake bottom that was to be displayed by an adventurous lover in a window for the climactic hot poker treatment ('And Nicholas is branded on the bum,/ And God bring all of us to Kingdom Come' as Coghill re-phrased it) – provided a running gag when it went missing. A volunteer body double stepped forward only to be repulsed with a cry of 'Who'd want to kiss that big hairy arse?' and a firm riposte by director Snell: 'I'm sorry, but if nobody else steps *into* the breach, I'm afraid Nathan is going to step *out* of his breeches.' And grumpy old Simon/Justin had an actor's tiff with his director when he protested that friars were just as concupiscent as the money-grubbing summoner he was lumbered with, pointing out that, in the original, the devil 'hoisted up his tail and 20,000 friars flew from his arse like bees'. 'That's enough!' snapped Snell. 'But it's in Chaucer!' 'It's not in Snell!'

Ambridge amdram sounded lively and smoothly competent. The cast party duly followed, with an awards ceremony honouring Best Man in Tights, Most Medieval Make-up and Lustiest Wench. But the most touching moment was when David Archer (played by Timothy Bentinck, the 12th Earl of Portland, forsooth) congratulated Lynda – often viewed as a pushy, overweening urbanite intruder – on her 'absolutely brilliant' achievement, proud that his barn had been at the centre of so binding and enjoyable a community experience.

This all served, ironically, to undermine Simon Williams's point when he averred, with a touch of sarcasm, in that same *Telegraph* article: 'Acting is just so easy – anyone can do it. All over the country ordinary, sane healthy civilians with proper jobs and planned holidays and pension schemes and all

that other guff, devote their spare time to amateur dramatics.' He opined
that amateurs 'haven't a clue what it's like doing a matinée in an empty
theatre two hundred miles from home, during a heatwave, when you've had
a dodgy curry the night before'. He implied a false virtue in such deprivation,
as if his galley-slave conditions at work should be more profoundly
appreciated by people who undertake what might be deemed proper jobs to
pay their rent and raise their families before going out to make up theatre in
the evenings.

Even so, the Williams view of the amateur as a laughing stock, it must be
said, is not necessarily without foundation, although foundation itself is a
rarity in most make-up boxes these days, along with Leichner's 5 and 9 and
a tube of dark Egyptian tan. I once knew an amateur actor who moved
about and talked quite naturally until the minute he stepped upon a stage
when, in whatever the role, he hunched his shoulders up to his ears, turned
glassy-eyed and started talking in a weird voice pitched somewhere between
Charles Laughton as Captain Bligh and Vincent Price in a horror movie.

But it is a condition of some professional actors, too, that they do not
have any idea of how bad they really are. Even good ones can be laid low
by misfortune. In a long-ago professional production of *King Lear* in
Cardiff, in which Lear was played by the notable leading actor Joseph
O'Conor (he alternated as Othello and Iago with Donald Wolfit and was
Mr Brownlow in Carol Reed's film of *Oliver!*), Lear's beard fell off –
unnoticed by him alone – while he cradled the dead Cordelia. In an earlier
scene in the same production, Kent, having been thrown a gratuity for his
pains in tripping over the insolent Oswald, watched the money-bag sail high
between his upraised arms, like a rugby ball between the posts. No way
daunted, he turned smartly on his heel into the wings, where the bag had
landed, retrieved it, and returned briefly to signal his thanks to the king with
a thumbs-up.

Even at the National you sit tight whenever an onstage telephone rings,
hoping against hope that it will stop ringing when the actor plucks it from
its cradle; even better, of course, if he plucks it just *after* it has stopped
ringing. It takes a real pro to extract him or herself from a phone disaster, as
did Sybil Thorndike when she stepped confidently downstage to answer a
rogue phone that should not have rung at that point, picked it up, and
turned upstage with an arm outstretched towards Gladys Cooper saying,
'It's for you, dear.'

Coarse theatre mishap, telephone-wise, is elevated to sublime comedy in
Michael Frayn's *Noises Off* (1982), arguably the funniest English play since
the war, when Dotty the diva, in the role of Mrs Clackett, the slovenly housekeeper in the play-within-a-play ('Nothing On'), gets in a rehearsal tizzy
over putting back the phone she's just answered and leaving the stage with

THE AGONY AND THE ECSTASY

a plate of sardines she's just come on with: 'It's no good you going on', she yells at the director at the back of the stalls, 'I've only got one pair of feet'. The delirium of *Noises Off* (the first act is set in a rehearsal, the second backstage, the third during a disastrous performance) lies in the deployment of rep cliché and incompetence in the cause of creating iron-cast, clockwork farce; ironically, and splendidly, the play is now an amdram staple.

And Dotty's 'sardines' have given their nomenclature, along with Mrs Clackett's iconic headscarf (worn successively on the professional stage by Lynn Redgrave, Patricia Hodge and Celia Imrie), to the artwork on the cover of amateur theatre's very own magazine, directory and social network centre. Like sardines in the tin, an awful lot is crammed into eighty-odd pages of *Sardines* four times a year.

(The other significant sardines check in modern British theatre is that of Alan Bennett as the sermonising vicar in the game-changing 1960 revue *Beyond the Fringe*, opining that life is like a tin of sardines: 'There's always a little bit in the corner you can't get out. I wonder . . . is there a little bit in the corner of your life? I know there is in mine.')

Two years after *Noises Off*, Alan Ayckbourn created his spirited response to Frayn, *A Chorus of Disapproval*, which in the original 1985 National Theatre production featured no less than three great male actors who had each first made his mark in amdram: Michael Gambon as the harassed Welsh director Dafydd ap Llewellyn of the Pendon Amateur Light Operatic Society (PALOS) putting on *The Beggar's Opera*; Colin Blakely (who succeeded Gambon on the West End transfer) in his last ever stage performance; and Bob Peck as the bereaved office worker cast as Macheath in the Gay play (with music), and an unlikely sex god torn between the director's distraught, unhappy wife and the company's voracious, married 'swinger'.

Gambon, an apprentice engineer, had acquired the confidence to go forward into the profession by appearing in several productions with the Geoffrey Whitworth Theatre in Crayford, Kent, where he attended the local secondary school, before joining the left-wing amateur Unity Theatre in London, first as Buck Mulligan in James Joyce's *Bloomsday*. Blakely was a stalwart of his home-town Bangor Drama Club in County Down, Northern Ireland, before turning professional in Belfast. And Peck appeared with amateurs in the Leeds Civic Theatre when he was an art student in the city. This binding of the amateur and the professional stage in the careers of such actors is far more the norm than the exception. The catalyst is often, though not always, Shakespeare, as documented by the scholar Michael Dobson in his *Shakespeare and Amateur Performance*.

Many of our leading actors – sometimes I think almost all of them – have toiled in amdram, often while holding down proper jobs, and then become notable stars. Leonard Rossiter worked in insurance, and amdram, for years before turning professional in his late twenties. Freddie Jones left school to work in a home appliances store, then for ten years as a lab assistant at a chemical factory in Tamworth, while immersing himself in amateur dramatics at the old Shelton Rep and other companies around Stoke-on-Trent. He was well into his thirties by the time he trained at Rose Bruford and made his London debut with the RSC in 1962.

When Anthony Hopkins and Ian McKellen played in Richard Eyre's fine television production of Ronald Harwood's *The Dresser* in 2015, the backstage milieu of the play was supplemented with a BBC on-line feature recording the stars' debt to where they started. McKellen mentioned the Bolton Little Theatre. Hopkins said he found himself, by accident, in an amateur dramatics class at his local YMCA in Wales. Ben Kingsley, the son of a doctor, joined his local amateur society, the Salford Players, where he performed while working as a lab technician. He was so 'transported' by the thrill of the audience response that he joined a children's theatre company in London. Glenda Jackson's first job on leaving school was in a local pharmacy and she got involved in amateur theatre in her home town of Hoylake in Cheshire, 'usually playing maids and things like that'.

Brenda Blethyn recounted how she worked as a secretary for ten years before finding her feet with the Euston Players, British Rail's amdram group. She even remembers the first line she ever uttered on stage: 'It's a real dirty old night. Evans the post says the mist is right down to the path, quite thick it was.' The more she did, the more she loved doing it, being part of the whole operation of 'putting on a show'. So when she learned that the Young Vic needed a volunteer to type thousands of envelopes, she offered her services. 'I found I could sneak out and watch *The Taming of the Shrew* with Jim Dale, Jane Lapotaire and Nicky Henson from the balcony. How could I possibly know that six years later [in 1976] I'd be performing there as Cassandra in *Troilus and Cressida*?' She moved with her then husband to Sussex, joined the amateur Chichester Players whose director insisted she take up acting professionally. She applied to, and was accepted by, the Guildford School of Acting in 1972. This is how careers in the theatre often, almost usually, happen. Mind you, I did once ask Toby Jones, Freddie's son, if he had ever worked in amateur theatre. 'Why, does it look as though I have?' was his half-serious, self-deprecating riposte.

The story of many even younger prominent actors is incomplete without reference to amdram. Jude Law's induction into his profession was no doubt inevitable – his parents, both theatre enthusiasts – met as students at Goldsmith's College in London and took along their son, and his elder sister, Natasha, now a successful painter and graphic designer, to their local amateur theatre in Eltham, south east London, in the late 1970s. While Mum directed and Dad acted, young Jude watched, listened and joined in. He recalls that nobody in the Eltham Little took the work anything but seriously.

He was part of the youth group, the New Stagers, for several years, during which time the theatre was re-named (in 1982) the Bob Hope Theatre for the great comedian who was born locally and funded the theatre through his Pro-Am Golf Classic. For Law, amdram was part of his training which continued when, as a fifteen-year-old schoolboy at Alleyn's, he joined the National Youth Music Theatre in 1987. His great friend and contemporary in the NYMT was another future star, Jonny Lee Miller, and they were soon followed by comedian Matt Lucas and such other rising talents as Sheridan Smith and Eddie Redmayne. 'It was more than song and dance', says Law, 'I learned almost everything I know about acting, and ensemble work, at the NYMT under Jeremy James-Taylor. And when I was asked recently to write about the Bob Hope in my time there, I was literally overcome with emotion at the memory of it all. It all meant a great deal to me, and the level of professionalism in that experience of amateur theatre was as high as anything I've subsequently known.'

It is the social nexus of the amdram and light opera societies that has sustained the professional repertoire just as much as the old professional repertory system. And while professional actors move on from one engagement to the next, forming new families and friendships as they go – unlike actors in the Russian and Eastern European theatres who stay in one company for life – amateurs often spend decades in the haven of one company that becomes the social centre of their world. Friendships – and animosities – run deep; short-lived and long-term affairs flourish and crumble; marriages, divorces and other ructions occur, all exacerbated by the intensity of the performance schedule at the end of a leisurely, part-time preparation.

Such a fabric, woven from performance and reality, comradeship and rivalry, sex and sublimation, is perfect material for popular crime fiction – and the theatrical wing of this genre has some notable examples. The title of Simon Brett's *An Amateur Corpse* (1978) has the double implication of an actor 'dying on stage' (i.e. failing miserably to please an audience) and of the moment of uncontrolled hysteria when, because of a mishap or a missed cue, an actor breaks up, or corpses. Even the most seasoned professional spends time trying to corpse his fellows: the late Michael Bryant, playing Enobarbus in a National Theatre production of *Antony and Cleopatra* on the night when Judi Dench (Cleopatra) was nominated a Dame of the British Empire, hissed upstage to her in a whisper that carried over the front ten rows of the Olivier stalls, so perfect was his muted articulation, 'I suppose a quick fuck's out of the question, then . . . .'

When Brett's victim, the actress playing Nina in a production of Chekhov's *The Seagull* for the suburban thespian ensemble the Breckton Backstagers is found strangled in a coal-shed, the investigation unravels a slew of romantic, obsessive and downright nasty possibilities. Nina had no friends and an unhappy marriage, and had joined the back-stabbing Backstagers to meet people and perhaps –here's the clue – rekindle a misfired professional career she'd embarked upon in 'the real theatre world'.

The great thing here about Brett's amateur sleuth, Charles Paris – given a wonderful, laconic world-weariness by Bill Nighy in the long-running spin-off series on BBC Radio – is that he is himself a moderately unsuccessful professional character actor with a borderline drink problem who has been invited out to the suburbs to give a critical assessment of *The Seagull*. Of course, he only empties both barrels, in his cups, to us, the readers, not to the actors themselves (tread softly, because you tread on their dreams): 'Such a pity that amateurs are always tempted by classic plays . . . amateurs should stick to what's written within their range – Agatha Christie, frothy West End comedies, nothing that involves too much subtlety of characterisation. Leave Chekhov to the pros.'

This, again, as Brett is fully aware – as a quondam member of Questors himself before going on to Oxford theatre and a notable career in light entertainment at the BBC – is a gross, prejudicial exaggeration, however applicable it may be in the particular case of the Breckton Backstagers. 'Frothy West End comedies' are harder to do really well than *King Lear*. Or, at least, the problems are as great, only different. Paris himself is allowed by Brett to recognise the irrationality of his views, putting them down to the insecurity he feels within himself, as if the very existence of amateur dramatic societies seemed to threaten or even undermine the seriousness of his own profession.

This ambivalence about the proximity of amateur and professional is more comically developed in the *Midsomer Murders* television writer Caroline Graham's novel *Death of a Hollow Man* (1989), in which the onstage murder (or suicide) of the actor playing Salieri in the Causton Amateur Dramatic Society (or CADS) version of Peter Shaffer's *Amadeus* prompts a vitriolic attack on 'amateurishness' in the props department; the protective film of tape on the blade of Salieri's knife has been inadvertently (deliberately?) removed.

This does not impress the grandiose director, Harold Winstanley, a refugee from the business who, twenty years earlier, had acted at Filey, produced a summer season at Minehead and appeared in a Number One tour of Agatha Christie's *Spider's Web*. As a CADS irregular remarks, without sarcasm, 'You couldn't argue with that sort of experience.' Harold's young protégé is leaving CADS to take up a place at a drama school in London: 'I want to go into the theatre' says the wannabe. 'But – you're *in* the theatre!' squeals Harold. 'I mean the real theatre.' Harold explodes onto another plane of Gloria Swanson when embroiled in the fetid atmosphere of accusations and informed that the Press has arrived. 'That pot-bellied idiot from the *Echo* . . .?' 'No, the real Press. *The Times. The Independent. The Guardian*. Michael Billington.'

'*Michael Billington!*' The blaze of hope in Harold's eyes dazzled, we are told ('Cover her face. Mine eyes dazzle. She died young,' says Ferdinand of his sister, the Duchess of Malfi) . . . 'Is it really true . . . At last! I knew it would come. I knew they'd remember me . . .' And he's ready for his close-up. This low-grade Hollywood camp is enjoyably ludicrous, but contains a grain of reminiscent truth in the lower reaches of old-style rep and some areas of aspirational amateur theatre. I once knew of a company manager in a Butlin's holiday camp weekly rep company in Bognor Regis who had changed his surname to 'Garson' in honour of Greer and was dazzled, like Harold, by attention and follow spots when hauled away on suspicion of having tampered with the company's wage packets every Friday afternoon during the summer season.

The amateur theatre has no wage packets, though some of the leading companies actually reverse this non-process by charging an appearance fee to certain required visiting actors, as well as the usually modest membership fees. There are no processed figures to imply the demographic constituency of amdram participants, but it is clear that the pastime is as widespread and popular in Great Britain as are fishing and football. Helen Nicholson, a professor at Royal Holloway College in London, who has researched many aspects of amateur theatre, has said that she is confidently certain that everyone in this country lives within three miles of an operating amateur theatre.

It is an extraordinary fact that the emotionally reticent and undemonstrative British are at it like knives, both onstage and behind the scenes – *An Amateur Corpse* contains a scene of steamed-up sex in the lighting box between shows in a darkened theatre. And the social network of theatre in this country, the extent to which the professional and the amateur, the student and the enthusiast, the technicians and the costumiers, all overlap and intermingle is far more profound and pervasive than is generally acknowledged. It is in the nature of theatre that audiences are as involved in the art form as are practitioners. Without an audience, there is no theatre. You could easily say that the audience *is* the theatre. 'Amateur' means very little in such a context.

Also – there's no way round this – people of colour are sadly few and far between in amdram, as they are equally rare in our orchestral and choral societies. We are dealing here with cultural realities, not theories, and we await developments. Amateur theatre tends to thrive in white, middle-class, suburban environments. Where the social demographic has changed significantly in the past fifty years – as, for instance, in Ilford in Essex (now designated as being in East London), an area transformed by its vibrantly expanding Asian and Bangladeshi community – the local amateur theatre scene is in steep decline.

The demarcation lines between professionals and amateurs, once blurred, are under pressure once more, as major professional theatre companies become as engaged with their outreach, educational and community work as they are with their headline product. The RSC has an Open Stages policy, collaboration with several regional theatres and centres and a thriving schools programme. And, for the past ten years, the company has been actively committed to transforming the relationship between amateur and professional theatre. Why? Surely the main task of the RSC is to continuously renew itself as a leading company in the land, with the best actors and a more heightened profile in London, as well as across the UK?

The RSC's answer to this, not unreasonably, is that the company *is* renewing itself in these outreach programmes, which are hard-wired into the most important people of all – the audience – or at least the potential audience. Erica Whyman, the RSC's deputy artistic director, sees the division between amateur and professional theatre as essentially false, suggesting that the establishment of the Arts Council in 1946 drove a divisive wedge through the nation's 'serious' club and repertory theatres, where actors had, prior to that date, moved easily and freely between paid and unpaid work.

To this day, the Arts Council refuses to recognise amateur theatre in its dispensations, with the exception of a few notable capital project investments. The Little Theatre Guild, the body representative of all amateur companies

FIGURE 2 *Ayesha Dharker and John Chapman in the RSC's pro-am* A Midsummer Night's Dream: A Play for the Nation *in 2016, with amateurs playing the mechanicals. (Photo: Topher McGrillis © RSC.)*

who own their own theatres, is becoming, understandably, increasingly vociferous on the subject; the wind of change is definitely in their favour.

Michael Boyd, the former RSC artistic director, was the driving force behind the Open Stages initiative, recognising the huge energy particularly with regard to Shakespeare in the amateur theatre. He was committed to opening out the company into the community. His successor, Gregory Doran, took it all one stage further in 2016 when he announced a production of *A Midsummer Night's Dream: A Play for the Nation*, to be directed by Erica Whyman. This would involve fourteen amateur groups throughout Britain providing the actors to play Bottom and his fellow mechanicals in each regional stop-off – 'hard-handed folk' (amended from Shakespeare's 'men'; there were two female Bottoms and several Quinces with quims) – culminating in a performance on the main stage in Stratford-upon-Avon.

While it is true that we now look at the rehearsals and performance of 'Pyramus and Thisbe' by the mechanicals in *A Midsummer Night's Dream* as a love letter to amdram, Michael Dobson points out that Shakespeare almost certainly didn't. At the time of the play's composition, 1595, the days of guilds mumming the Mystery plays had long vanished. But at the Restoration of the monarchy, amateur theatricals revived and a script published in 1661 as fuel for the theatrical energy of young tradesmen forbidden to marry before completing their training was titled *The Merry Conceited Humours of Bottom the Weaver*, a version of *A Midsummer Night's Dream* as if edited by Nick Bottom.

As Dobson concludes, 'Amateur theatricals as we know them – especially amateur theatricals involving Shakespeare – start here.' We know that Shakespeare anticipated many social developments and phenomena in his work – at Oberon's command, Puck says he'll put a girdle round the earth in forty minutes; the first Sputnik encircled the globe in thirty-eight – and now we know, says Dobson, that he anticipated, perhaps even accidentally produced, through this work, our national obsession with the activity.

It is perhaps harder to see how the experiment could be extended into the rest of the RSC's repertoire, though the RSC Amateur Ensemble had emerged in 2012, when a cast entirely made up of amateurs across the Midlands in Birmingham, Coventry and Leamington Spa worked with RSC directors, designers and technicians to produce *Pericles* as part of the World Shakespeare Festival in the company's Courtyard Theatre (the temporary venue before the refurbished main house re-opened) in Stratford-upon-Avon. The title role was impressively played by the young amateur Sope Dirisu, and he has since gone on to forge a professional career, playing the lead role, with some success, in *Coriolanus* at the RSC in 2017. It was surely no coincidence that, in 2018, the National chose the same play, *Pericles*, in all its epic romantic glory, to launch its Public Acts initiative involving over 200 amateurs of all ages across London, working with professionals on a production given on its main Olivier stage.

There is no let-up in the intensity of the RSC's Open Stages and schools programmes. The company hosts a 'Big Amateur Weekend' each year attended by up to 100 people from all round the country paying £200 a head for the privilege of participating in workshops related to RSC's production practice in voice, movement, technical support work and playwriting. These events must surely be of more benefit to the amateurs than to the RSC itself, and can be seen as part of a sustained campaign by the company to permeate the consciousness of the nation at a time when its lustre has dimmed and its pre-eminence in Shakespeare production ceded, in London at least, to Shakespeare's Globe, the most popular theatre in the capital. The Globe has operated each year since 1997 between May and October, under the successive artistic directorships of Mark Rylance, Dominic Dromgoole, Emma Rice (briefly) and, currently, Michelle Terry.

Apart from, as Erica Whyman insists, needing 'to have a tangibly national experience every year', the RSC hierarchy is trying to recover lost ground and stake out new territory at the same time. One particular success story is claimed for Blackpool, Lancashire, a town where 40 per cent of the adults, it is alleged, have a reading age of eleven. *A Midsummer Night's Dream* played for a week in the Grand Theatre to packed audiences of 700 people a night, 48 per cent of whom had never been to this venue on their doorstep – a magnificent Victorian design by the greatest theatre architect of the era, Frank Matcham – nor been to London, nor read or seen anything by Shakespeare. There are always inevitable barriers between people and the arts, partly because of the commodification of the material, partly because of class prejudice, partly because people think that the arts, and especially the theatre, are not for them, not part of their entitlement. Amateur theatre can do, and does, a lot to assist in the dissolution of these false partitions.

At the RSC, Jacqui O'Hanlon, director of education, says that 'everything' started with Cicely Berry, the renowned voice coach at the company between 1969 and 2014, who developed a range of work connecting actors to the words. Berry launched this campaign with young people and people in prisons, highlighting the magnetism of language, and Shakespeare in particular, for audiences of all ages and social backgrounds. This, says O'Hanlon, is a growing part of how the RSC understands its role in fulfilling its own remit, nationally and internationally, and its duty in terms of both 'artistic excellence' and engaging an audience 'very directly' in its work. The amateur theatre comes into play in the avowed policy of 'extending the parameters of who we make theatre with', from partner theatres to primary schools in Middlesbrough and amateur companies in Blackpool; these factions are 'all part of the RSC'.

It is interesting that when the RSC cast an unknown 24-year-old, David Warner, as its 1965 Hamlet, he made his mark as an unexpected, though fully professional, intruder in the ranks (he hadn't been in rep; he'd failed to get in) even though he had already played Henry VI and Richard II for the company. Doubly interesting, too, that the diffident, brilliant Warner, had shuffled through RADA training into the RSC because of his almost accidental tumbling into amdram in Leamington Spa where, in his occasional day job during his unhappy teenage years, he sold newspapers to a short-trousered Michael Billington in the department store, Burgis & Colbourne.

At school, encouraged by a teacher, Warner played Lady Macbeth ('the tallest in British stage history', he suggests) and Shylock, and started going to watch theatre in Stratford-upon-Avon and Coventry not because he was theatre-struck – 'Home life was such that I didn't want to be in the house much' – but for something to do. This reminds me of the critic Irving Wardle, who has connections with the Bolton Little Theatre, saying that the appeal of amdram for many was the licensed exit it offered from sitting at home with the beloved every night. Amdram gave Warner somewhere to go. He wasn't in it for the social life – though he certainly enjoyed going to the bar – and he doesn't remember making any friends.

When he finally got going, Warner oscillated between performing at the Loft in Leamington Spa and the Talisman in Kenilworth, and remembers in particular two performances by a postman, Joe Rowlands, as John Proctor in *The Crucible* and Lord Goring in Wilde's *An Ideal Husband*. At the Loft in the early 1960s, a travelling group from Birmingham University visited with a production of *Hamlet* for which they required a few amateur spear carriers. Warner volunteered, then withdrew, because he was 'too nervous'. He learned later that the Hamlet was Geoffrey Hutchings, and the Claudius, Terry Hands – future distinguished colleagues of his at the RSC, one a fine second lead actor, the other an important artistic director.

Warner looks back on his amdram days with unalloyed affection. He says that if he hadn't gone to RADA, 'amdram would have been a bit of a life-saver. Nobody expected me to do anything. The fact that I have is such a surprise, the gravy in my life. I have had to live with the comments of actors over the years who just don't think I'm worth it. I won't mention names. There are always detractors.'

Admittedly Warner, a most sensitive soul, takes his modesty and self-deprecation to unnecessary extremes, but even as an amateur, he was excoriated in the local press when he played Marchbanks in *Candida* ('To give him some credit . . . he did know his lines') and was so irritated by the initially bad reviews for his RSC Hamlet ('I'd as lief the town-crier spoke his lines as David Warner') that he insisted on a collection of them being printed in the Aldwych Theatre programme when the production sailed triumphantly into London as the hottest ticket in town, with Janet Suzman succeeding Glenda Jackson as his ground-breakingly neurotic/psychotic Ophelia.

The RSC's *Dream* project wasn't a calculated attempt to uncover a new Warner, or any other relatively untried actor who might refresh and enliven its ranks (though, as it happens, no less than five of the eighty-four amateur mechanicals have gone on to professional training), but a sort of glorified PR exercise in the interests of democratic outreach and diversity.

In Stratford, I saw the RSC share the stage with the Nonentities of Kidderminster and, at the Barbican, with the Tower Theatre of London. Hundreds of regular schoolchildren around the country were employed as fairy attendants, too. Neither group of amateurs was fazed or frightened by the experience and both the Bottoms I saw showed up pretty well, suitably over-pleased with themselves, suitably uncomplicated, though perhaps just missing out on the two revelatory aspects of Bottom's experience a good professional actor would exploit: his tumescent sexuality in the guise of a donkey and his subsequent deflation in the magical realisation of 'Bottom's dream' and most rare vision.

The Tower Bottom, John Chapman, ran a blog of his experience, documenting the bizarre rehearsal process in which the amateur groups were linked up on monitors with the RSC's rehearsal rooms in Clapham, south London. There would be a 'Bottom hub' on Saturday mornings there, too, joined by the director, the infinitely accommodating Titania (Ayesha Dharker) and the other thirteen, far-flung wobbly weavers. Whatever the gains of the project, the thirteenth production of the play in the history of the RSC, I can confidently pronounce, was not the best, not by a long chalk. And there was an added element of controversy surrounding the casting of amateurs in that Equity, the actors' union, had issues with the jobs not going to its under-employed members, though careful negotiation led to an agreement in the end. I rather cruelly concluded in a review that it was fairly hard to distinguish between amateurs and professionals in this production. That problem was no doubt my problem, but the show seemed to me to fall between two stools of professional competence and amateur good intentions. That said, I love the stories that emerged.

In rehearsal, all the Bottoms were given a special task by Erica Whyman, and that of Trevor Gill from the Belvoir Players in Belfast was to record a storm-tossed speech of Lear. He went out and found a blasted heath, in a storm, in the middle of the night, and fulfilled his brief with knobs on. The local Bottom in Stratford from the Bear Pit amateurs just across the river from the Royal Shakespeare Theatre was in fact the RSC's box office manager. The Bottom from Nottingham, Becky Morris, was probably the least experienced of all the amateurs, says Erica Whyman, and excruciatingly shy until she went on stage. Then she turned into Les Dawson, with 'a wonderful quality of gentleness', and volunteered to sing her 'tongs and bones' song while accompanying herself at the piano as Titania lay across the internal strings.

The Little Theatre Guild holds annual general meetings at one of the member theatres, and there are regional meetings, too, and a great sharing of advice and experience on issues such as health and safety, royalty payments to agents and publishers, new writing and training programmes, technical maintenance and innovation, international contacts and festivals, problems with local reviews coming out at the end of the week, not to mention the decimation of theatre coverage, not least reviews, in local and even some national newspapers throughout the land.

At the seventieth AGM of the LTG in 2016, hosted by the Crescent in Birmingham, I relished a colourful tapestry of updates and anecdotes provided by members and officials in their speeches and everyday chatter over lunch, coffee and drinks. Patricia Clough of the Bingley Little Theatre recalled an earlier conference where a mayoral party walked out in the interval of Arrabal's sexually explicit *Car Cemetery*. On another occasion at the Questors, an extravagant buffet laid out in the Stanislavsky room – a huge guffaw as the Russian master of motivational realism, who hailed from a family of obsessive amateur actors, is name-checked – was greedily scoffed by the resident actors before the guests arrived. Actors, amateurs no less than their professional counterparts, are always hungry. One delegate quoted John Wardle, Irving's father and founder member of the Bolton Little Theatre, who suggested that the conference he'd recently attended felt like 'an ordeal by hospitality'.

In between the socialising, however, there is important business, such as the announcement that Kenneth Branagh is to succeed Ian McKellen as patron of the LTG (Branagh was a member of the youth theatre at the Progress Theatre in Reading, where he remains a patron); a fundraising break-out in which we were informed that there are 3,000 trusts and foundations out there who give away £3 billion a year – delegates should know their criteria; and a renewed frustration at the continuing lack of interest from the Arts Council despite a recent capital grant of £100,000 made to a member theatre.

The seventy-first AGM was hosted by the Archway Theatre in Horley, Surrey, an amazing little set-up of 100 company members and 800 supporters housed in ten railway arches serving as rehearsal room, wardrobe, furniture store, workshops (the elderly set-builders are known as 'the scenery citizens') dressing rooms and a tiny studio. The Archway, founded in 1939, has been on this site since 1952, nabbing its original seats from the old Gaiety Theatre in the Aldwych which was closed in 1939 and demolished in 1956. In 1987, they rebuilt the main stage the other way round in the archway, increasing the capacity from sixty-five customers to ninety. Judi Dench is their patron.

There is something entirely 'honourable', as Ian McKellen says, about people putting on plays, after a hard day's work, for their fellow citizens and the rest of us to come and see. And you can as easily argue, with the actor/writer Michael Simkins, whose books about acting are at least as funny as Michael Green's, that professional actors are the ones beyond the pale 'because we've chosen to put ourselves ever so slightly outside the social norm'.

Acting is an odd profession in that the actor is required to substitute another reality for his own. This can strike the public as forming a bubble of pretence that is dodging the real issues of life, though of course that is another misapprehension that leads to cat-calls of 'luvvies', whether you are amateur or professional. As Michael Simkins says, 'The only absolute difference between them and us is that professionals are prepared to put up with the terrible uncertainty of it all. I've known some wonderful amateurs and some terrible professionals. Amateurs simply won't risk it full time.'

Derek Jacobi expressed it well, too, in an interview with *Sardines* magazine in 2016: 'Amateur actors who are successful ... they obviously don't need acting; they've got another life, a job. But you've got to think of life without acting, and if you can't conceive of a life without acting then you've got to be an actor. You've got to do it.' No good professional actor ever thought, except perhaps flippantly, that what he or she did was just a job. Jacobi insists it's a vocation: 'You've got to have the fire in your belly; you've got to need it. It's an extremely risky decision to take. It doesn't earn you a living but it can make you a fortune. It's a risk.'

But what if you are happy with the compromise and find a way of making of it a supreme virtue, as do many of the amateur actors I've spoken to? A life of risk and insecurity is bartered for a life in other, possibly more respectable, professions while retaining the appurtenances of a theatrical career: acting itself, the applause, the camaraderie, a sense of worth, even importance, in the community.

2

Mysteries, Fireworks and Students

The formulation of the amateur theatre phenomenon is a long and winding journey on a bumpy road, but there are signs and milestones along a route that takes us, essentially, from country house theatricals to the efflorescence of the undergraduate societies at the oldest universities.

Although the first so-called amateur dramatic society in Britain was formed at the very start of the nineteenth century – the Pic-Nic Society club opened in the Tottenham Street Rooms, on the site of the future (now gone) Scala Theatre, in 1802, with performances of French and English plays – there have been amateurs at the centre of more or less all theatrical endeavour since the middle ages: members of the guilds – who were apprentices, craftsmen and journeymen – performed miracle and morality plays on the streets of Wakefield, York and Chester.

The performances were given on wagons in the streets by this confederacy of tradesmen – merchants, tailors, drapers, ostlers, butchers, weavers and carpenters, precursors of Shakespeare's mechanicals, in fact. The York mystery cycle, recounting Biblical events from the Creation to Judgement Day, full of character, colour and demotic low speech, dated from the mid-fourteenth century and continued as popular, festival theatre until suppressed by the Tudors in 1569. The plays started to make a comeback in the twentieth century, notably in 1951 when, as part of the Festival of Britain, they were produced with amateurs in the enchanting stone ruins of St Mary's Abbey in the Museum Gardens of York by E. Martin Browne, at that time the director of the British Drama League.

Judi Dench, one of the greatest actors of our day, and a peerless Shakespearean, appeared in that 1951 production, aged sixteen, returning several times to this popular throwback in the abbey ruins and eventually 'starring' as the Virgin Mary before going on to train at Central School and make a 1957 professional debut as Ophelia with the Old Vic. The one professional in the cast – and this remained a tradition – was Jesus, played by the same Joseph O'Conor whose beard fell off as he cradled Cordelia in that ill-fated Cardiff *King Lear*.

Thereafter, the cycle was revived *al fresco* every three or four years until 1988, when the performance moved inside to the Theatre Royal in the city and, climactically, in a York Minster spectacular staged by Gregory Doran of the RSC in 2000. The plays returned to the abbey ruins in 2012 – with the help of 1,000 local volunteers and a rotating cast of 500 amateurs – before the cycle came full cycle and took once more to the streets on mobile wagons in 2018.

The medieval mystery plays with their origins in amateur theatre resonate not just through Shakespeare but through our entire theatre. They remain a cultural lode star. Perhaps the greatest of all modern productions was the version made of the York and Wakefield cycles by the poet Tony Harrison for the National Theatre in 1977, undoubtedly one of the highlights of the Peter Hall era on the South Bank in the production directed by Bill Bryden and designed by William Dudley (who started his career with amateurs at the Tower Theatre in Canonbury).

Then in 1984, the late Anthony Minghella, whose films included *The English Patient* and *The Talented Mr Ripley,* wrote a delightful and very funny stage play, *Two Planks and a Passion,* directed by filmmaker Danny Boyle, in which the community of fourteenth-century York amateurs prepare for a performance in front of King Richard II.

The third significant 'York cycle' modern play came from the Royal Court director Peter Gill who once averred, referring to the anonymous clerical author of the Passion plays, known as the York Realist, that 'if it hadn't been for [him] . . . Shakespeare would have been a second rate writer like Goethe'. Gill's play, *The York Realist* (2002), took a 1960s production of the cycle as the background to a love affair between a farm labourer involved in the show and a young assistant director from London, thereby also setting up a cultural tension between the bovine sincerity of provincial art and its metropolitan representation, a tension often reflected at the Royal Court in Gill's time there – he directed the famous rediscovery of the D. H. Lawrence trilogy in 1966- and in the 'work' plays of David Storey, which soon followed.

As the Mysteries remained hidden from public approval for three centuries, amateur performers, admittedly of a higher social caste, appeared in the masques and pastorals – not the plays – during the reigns of Elizabeth, James and Charles I. It's worth remembering that our first recognised comedy, Nicholas Udall's *Ralph Roister Doister* – actually about as funny as a prolonged session of root canal treatment – was written in 1552 by a schoolmaster for his pupils to perform and that our first serious tragedy, Norton and Sackville's *Gorboduc* – a *Lear*-like barbaric scenario of dissension, violence and revenge in a squabble over the royal succession – was played by the gentlemen of the Inner Temple in 1591.

When it comes to the country house private theatricals of the late-eighteenth century, it's useful to think of the distinction between the players and the gentlemen as analogous to that in cricket before the full professionalisation of the sport. It was the gentlemen – the aristocrats – who created what, in effect, became a national craze. This development is reflected in the history of the company that claims to be the oldest 'modern' amateur set-up, the Old Stagers in Canterbury. Since 1842, interrupted only in war-time, they have been presenting a play during Kent cricket club week in Canterbury. The gentlemen amateurs were often joined on stage by a professional actress (in cricketing parlance, a player) of the calibre and standing of Ellen Terry or Irene Vanbrugh.

John Milton's masque *Comus* was performed by amateurs in Ludlow Castle in 1634, but private theatricals were in abeyance in the years after the Restoration. According to their chronicler, theatre historian Sybil Rosenfeld, they returned with a vengeance, initially among families, around 1770. One of the pace-setters was Sir Francis Blake Delaval, the wild and dissipated owner of Seaton Delaval Hall, a Northumberland pile designed by John Vanbrugh in the style of an Italian palazzo. His London address was 11 Downing Street, nowadays occupied by the Chancellor of the Exchequer.

In 1751, Delaval, who was a friend of the similarly dissipated playwright Samuel Foote, and a few chums, had hired Drury Lane to perform *Othello*. Over 20,000 people wanted to see it, but attendance was restricted to 1,000 and all the tickets distributed beforehand. The House of Commons – Delaval was the newly elected member for Hindon in Wiltshire – adjourned two hours early to be there, and the Prince of Wales sat in a stage box. Delaval himself played Othello and his two brothers Iago and Cassio with Desdemona taken by a friend of Delaval's mistress. The prologue and epilogue were supplied by the mad poet Christopher Smart, who had been Iago's tutor at Cambridge:

While mercenary [i.e, professional] actors tread the stage
And lively scribblers lash or lull the age,
Ours be the task t'instruct and entertain
Without one thought of glory or of gain . . . .

None of this, or indeed the performance, washed with David Garrick, who told Foote, 'I never *suffered* so much in my whole life.' Even allowing for the fact that Garrick, like most professionals of the day, was contemptuous of the amateurs, you suspect that his misgivings were not without foundation. This would have been in spite of the actors having been coached by Garrick's friend and Drury Lane partner, Charles Macklin, an acclaimed professional Iago.

Not all reports of acting standards were so bad. Rosenfeld recounts the story of William Fector, a baker's son at Dover – not even middle-class, let alone a glitterato of the *haut ton* – acting from 1783 in a private theatre he had bought and fitted out with a seating capacity of 190. Its motto was 'Labor ipse voluptas' ('Pleasure is in the work itself'), not too far off an almost perfect definition of amateur theatre. Fector scored many hits, including one of Master Betty's great roles, Zanya in Edward Young's *The*

Revenge, in which one critic said that Fector 'acts in so easy, familiar, yet powerful a manner that I imagined I saw a second Garrick rising up to banish bombast and affectation'.

From this, you might easily conclude that Fector and other amateurs were caught up in the ground-breaking move towards naturalism pioneered at Drury Lane by Garrick and Macklin in the mid-eighteenth century. Certainly, Rosenfeld concludes, '[Fector's] concentration on tragedy was without parallel in the theatricals of his time, and betokens a passion for acting rather than the usual desire for amusement'.

The most famous of all the private theatres in the eighteenth century was that of the Earl of Barrymore at Wargrave, an expensively built arena attended by aristocrats and royalty watching Restoration comedy and Ben Jonson city satires punctuated by supper parties, balls and firework displays. Unfortunately, the party balloons were popped after just four years when, in 1793, the young earl, aged twenty-four, was killed by the accidental explosion of a gun while on duty with the militia. His death, like that of Don Juan, says Rosenfeld, seemed to leave the world bereft of some great dynamic vitality.

A similar sort of cachet was attached to the Duke of Richmond's theatricals in Priory Gardens, Whitehall, where an elaborate system of invitation was created in order to avoid what the host might deem 'the intrusion of improper company', names printed on tickets along with signatures and seals of arms. One of the great professional actors of the day, John Philip Kemble, defended the amateurs and praised the production of Arthur Murphy's Drury Lane comedy *The Way to Keep Him*. Lord Derby, he said, played a 'rather too rotund lover' in one play, 'but had so improved under tuition' that in *The Guardian* by Garrick he made such a hit that 'Garrick himself . . . would have rejoiced in his Heartley'.

Another outlandish aristocratic amdram character celebrated by Rosenfeld was the so-called Margravine of Anspach, 'a vain, egotistical creature whose entertainments, as writer and actress, were not intended principally for her friends, but for herself'. The producer and theatre design consultant Iain Mackintosh takes issue with Rosenfeld's curt appraisal in a talk about the Margravine titled 'Riding the Three Tygers of Sex, of Society and of Showbusiness,' which he has delivered in Oxford colleges and to the Samuel Johnson Society.

Drawing on research beyond Rosenfeld, Mackintosh paints a portrait of an extraordinary creature whose energy, wit and scholarship informed her theatrical ventures as startlingly as her 'voracious sexualism'. She had a hand in creating four private theatres, and her own plays were presented on the professional stage by the playwrights Sheridan and George Colman. As plain Lady Elizabeth Craven, she had been married while conceiving seven children and indulging in numerous affairs. She set about entertaining on a more lavish scale the minute she married the Margrave of Brandenburg-Anspach. Apart from his enormous wealth, the Margrave had family connections with several branches of European royalty and Lady Elizabeth thus settled quite happily into his grand house at Hammersmith.

There were fêtes, a supper theatre (on a different plane to a modern fringe theatre equivalent such as the old King's Head in Islington, where, in my experience, a bad dinner was invariably precedent to a good play and vice versa, or the more recently established Menier Chocolate Factory with its wittily themed bill of fare in Southwark) and finally a spectacular purpose-built theatre, which opened in 1782 with French comedies, Italian pastorals and historical interludes.

The theatre operated until the Margrave died in 1806 and anticipated the amateurs of the 1930s in presenting the sort of plays the public, or commercial, theatres did not provide: Beaumont and Fletcher's *The Tamer Tam'd*, for instance, the lively feminist reply to *The Taming of the Shrew* popular throughout the Restoration, and in revival with David Garrick, but not seen in the modern professional repertoire until the RSC's revival in 2003; or Marivaux's *Le jeu de l'Amour et du Hasard*, or Schiller's *The Robbers*, these two both now staples of the European classical repertoire.

Jane Austen and Charles Dickens, arguably our two greatest novelists, were enthusiastically attendant on the evolution of amateur theatre, Austen at first as a child in her family's private theatricals at Steventon rectory, and Dickens, half a century later, with his own touring company and as a vividly engaged audience member at the relatively insalubrious private theatrical dives around town as reported in his *Sketches by Boz* (1837):

> The principal patrons of private theatres are dirty boys, low copying-clerks, in attorneys' offices, capacious-headed youths from city counting-houses, Jews whose business, as lenders of fancy dress, is a sure passport to the amateur stage, shop-boys who now and then mistake their masters' money for their own; and a choice miscellany of idle vagabonds. The proprietor of a private theatre may be an ex-scene-painter, a low coffee-house-keeper, a disappointed eighth-rate actor, a retired smuggler, or a certified bankrupt. The theatre itself may be in Catherine-street, Strand, the purlieus of the city, the neighbourhood of Gray's-inn-lane, or the vicinity of Sadler's Wells; or it may, perhaps, form the chief nuisance of some shabby street, on the Surrey side of Waterloo-bridge.

It is delicious how down, dirty and pervasive these inner-city private theatricals had become by the mid-1830s. Interesting, too, how a pair of theatrically savvy contemporary writers, Paula Byrne and Simon Callow, have extrapolated the contrasting, respective theatricality of both Austen and Dickens in considering the core of their fictional work, and not just in the obvious manifestations in *Mansfield Park* and *Nicholas Nickleby*. Byrne argues persuasively that Austen's passion for the theatre informs almost every scene in every novel in some way, while the novelist certainly exploited the widespread moral disapproval of the stage and its 'goings-on' in the famous theatrical sequence in *Mansfield Park*; the heroine, Fanny Price, is prissily reluctant to join in what the critical Edmund Bertram deplores as 'the raw efforts of those who have not been bred to the trade – a set of gentlemen and ladies who have all the disadvantages of education and decorum to struggle through'. Bertram is pre-echoing the sentiments of Henry James, a great novelist but failed playwright, who was appalled, in 1876, at the effect, as he saw it, of country-house private theatricals on a social life in London possessed by theatrical mania:

> If you go to an evening party, nothing is more probable than that all of a sudden a young lady or a young gentleman will jump up and strike an attitude and begin to recite a poem or speech. Every pretext for this sort of exhibition is ardently cultivated and the London world is apparently filled with stage-struck young persons whose relatives are holding them back from a dramatic career.

As implied in James, there was always, from the start, an element of puritanical opposition to the private theatre, aristocratic or low-born – the example of the great houses, says Rosenfeld, spread to the tenants 'who spouted their heroics in barns' – while the Pic-Nic amateurs were derided for their pretentiousness in competing with the patent theatres, where plays were licensed for performance by professionals. But even some objectors conceded that play-acting might be a form of amusement preferable to gaming and drinking, following the lead of an editorial comment in the *Morning Post* of January 1792 that the experience of theatre-going, if the right plays were selected, might even be elevating. To that end, private theatricals might even be considered a national benefit. There was still another century to go before that seemed even remotely possible.

While Rosenfeld suggests that private theatricals petered out in the first quarter of the nineteenth century, another historian, David Coates, in a lecture delivered to the Society of Theatrical Research in April 2017, revealed evidence of country house theatricals right through to the mid-nineteenth century. In London, meanwhile, the Dramatic Institute in Gough Street, noted in the *Morning Chronicle* as a den of vice and immorality until about 1830, was succeeded ten years later by Miss Kelly's more high-minded and purposeful school and theatre in Dean Street, hired by Charles Dickens and his friends for a performance of Ben Jonson's *Every Man In His Humour* in 1845.

And by the end of the nineteenth century, amateur theatre is a serious business in schools, the armed services and the universities. One of the most interesting battles against stuffiness, snobbery and puritanism was waged in the formation of the Oxford University Dramatic Society, the OUDS, in 1885. Professional actors had visited Oxford after the Restoration, but the authorities remained hostile for over a century, only lifting a ban on theatrical performance of any kind in the 1790s. By 1850, undergraduates were putting on plays in their own colleges. A group based in Christ Church, the

Philothespians, presented an 1881 production of *The Clandestine Marriage* by Garrick and George Colman in which, unfortunately, one of the actors was reported to have 'carried on far too animated a conversation with the prompter, even for amateur theatricals'. Just as the Philothespians were lapsing into becoming just another debauched dining club for undergraduate hedonists and louche aristocrats, along came a key figure in our early twentieth-century theatre: Arthur Bourchier.

Bourchier arrived at Christ Church from Eton already committed to a life in the theatre. He shook up the Philothespians and then advocated the idea of a separate dramatic society to be supervised by the Varsity itself. He was aware that Cambridge University had beaten him to his own idea, with the founding of the ADC Theatre in 1855 (though the academically driven, RSC-formulating Marlowe Society was not created until 1907). There is no doubt, however, that Bourchier struck the crucial deal – with one or two colleagues – that placed university theatricals in close collaboration with the professional theatre, and that deal has persisted informally through the subsequent years.

In May 1885, the first OUDS production opened in the Town Hall in Oxford and was reviewed by Oscar Wilde. The play was Shakespeare's *Henry IV, Part One*, with titled ladies in the locality playing the hostess Quickly and Lady Mortimer (there were no women as yet in the university) and Bourchier as Hotspur. In his essay for the *Dramatic Review*, Wilde eulogised the OUDS, the city of Oxford, the play itself, and, especially, the new star: 'Mr Bourchier has a fine stage presence, a beautiful voice, and produces his effects by a method as dramatically impressive as it is artistically right . . . [he] has the opportunity of a fine career on the English stage, and I hope he will take advantage of it'.

He did. After staying on for a couple of years after graduation, helping and subsidising the new adventure – he played Feste when the OUDS opened the New Theatre (now the Apollo) in George Street in 1886 – he made a professional debut as Jaques ('All the world's a stage . . .') opposite Lillie Langtry in *As You Like It* in 1899. Thereafter, through to the 1920s, he acted and managed theatres with all the great names of the day – Charles Wyndham, Herbert Beerbohm Tree, H. B. Irving and Frank Benson. (As with any prominent actor, there were those who took a view of Bourchier's acting style different from Wilde's; W. S. Gilbert said of his Hamlet, 'At last we can settle whether Bacon or Shakespeare wrote the plays. Have the coffins opened and whichever has turned in his grave is the author.')

Bourchier's career, launched with the OUDS, has been an example down the decades and one followed by hundreds of aspirant Oxford actors and directors, from Nigel Playfair, Gyles Isham and Emlyn Williams right through to Kenneth Tynan, Sandy Wilson, Richard Burton, Diana Quick (the first woman president of OUDS), Katie Mitchell (the second) and Imogen Stubbs. The same sort of pattern emerged in Cambridge, and other colleges and universities, soon afterwards. But while the modern theatre was evolving at the turn of the century through the spread of the amateur theatre movement, the energy of students and the emergence of a socialist and New Woman agenda both here and in Europe, there was still time – just about – for a few late flurries of the old-style private theatricals.

And none were more flamboyantly executed than those of Henry Cyril Paget, fifth Marquis of Anglesey, in his converted chapel on the family estate at Plas Newydd. For two years from 1899, the bill of fare was mostly a sort of variety bill featuring local amateurs and some touring professionals for the benefit of tenants, guests and local notables. In 1901 he fitted out the theatre with electric stage lighting, re-opened the place as a public entertainment venue and lured, with huge payments, an entire professional company who had been playing in Llandudno. For the next three years he toured with his own company around Britain and Europe, appearing himself in pantomime and musical comedy in costumes so lavish and bejewelled that he needed an army of dressers all of his own. According to the historian Christopher Simon Sykes he and his company travelled with specially painted scenery in five trucks, their own orchestra, and with props made as exact copies of furniture in the Anglesey castle.

By 1904, according to another historian, Viv Gardner, Paget had bankrupted the estate, 'spending thousands of pounds on jewels, furs, cars, boats, perfumes and potions, toys, medicines, dogs, horses and theatricals on a scale unimagined even among the profligate Edwardian aristocracy. Everything was sold to meet his debts, down to the contents of the potting shed and a parrot in a brass cage.' The marquis himself used to parade through London carrying a poodle decked out in pink ribbons. Shortly after being declared bankrupt, and six months before he died in 1905, aged 29 in Monte Carlo, he told the *Daily Mail*, 'I must apologise for not appearing before you in peacock-blue plush wearing a diamond and sapphire tiara, a turquoise dog-collar, ropes of pearls and slippers studded with Burma rubies; but I prefer, and always have preferred, Scotch tweed.'

The antics of the Marquis signal the highwater mark of private theatricals and also their demise. The theatre generally, thanks to the inroads at the Royal Court made by Bernard Shaw, Harley Granville Barker and their colleagues, was changing, and the reinvented modern amateur theatre was endemic to that process. Fêtes and fireworks were a thing of the past, except on special occasions, and then for all to share, and in public. The archives of the Old Stagers in Canterbury contain detailed information of amateur theatricals, or 'spouting clubs' as they were sometimes called, proliferating across the country. And with this wresting, as it were, of the amateur dramatics of private theatricals – both high and low – from what in many respects were secret societies, the great national enterprise began. The campaign for a National Theatre was a symbolic statement of public intent, seriousness and social diversity.

3

Whatever Happened in Ilford?

My first experience of amateur theatre was in the town where I grew up in the 1950s and 1960s, Ilford in Essex. It seems therefore the best place to start a journey of discovery, and recovery, in my salad days when, like Shakespeare's Cleopatra, I was green in judgement, cold in blood ... and highly susceptible to the roar of the greasepaint, the smell of the crowd. It was glamorous – it was all I knew – and I was drawn to the activities of a small amateur company, the Renegades, and its eccentric, charismatic leader, like a moth to a flame.

For me, as a pupil at the local Catholic primary school, my life in the Ilford, Goodmayes, Seven Kings and Chadwell Heath area was bounded by football, school plays, more football and weekly piano lessons. The latter were dispensed by a large, handsome German mezzo soprano called Mrs O'Keeffe, married to an Irish railway worker, who lived two or three doors along the street. Although Mr O'Keeffe worked on the tracks in orange overalls, he set off to work each morning in a pin-striped suit and bowler while his wife, the Kirsten Flagstad of Seven Kings, bullied and cajoled her pupils whose parents had no idea of the landscapes she was conjuring for them.

As far as my folks were concerned, Mrs O'Keeffe offered a convenient (and fairly cheap) way of getting my brother and me out of their hair for a couple of hours each week. They acquired a fuzzy-toned second-hand upright piano for £5 and several books of arpeggios, scales and pieces for beginners as directed. Even when I crossed town every day to a north London grammar school in September 1959, I continued my piano lessons until I was competent enough to accompany Mrs O'Keeffe heaving her vast bosom through 'Softly Awakes My Heart' from *Samson and Delilah* in the annual pupils' concert in the Seven Kings library hall. Mr O'Keeffe was odd enough, but I harboured even odder feelings for Mrs O'Keeffe, whose strict, lustrous, heavily-scented tutorial proximity to me at the keyboard brought on my first pre-adolescent hot flushes.

The Ilford Palais and the Room at the Top in Harrison Gibson's department store were renowned night spots just beyond the East End in this first Essex staging post en route to Romford, Hornchurch, Billericay and Southend-on-Sea. And situated just behind Harrison Gibson was, for fifteen years from the mid-1950s, the Little Theatre, home of the Renegades, Ilford's leading amateur theatre company.

By the mid-1960s, theatre had joined football and piano-playing as a third time-consuming enthusiasm: my brother and I started going 'up to town' via Liverpool Street Station for as many as three shows a day on a Saturday. Sample outing in December 1966: 2.15pm, Maggie Smith and Robert Stephens in *Much Ado About Nothing* at the Old Vic (Ian McKellen as Claudio); 6pm, Joe Orton's *Loot* at the Criterion; 8.30pm, *On Approval* by Frederick Lonsdale (Edward and James Fox's grandfather) with Michael Denison and Dulcie Gray at the St Martin's.

Our father had taken us to see the RSC's *Wars of the Roses* and the David Warner *Hamlet* at Stratford-upon-Avon in 1965. And so, of course, we joined the Renegades, which presented one play a month and met, as a club and for rehearsals, three nights a week, under the direction of James Cooper, one of the most extraordinary, cantankerous, dedicated and inspirational people I have known.

Harrison Gibson was virtually opposite the Ilford Town Hall, one of a few fine Victorian buildings in the town, where, in November 1948, aged thirty-two, James Cooper played Hamlet and was noticed in the national press by the *News Chronicle* as a worthy pioneer, taking good theatre 'to the outskirts.' The critic Alan Dent, a fairly hard-to-please Scotsman and friend and colleague of James Agate, the great critic who had just been succeeded on the *Sunday Times* by Harold Hobson, declared that Cooper was by no means the least considerable of the eight Hamlets he had seen that year, an octet that included Paul Scofield and Robert Helpmann alternating in the role at Stratford-upon-Avon. And he concluded: 'This is a capital amateur company. They are young and zestful and, unlike some professionals, they make a point of audibility.'

Cooper had worked as a dancer on the south coast and as a stage manager for Noël Coward in the war when he, Cooper, was running a theatre in Nairobi. He was the scion of a family brush business in Barking, next door to Ilford, and he headed straight back there on being demobbed. He acquired three blue pin-striped suits in Morris Angel's, the theatrical costumiers, treated himself to a few days in the Strand Palace Hotel and took a letter of introduction from Coward himself to the all-powerful producer of the day, Binkie Beaumont of H. M. Tennent.

This resulted, he said, in an understudy role in *The Man Who Came to Dinner* starring Robert Morley at the Savoy Theatre, though as Morley had finished with the play in London and on tour by 1943, Jimmie – as he was generally and affectionately known – was perhaps getting his dates and details muddled, not for the first or indeed the last time.

The main point, though, was that the role of understudy was simply not in his repertoire. In later life he indeed played the Morley role in *The Man Who Came to Dinner*. But as Ilford's leading theatre personality and its biggest fish in a fairly small pond, he was not only the man who came to dinner, he also sat at the head of the table, supervised the guest list, prepared the menu, cooked the meal, washed the dishes and locked up when everyone else had gone home.

He ran the Renegades from 1947 until its dispersal in 1984, three years before his death in 1987, directing every single play (over 400 of them all told, one a month), in which he invariably took the leading role; built and painted the sets; manned the box office; did the lighting and soundtrack, the posters and the programmes.

Cooper set about creating theatre in a town that had lost its sole remaining dedicated theatre space when the Ilford Hippodrome was hit by a bomb in January 1945, blowing Renée Houston, busy slapping her thighs in *Robinson Crusoe*, clean off the stage, though the band played on while the audience filed out to the street. Cooper, born during the First World War, and his family, would have visited more than once this great 1909 Frank Matcham palace of varieties on the Ilford Broadway, a sister theatre to the Lewisham Hippodrome and the London Palladium, with seating for 2,500. The bill of fare included names such as Max Miller, Vera Lynn, George Formby, Tommy Trinder, Richard Tauber and Gracie Fields, though it operated as a cinema between 1924 and 1938.

The Hippodrome stood as an empty shell for a decade before being demolished in 1957 after pieces of falling masonry hit a passing bus. By then, Cooper had opened Ilford's new and only theatre. This one was the extreme opposite of anything designed by Frank Matcham: a disused reading room half a mile or so further along the High Street. The age of the big popular Victorian theatres in the provinces was coming to an end. In Ilford, as in so many places, the torch was taken up by the amateur theatre and that meant idealistic intervention by theatre-loving individuals in consort with sympathetic local councils.

Cooper was very different from many of the other amateur theatre champions around the country, who tended to be middle-class, educated men (and women) of letters driven by, broadly speaking, socialist principles. Cooper was relatively uneducated, deeply opposed to the tenets of state-funding as represented by the newly formed Arts Council and not particularly interested in the new European theatre of Brecht, Pirandello, Karel Capek, Bernard Shaw and so on, who feature prominently in the early repertoire of the Little Theatre Guild members.

He sought exemplary sustenance instead from the old-style actor managers, West End hits and careers of his heroes: Olivier, Coward and the brilliant American Jewish entertainer Danny Kaye, to whom he bore an uncanny resemblance in physical fluency, high-cheek-boned facial mobility and a wavy, Brylcreamed hairstyle. And, like Kaye, Olivier and Coward – indeed like all the stars in those days – he smoked cigarettes, the first and most consistently present of his personal properties onstage and off.

I've never known anyone else who smoked Cooper's preferred brand of cigarettes, Perfectos. Certainly no-one else in Ilford did. But then, no-one else in Ilford swanned along the Cranbrook Road to Planter's coffee emporium wearing a barathea blazer, beautifully tied silk cravat and a camel hair overcoat draped casually over his shoulders and staying there while he weaved through crowds of shoppers in a fast, unbroken ambulation as though heading for a perfectly timed downstage entrance.

All the world really was a stage to Cooper. Continuing past Planter's and heading towards Valentine's Park – where he and his actors rehearsed in the open air in the first days of the Renegades – he would now, were he alive, pass a pub called the Great Spoon of Ilford with a prominently displayed statue of Shakespeare's clown Will Kemp in the front bar as he started out on his nine-day jig to Norwich.

Kemp wrote in his account of the expedition that, on the first day, he had fled an over-subscribed bear-baiting in Stratford and arrived in Ilford

> where I again rested, and was by the people of the town and country thereabouts very well welcomed, being offered carouses in the great spoon, the whole draught being able at that time to have drawn my little wit dry, but being afraid of the old proverb – He had need of a long spoon that eats with the devil – I soberly gave my boon companions the slip.

Although he was generally known, and without any hint of wry deprecation, as Ilford's Mr Theatre, Cooper's struggle to achieve his goal – run his own company in a theatre he controlled – was as titanic, and as much a test of his endurance, as the higher-profile campaigns of Joan Littlewood at Stratford East or Peter Hall at the National Theatre. It was uphill all the way, and not made any easier by the fact that his default mode with authority figures, and especially town councillors, was abrasive to put it mildly.

He decided to leave his brother to look after the brush business while he set about his task, and he started off as a critic. He bought a two-shilling ticket at the Town Hall to see the Plessey Dramatic Society (the Plessey electronics company had their headquarters in Ilford) in Gerald Savory's comedy *George and Margaret* and was so incensed by its inadequacy as a production, and its anodyne marks-out-of-ten reception in the local press, that he wrote a scalding letter to the *Ilford Recorder*. He caused ructions on the letters page and was promptly invited to be the paper's theatre critic.

This tactic of self-promotion was uncannily echoed a few years later when Kenneth Tynan, just starting out, and appearing as the Player King in Alec Guinness's 1951 production of *Hamlet*, responded audaciously to a review by Beverley Baxter in the *Evening Standard* – 'I am a man of a kindly nature, who takes no joy in hurting those who are without defence, but Mr Ken Tynan would not get a chance in a village hall unless he was related to the vicar. His performance was quite dreadful' – with an open letter declaring that his performance was 'not quite dreadful but, in fact, only slightly less than mediocre.' This splendid bit of cheek led almost directly to Tynan's appointment as Baxter's successor; he had already targeted Baxter, while still at Oxford, for being over the hill and beyond the pale.

Cooper wrote under the name of Aeacus who, in Greek mythology, was the son of Zeus and a fearsome judge in Hades. But he soon swapped writing for doing. He advertised for actors in 1946 and one of those who responded, and stayed with him for the full forty years, Lila Myra, Ilford's answer to smoky-voiced Betty Marsden, doyenne of radio comedy in the 1960s, consulted an oracle. 'Myra has been to a psalmist,' wrote another founder Renegade, Gladys Lee, in her diary, 'who told her the company will be a big success; she has much faith in things psychic being mildly mediumistic herself,' and she would, of course, duly play Madame Arcati in Coward's *Blithe Spirit*.

Cooper declared the Renegades open for business with a production of Terence Rattigan's *Flare Path* in a Quaker meeting house in Barking in January 1947. The programme carried good wishes from Rattigan and Coward, and a personal post-war manifesto: 'This theatre was born out of the recent conflict, and in the knowledge that every community needs a centre where they and their children can enjoy the best in entertainment.'

Unfortunately, according to Gladys, the sound effects went wrong and the curtain got caught up on a hook, but the audience of about 200 put £6 in the plate, half of which went to the local Dr Barnardo's orphanage. Jimmie cheered up, too, said Gladys ten days after the opening, 'much brighter after lunching on five gins,' and the Renegades made what was technically their Ilford debut with the same play at Ilford County High School in February.

The cast included a vivacious, dark-haired schoolteacher at my future primary school, Roma de Roeper, who before long became Cooper's lover. The company was peripatetic around Barking and Ilford for several years, but Cooper found some abandoned garages next to the Thompson Rooms (the reading room, later the Little Theatre) where he could at least build and store scenery and props. He was married at the time to Mary Powell, also a budding local amateur actress. They lived over a shop with their daughter, but Jimmie jumped ship with Roma, just as he cut all ties with his family firm, and moved into a converted hayloft at the rear of Ilford Station where the dried grass had once been stored for the railway horses. Mary, in turn, and much later on, in 1972, formed a rival amateur group, the Redbridge Stage Company (or the 'other RSC,' as it became known) with one Graham Wright whom she married. Cooper dubbed his loft, which you climbed into like some theatrical bivouac after ascending a very rickety staircase in a mews by the station's back entrance, The Stables; it would remain his home, as well as the Renegades' meeting place, for the rest of his life.

For seven years, the company continued to perform in halls, schools and even hospitals in the area. For a production of *Antigone* in Seven Kings

FIGURE 3 *Roma de Roeper and James Cooper in John Patrick's psychological thriller* The Two Mrs Carrolls, *presented by the Ilford Renegades in their inaugural season in 1947.*

library in 1951, Jimmie wanted a very young heroine and asked Roma's advice. She knew of a startling young schoolgirl actress at the Ilford Ursuline Convent School she herself had attended. They went along to see Yvonne Haesendonck in a school play and Cooper not only found his Antigone, but also his future leading lady, and lifetime boon companion, once she had completed her schooling and spent a year in France as an *au pair*. Roma was considerably put out by developments, not to say heart-broken – Jimmie was undoubtedly the only true love of her life – though the two women rubbed along together with Jimmie for several years until Roma decamped to the Midlands and became a leading light at the Crescent Theatre in Birmingham.

John Woodvine, the future RSC 'heavy' and an actor of great voice and gravitas, was the Chorus (Jimmie was Creon) in *Antigone*. He had previously been Claudius – Roma was Gertrude – in the Town Hall *Hamlet*. After six or seven years of solid campaigning, and a growing undertow of local support, Cooper succeeded in his suggestion to the council of converting the Thompson Rooms into the Little Theatre at a cost of £10,000 with a seating capacity, on one level, of 212. The only drawback, as far as he was concerned, was that he was obliged to share the new facility with other amateur companies.

Still, the Renegades opened the theatre in May 1954 with Thornton Wilder's *Our Town*, one of Jimmie's favourite plays. The cast included Dudley Stevens (later a renowned character actor in West End musicals and at the Players in Charing Cross) as the young boy developing into manhood; Jimmie as the stage manager (obviously); and Roma and the equally formidable, though less stylish, Lila Myra as the two mothers.

The show, which came with good wishes from the author, Sybil Thorndike, Olivier and John Gielgud, was a smash, and the local press saluted the Renegades as 'the inspiration and powerhouse of local theatre.' There was only one mishap on opening night: the tank for the toilets had been placed in the rafters above the auditorium and, during the mayor's welcome speech, there was heard a continuous loud flushing noise as opposed to a more desirable quiet 'hushing' noise in the stalls. The tank was turned off before the play started. Queues for the interval loos were as long as those soon forming at the box office.

The Little Theatre was owned and operated by the council, who made the premises available to some ten established amateur companies, while the existing musical and operatic societies, including the illustrious Ilford Operatic and Dramatic Society, which had presented big musical shows at both the Hippodrome and the Town Hall since its formation in 1919, continued to use the Town Hall.

An Ilford Theatre Guild was formed in order to try and control the programme from repeating or doubling back on itself and foster cooperation and camaraderie. Cooper rapidly grew impatient with any cooperative or indeed comradely spirit that came his way. He rescinded the membership of the Renegades in 1958, cocking a snook and asserting his independence by presenting, in February 1959, the European stage premiere of Reginald Rose's *Twelve Angry Men*, originally a television play before becoming the movie starring Henry Fonda – whose character was played by Cooper, who else, in Ilford.

Apart from the outstanding annual pantomime – he was always an expert dame – Cooper regularly pulled special rabbits out of the hat throughout the 1960s. In 1964, the playwright Duncan Greenwood –who wrote a string of successful West End farces with Philip King (sole author of *See How They Run*, one of the greatest of all British farces) – was travelling home to London from Southend when he saw a Renegades poster, stopped off to see the show, liked it, got talking to Cooper and went home to write *No Time For Fig Leaves*, a comedy about women running the world after an atomic accident. The Renegades presented the world premiere in August 1964. In the following year Greenwood gave them another play, *In at the Death*, a comedy thriller, which I saw shortly afterwards at the Phoenix Theatre in the West End starring Terence Alexander, Jean Kent and Charles Stapley (Stapley, as it happens, was born in Ilford and educated at Ilford County High School).

It was around this time I gravitated towards the centre of the Renegades myself, on the brink of going up to Oxford while working my way through a preparatory reading list. My brother Martin, who later trained as an actor at the Guildford School of Dance and Drama, in the same 1969 intake as Celia Imrie and Bill Nighy, had already appeared in a Renegades pantomime and, most memorably, as young Ronnie Winslow, accused of stealing a five-shilling postal order, in Rattigan's *The Winslow Boy*. I tagged along, making myself useful for the Old Tyme Music Hall evenings on the piano and proving my unsuitability for the stage as an actor by making a hash of the tremulous young Geordie radio operator in Willis Hall's superb Malaysian jungle play, *The Long and the Short and the Tall*.

Before I decamped to gad about among the dreaming spires, Cooper staged one of his very finest productions – the 1945 Appalachian Mountains ballad melodrama *Dark of The Moon* by Howard Richardson and William Berney – for the Redbridge Arts Festival of 1967 (the enlarged borough of Redbridge, encompassing Ilford, Wanstead, parts of Dagenham and Chigwell, had been created in 1965). The play had been first and famously directed in London by Peter Brook in 1948 as a sort of folksy dry run for his brilliant *Marat/Sade* at the RSC in 1964, another outbreak of mass hysteria, only this time in an asylum, not a religious outback.

Dark of the Moon contains an element of hocus pocus in the tale of Barbara Allen (as in the folk song) and the witch boy, John, who falls in love with her. The cast is huge, so Jimmie roped me in to play a young lad who owns up to an episode of adolescent lust, along with his girlfriend, in a revivalist meeting. The energy and rhythm of the play is so strong that I can quote to this day my confession speech – I suppose I'd had years of humiliating practice while going to weekly confession in the Catholic church.

My penitent girlfriend was played by a gem of an actress, Angela Groombridge, married to John Wallbank, a jazz musician and professional technical operations manager for Joan Littlewood at nearby Stratford East, and later production manager for the impresario Eddie Kulukundis. The 'dirty old man' of the community, Uncle Smellicue, was played by Leslie Robinson, father of Baldrick in *Black Adder* actor and Labour Party activist Tony Robinson, one of several members of the Wanstead Players, reputedly the oldest amateur theatre company in Essex and East London (founded in 1929). He, and other non-Renegades, were cast by Jimmie to fulfil – reluctantly, as far as he was concerned – the brief of providing a festival production more fully representative of the new borough than just his own company.

The witch boy himself was played by the distinguished Australian dancer and choreographer Noel Tovey who brought a vibrating physicality and spiritual 'otherness' to the role. Noel was between professional engagements and had answered an advertisement in *The Stage*, renewing an earlier contact with Jimmie when the latter directed him as the lunatic Renfield in *Dracula* at the Little Theatre Club in Garrick Yard, off St Martin's Lane in the West End. This venue – which became a stronghold of small fringe companies at the end of the 1960s – had been founded by Valery Hovenden in the 1940s as a place for professional actors to work when out of paid employment. She always laid on a supply of apples and red wine.

This led to Noel's first performance at the Renegades, in a stage adaptation of Alfred Hitchcock's *Shadow of a Doubt* in 1962 – adapted from Thornton Wilder's screenplay – in which he appeared with Jimmie and Roma de Roeper. Noel said that *Dark of the Moon* was 'one of the most rewarding experiences that I'd had in London' – and he worked successfully here for thirty years before returning to Australia as a trailblazer for indigenous people. His searing account, *Little Black Bastard*, of his trials and tribulations in an abusive Aboriginal childhood was part of his advocacy for underprivileged artists and non-artists alike.

Noel was unusual in coming into the Renegades from the professional theatre, though he made no differentiation in his approach to work, amateur or professional:

> Everything that I did I approached as a professional, even working with Jimmie, who always paid my bus or train fares. I worked with some very talented people in amateur theatre. The difference between them and me was that it was the only career I wanted. I cannot begin to even tell you how difficult it was for me but regardless I pressed on.

More typical, perhaps, was the participation of John Woodvine, starting out with Jimmie, or of local lad Ken Campbell, founder of the kamikaze fringe theatre group The Ken Campbell Road Show, and mad monologist extraordinaire, continuing his association with Renegades while studying at RADA. Campbell also brought along some of his contemporaries at the drama school – Larry Linville of *M*A*S*H* fame, Bernard Lloyd of the RSC (then plain Bernard Gibbons) and John Alderton all played roles in *The Merchant of Venice* with Jimmie as Shylock.

Jimmie introduced his RADA protégés at the curtain call, announcing Bernard Gibbons as 'Bernard Cribbins,' which drew a puzzled round of applause from the audience (Cribbins had recently had two top ten songs in the pop charts, 'The Hole in the Ground' and 'Right Said Fred,' and was already famous; this unknown Cribbins, listed as Gibbons in the programme, was an imposter). Liz Robertson – daughter of an Ilford bobby, herself a West End musicals star and eighth wife of *My Fair Lady* lyricist Alan Jay Lerner – featured in several Renegades pantomimes as lead dancer with the local Betty Finch Stage School. And West End producer and casting director Denise Sylvey caught the bug big-time both on stage and in The Stables where the company assembled on the Monday after the previous show's last night.

Those of us who had not appeared in the show were required to read out a written account of what we'd thought of it. And that is how I first stumbled into being a critic. There were two hard lessons to learn and I've never forgotten them. First, a critic can rarely tell a writer, director or actor something they do not know already or hadn't at least secretly acknowledged (this does not necessarily apply to the most delusional of writers, directors and actors, who tend to be more prevalent in the amateur theatre, just about, than in the professional ranks). So don't think, ever, you're giving 'notes'. Second, learning how to say exactly what you think to the faces of those involved in the show, which means bolstering praise and dispraise equally with good argument, in order to undercut the embarrassment of gush on the one hand and unwarranted abuse on the other. There was nothing wrong with a good old dose of rudeness, as long as it was funny and well expressed. That became my mantra, of necessity, really, as I was incapable of aspiring to the admirable example of Irving Wardle who always advised putting in print only what you could say, without squirming, to the face of the person or people involved.

I think Jimmie encouraged these in-house reviews partly because he loved to take issue with them and partly in the hope that his actors more readily understood that it wasn't just him who could give them a hard time. And he sportingly allowed the rank and file to give *him* a hard time. No-one excelled at this more than did the cheerful and combustible red-faced house manager, Blagdon Mansfield, whose marvellous name was surely some compensation for the fact that, in real life, he was a milkman. The Renegades of the 1960s was awash with striking and original personalities, and the memory of them huddled together in that smoke-filled garret, reading and rehearsing plays, or discussing world affairs, has never faded.

Jimmie, who was troubled with stomach ulcers, and often visibly racked with pain, lay on his chaise longue, smoking his Perfectos and sipping milky coffee, while everyone else in the room vied for attention, hoping not to be, as often happened, cut down at the knees. Yvonne – who ran a highly successful career as a top-ranking company secretary at Simpson's in Piccadilly – would potter about upstairs, ministering to Jimmie's needs, while brave company members like Leonard Charles, a senior civil servant, and Frank House, the amiable stage manager who worked in the health service and smoked like a chimney, took issue with the more outlandish of their leader's assertions.

Noel Tovey certainly enlivened and entertained the gathering while he was there, and another Australian, the flame-haired Margot Kenrick, was the nearest we had to a Scarlet Woman, in manner and style at least. She oozed sex appeal, frankly, and took up with (and married) a much younger Renegade, Stephen Knight, a local journalist who wrote a best-selling fiction about Jack the Ripper and died tragically of a brain tumour aged just thirty-three in 1985.

As I drifted away, these vignettes only sharpened in retrospect, just as other Renegades in my time there relished the stories and myths of Roma de Roeper and other earlier star turns. There was the mysterious Francis Dalvin, a man of apparently limitless independent means, who collected African sculpture and lived in the only orange-painted house in nearby Manor Park, which in turn featured the only sunken bath and black bedroom in all of Essex. He also had a manservant – an even more exotic rarity in those parts. Dalvin's manner was aloof bordering on the humorously disdainful. Turning up for a rehearsal one evening, a fellow Renegade greeted him with, 'Hello, Francis, me old fruit . . .' to which he replied, 'I am not yours, I am not old, and I am not . . . well, you may have a point . . .'

Most extraordinary of all were Jimmie's favourite Ugly Sisters, the double-act of tall, suave Milton Cats, the manager of a local underwear business, and short, busy little Tod Hunter, a professional chicken-sexer, a highly specialised job which involves somehow identifying a chick's gender at birth. Cats, who hailed from Zimbabwe, was an excellent cook and a dab hand at whipping up a dress at the last minute if needed. His partner ran the Piccadilly Theatre and, when Shirley Bassey did a show there, Cats worked as her dresser. He was, as he exclaimed to anyone who'd care to listen, 'in seventh heaven'. He ended his days cooking for an old people's home in Wales. Toddy was a bitch, Jimmie told me, 'but you couldn't help liking him – except if you had to be on the same stage with him!'

Roger the Renegade, a cautionary and diversionary tale

Another of the regular Renegades who juggled his appearances with a professional career is Roger Sansom, an enchantingly committed old-school actor who knows what he's talking about and respects the traditions of his craft. He has, for many years, occupied a sort of twilight zone of touring, fringe and amateur work, all of it conducted in a professional spirit and with an appealing seriousness, by which I mean Roger takes himself seriously, even if other people might not.

Every actor, to a greater or lesser extent, has to cope with the hidden, usually unstated, ridicule of those who think what he does is essentially futile and self-regarding. Even Kenneth Branagh has defined his job as 'shouting in the evenings,' and the fine Irish actor James Hayes used that phrase as the title of his memoir of fifty years on the professional stage. Highs, lows, the elation and the indignities really are common to professionals and amateurs alike.

What is less common in someone like Roger Sansom is his encyclopaedic knowledge of the business and of Shakespeare in particular. In 1994, he won the title 'Bard Brain of Britain' in a BBC 2 television quiz chaired by Robert Robinson on which his fellow finalists were seasoned academics. All the same, Roger has only ever understudied in the West End, his name never remotely in lights and, in 1995, spent a whole year clocking in and not 'going on' in three separate productions – his roles were taken instead by George Cole in *Theft* by Eric Chappell, Sam Kelly in *Dead Funny* by Terry Johnson at the Savoy and Gerald Harper in a revival of Barry England's *Conduct Unbecoming*. The interesting thing here is that Roger was not really suited to any of those roles, but he loved being part of the show. The producers knew that, if he had had to go on, he would have done so competently enough.

And the audience would have heard him. For Roger has a voice. Some say that is all he has, and he is the first to point out that physical suavity is not his strongest suit. It's not even his everyday jacket and trousers. The critic James Agate once said that, when playing Romeo, John Gielgud – *the* voice of theatre in our time – had the most meaningless legs imaginable. Kenneth Tynan added insult to injury by declaring that Gielgud was the best actor in England . . . from the neck up. 'He says I've only two gestures,' moaned Sir John, 'left hand up, right hand down. Right hand up, left hand down; what does he want me to do, bring out my cock?'

Like Gielgud's voice, Roger's is strong, mellifluous, well-modulated and expressive. And he developed his passion for verse-speaking with one of his chief mentors, Kenneth McLennan, a jobbing actor over several decades, son of a theatre manager, who ran Shakespeare classes in his mildewed and untended flat in Battersea for many years. Roger thinks he probably took things too far with his insistence on the paramount importance of the verse but reckons you have to know the rules before you can claim to make them work for you as an actor.

Part of the tragi-comic side of Roger's story is that, although he was, he thought, a born actor, he was at first rejected by the profession he insisted on joining. At the age of seventeen, and after just one year's training, he was thrown out of RADA. One can only imagine the effect this had on him. An only child in Ilford, he had spent most of his Saturday afternoons at the Old Vic watching Shakespeare and learning cast lists off by heart – cultivating his obsession otherwise with television broadcasts such as 'Scenes from the Dream' performed by Robert Atkins and his company. He still possesses the programme of an Old Vic *Julius Caesar*, the first play he saw, and reels off the names: Jack May as Caesar and Octavius ('a semi-traditional casting double in those days'), John Phillips as Brutus, Michael Hordern as Cassius, Derek Francis as Casca, and Edward Hardwicke as Flavius uttering the first lines in an actor's voice he ever heard in a grown-up play – 'Hence! Home, you idle creatures, get you home. Is this a holiday?'

At school, he wrote to RADA and was accepted after delivering audition speeches of Richard II (still his favourite role and Shakespeare play) and, for comedy, one of the impostor Khlestakhov in Gogol's *The Government Inspector*. At RADA, Roger admits, he was a gangly seventeen-year-old who didn't know his left foot from his right, but that was no excuse or consolation for what happened to him, along with several others in his term's intake. They were unceremoniously 'dropped' as part, he now thinks, of a clearing-the-decks operation towards the end of John Fernald's tenure as principal. Nothing like this, they were told, had happened before, and it certainly hasn't happened since, except for the occasional disciplinary measure.

One of his dropped classmates, Letty Ferrer – the daughter of Jose Ferrer and Uta Hagen, one of the power couples of the modern American theatre – camped on Fernald's doorstep, demanding to be reinstated. (She wasn't, but has pursued a successful career anyway, as an actress and teacher, in the States.) His confidence shattered, Roger was in no mood to apply straight away to some other drama schools. Instead, he continued in the part-time job he'd begun as a student, dressing RSC actors backstage at the Aldwych Theatre. He even managed to convince himself he'd joined the company when he took part in a few RSC 'fringe' events, notably, he recalls, playing one of Herod's soldiers in a cycle of medieval Mystery plays in Southwark Cathedral (Ian Richardson was Herod; Peter Jeffrey, Jesus).

After three or four years of appearing with the Renegades he felt once again that he should be an actor 'in the larger scene' and resumed his career of fits and starts at Barrow-in-Furness Rep, where he earned his Equity card. In a year's work there, he played the first of the three roles he has taken in *Charley's Aunt* and appeared in an *Oliver Twist*, which had the distinction of being reviewed in the local paper by the woman who had made the adaptation (she liked it). When the panto season came round, he played the royal schoolmaster in *Sleeping Beauty*. At one performance, he was smoking quietly in the wings – couldn't happen now – and must have been partly visible from one side of the auditorium as the whole theatre was regaled with an exclamation from a small boy: 'Look, mum, the teacher's smoking!'

He never played romantic leads, and not a single young part until his late twenties. He had been told, correctly, that he would grow into his age as an actor, and that kept him going while he worked in a bank throughout the 1980s and resumed his other life as an amateur. As a professional – or, in his case, 'occasionally paid' actor and more usually very low-paid – he has worked with the late Richard Griffiths in *Under Milk Wood* at the Arts in Belfast after playing in a schools' tour of Northern Ireland; played Leonato in *Much Ado* for the Guildford Shakespeare Company; Pastor Manders in *Ghosts* at the Wimbledon Studio; and many other leading classical roles in a number of more marginal London fringe venues – the Drayton Arms, Teatro Technis, Camden People's Theatre and the Pentameters in Hampstead.

This latter venue, at the top of a pub in the middle of Hampstead village, is one of the oddest places of all. It is run by a delightfully scatty survivor of the 1960s, Léonie Scott-Matthews, and her partner Godfrey Old, a long-haired elderly jazz musician usually decked out in a tatterdemalion black suit and topper, giving him the curious appearance, as he silently leans forward proffering programmes, of a cross between Tiny Tim and Uriah Heep. Léonie has put on poetry readings and plays around several Hampstead pub venues over the years, counting such luminaries as Harold Pinter, Edna O'Brien, Dannie Abse and Roger McGough among her early performers and supporters. She operates entirely without subsidy – not much of what she puts on would tick too many Arts Council boxes anyway – and greets all patrons personally at the box office, taking names and emails to comply with her licensing conditions. Godfrey designs posters and T-shirts for the theatre, which Léonie has stuffed full with old playbills, photographs and art work, dolls' houses and cuddly toys, and unidentifiable bric-a-brac of all kinds. There's a curious conjunction here between the oddness of the setting and the badness of the acting, which makes for a strangely refreshing experience. And then someone like Roger comes along who can put in a decent claim for the serious theatre even when playing a tiny part of a judge or court usher, though he has also played Robert in Priestley's *Dangerous Corner*, Boss Mangan in Shaw's *Heartbreak House* and Malvolio in *Twelfth Night*.

Roger doesn't have an agent, but does have several loyal colleagues who often employ him – directors Harry Meacher (a former National Theatre player and, indeed, Renegade) and Bryan Hands (who was the stage director at Barrow in Roger's time there). He is also on the books of the Professional Casting Report (PCR), a contact service that doesn't charge clients for the jobs they obtain through them. 'A good many jobs I've done,' he says, 'have in fact been sub-jobs in that they are paid, but not anything like Equity rates.'

Increasingly, professional actors on the fringe are unprotected by Equity and work for no wages, minimal or token wages, or sometimes a bus fare. This is where the professional and amateur worlds really do find common ground, but there can be a sense of hostility and misunderstanding on both sides. The great differences persist in the conditions of work and the approach. I was shocked to learn at a Little Theatre Guild conference that virtually all of the delegates hardly ever had a complete cast together over the whole length of the rehearsal period until the final weeks. The intensity of amateur theatre is concentrated into the performance and rarely in rehearsals on two or three nights a week over a period of months.

If an actor in a professional show takes a prompt early in the proceedings, it unsettles the evening, but I have noticed that audiences at amateur theatre don't seem to mind this at all. Roger concurs:

The culture of amateur theatre tends to take 'drying' in its stride and considers that the solution is the shout-out from prompt corner, and that's that. I do think that the idea of an audience hearing a prompt is a sort of line in the sand between amateur and professional theatre, much more so than the issue of non-payment. I have never taken a prompt myself and I suspect that, were I to take one, I should probably give up altogether on the spot.

Which is not to say that I have never been in an awkward situation on stage. Once, playing Gaev in *The Cherry Orchard*, I returned in distress from the auction, but had to make an entrance down a small flight of stairs in the Wimbledon Studio [the room where, in the 1920s, Fred Astaire and his sister Adèle rehearsed their West End revues]. I was probably too bound up in my feelings of loss and sadness and I stumbled badly, but the actress playing my sister, Carola Stewart, rushed to my aid. And comforted me with a helpful ad lib, which was absolutely right. Other actors might have ignored me and let me end up sprawling on my backside in tears.

Roger sympathises with my reaction that I would have paid good money to see such an entertaining catastrophe, the point at which we can relish amateur theatre for conforming to its own stereotype as a source of masochistic fun and disaster. We all relish such mishaps, but this does not prevent us acknowledging the serious side of things, too. And for an actor like Roger Sansom with an indefinite status in the world of theatre, the amateur stage allows him to play the sort of roles not so easily come by in the professional ranks.

At the end of the day, the theatre is about actors and audiences whichever way you slice it, dress it up, or dress it down. Survival is a relative virtue, perhaps, but the main thing for most serious amateurs, and for their slightly more exalted colleagues in the twilight zone, is that they continue to do something in the theatre, anything at all. That may sound vainglorious, but if you don't understand this much about the theatre, I'd suggest you don't understand anything at all about it.

Even as it happened, the history of the Renegades was a kind of time capsule. The core Renegades repertoire was rooted in the first half of the twentieth century of popular theatre before the advent of kitchen sink drama and the embryonic fringe. So, it was always Terence Rattigan, never John Osborne; old warhorses like *Maria Marten* and *Peg of my Heart*, never young fillies in the Royal Court stable. There was the occasional Ibsen, Arthur Miller or Tennessee Williams, but Jimmie's instincts and preferences were at one with those of the Ilford audience in their thirties and forties who, like him, had survived the war and wanted to reaffirm their lives in the theatre culture they understood best.

And that meant plays like *Blithe Spirit*, *The Happiest Days of Your Life*, *Gaslight*, *The Diary of Anne Frank*, *Arsenic and Old Lace*, *Sailor Beware* and, especially, *See How They Run*. Philip King's farce was a staple of the repertoire in both amateur and professional weekly rep after the Second World War, not just because of its brilliance, but because of its nostalgic evocation of war-time entertainment. The village idyll – the fictional setting is Merton-cum-Middlewick – is submerged in the consequences of the hapless vicar's cheeky wife (she wears trousers, for heaven's sake) resuming a war-time dalliance with an actor in uniform; and the rekindling of that onstage passion in Coward's *Private Lives*, the hilarious 1930 comedy, which lit up the war-time gloom in a famous 1944 revival starring John Clements and Kay Hammond.

In her entertaining book of weekly rep anecdotage, *Exit Through the Fireplace*, Kate Dunn (niece of actor Simon Williams, scourge of the amateurs) recounts how one old-school actor manager in a rep revival of *See How They Run*, Charles Denville, greeted the audience like long-lost friends as they turned up before the show and chatted away to them in the two intervals before arriving on stage as the third-act police sergeant. He didn't know a single line, but kept clapping his hands together and saying, 'Now, what shall we do?'

Even the lowliest of amateur revivals, and certainly at the Renegades, do better than that with a play that hovers tantalisingly around the likelihood, as in *Noises Off*, of things going wrong once the play-within-a-play is underway. When the soldier and vicar's wife, Penelope Toop, re-enact Coward's second act fight scene, all hell breaks loose, leading to the climactic line about arresting most of the vicars on the stage. The command is issued by a bishop dressed in pyjamas, while the nonplussed police sergeant (though much less nonplussed than Charles Denville's version of him) tries to establish who's who – 'Which one of you lot is the vicar 'ere?' – as by this time the place is crawling with an escaped German prisoner, the various vicars, a bendy-limbed spinster who's been hitting the sherry bottle and an innocent housemaid who is accused unfairly of being 'an accelerator before the fact'.

Another of the most popular plays at the Renegades was Wynyard Browne's *The Holly and the Ivy,* which had become a 1952 movie starring Ralph Richardson and Margaret Leighton, in which yet another vicar's divided responsibilities towards family and parishioners are resolved in a Norfolk parsonage on Christmas Eve. And still another Renegades' staple, and one containing Yvonne's favourite role of a plain, sex-starved young girl, Fairy May, who sees herself as a great beauty, was a 1950 play called *The Curious Savage* by John Patrick, a whimsical but touching comedy, which on Broadway had starred Lillian Gish as an old widow signing on at a sanatorium with a $10 million fortune, pursued by her grasping stepchildren and finding consolation only with the other inmates.

Jimmie was adamant that *The Curious Savage* was a great play and produced it at least ten times over the years. He was fond, too, of quoting the playwright's epigraph taken from Lord Byron's *Don Juan*: 'And if I laugh at any mortal thing, 'tis that I may not weep.' These titles, many of them referencing war-time and chiming, albeit obliquely, with the experiences of the audiences, while mixing new concerns about relationships between the generations in an often unashamedly nostalgic glow, recur throughout the Little Theatre years, in stark contrast to what many amateur theatres were doing.

And, for the Renegades of my generation, they taught us something of our recent history on both sides of the Atlantic. There was also an intensity of cultural identification in these now mostly derided or forgotten plays, as they spoke directly to audiences, with no need to lecture or harangue. As far as I was concerned, I had plenty of time to come up to date later on with the great upheavals in the American and European theatre, as well as in our own subsidised sector.

Jimmie was fairly well supported in the local press, but it's fair to say that any effective publicity was best generated by Cooper himself kicking up a stink about this or that, finding yet another way of denouncing the council, of biting the hand that more or less fed him. The main commentators on the Renegades in the *Ilford Recorder* were a columnist called Basil Amps and a little Welsh theatre critic, a retired schoolmaster, called John Bright. Neither Amps nor Bright supplied much wattage or shone much of a radiant beam on theatrical matters, but at least there was a healthy non-stop stream of column inches, and Cooper was always good value for copy. He made sure of that.

Things started to change at the end of the 1960s, forcing Jimmie back on the offensive. His next decade began with the loss of the Little Theatre in 1969. Since the creation of the much larger Redbridge borough, the population of Ilford had increased by 40 per cent and the new borough of Redbridge had a total of 250,000 residents.

The Little Theatre was in use forty weeks of the year, often playing to 'House Full' notices. But many of the companies (not the Renegades) felt cramped and frustrated and sensed an opportunity to campaign for a new and bigger purpose-built civic theatre. The idea met an even more sympathetic response from the council when Sainsbury's offered to develop the site of the Little Theatre thus supplying the finance for what became, in 1974, the Kenneth More Theatre, right next to the Town Hall, at a cost of £500,000.

James Cooper wasn't the only person in Ilford who thought that a more appropriate appellation would have been his own name. Meantime, at Jimmie's suggestion, the interim period between the end of the Little and the start of the Kenneth More would be spent in the deconsecrated Wycliffe Congregational Church on Cranbrook Road, near Valentine's Park. The council arranged a seven-year lease with the church authorities, and the venue, now re-named the Cranbrook Theatre, opened in November 1969 with the Renegades' production of Pinero's *Dandy Dick*. The repertoire continued with old favourites such as J. B. Priestley's *Dangerous Corner* and *An Inspector Calls*, *The Diary of Anne Frank* and *The Merchant of Venice*.

As at the Little, the Renegades shared the theatre with the other companies, waiting for the day when they would all go away into the Little Theatre's replacement, which, it now emerged, was to be shared with professional companies. Jimmie had no intention of joining them there. The Kenneth More opened on New Year's Eve 1974 with a production of *The Beggar's Opera* by the KMT's general manager, Vivyan Ellacott, an experienced professional with Welsh National Opera and the renovated Grand Theatre, Swansea, who had been appointed to the post in 1972. Cooper objected most of all to the dilution of the KMT's demarcation line between amateur and professional, and could point defensively to those of his own colleagues who brought their outside professional experience to bear on the seriousness of an essentially amateur enterprise.

This purity of amateurism tempered with the amateur's experience in the real world is what defined the Renegades' character: they included – as well as a smattering of eager youngsters en route to college or drama school – an architect, audio-visual engineer, a lighting engineer, dress designer, company director, deputy headmaster, senior civil servant and an MP's secretary. The latter was Yvonne, who had moved on from Simpson's to work for Jeffrey Archer before he achieved notoriety as a best-selling novelist. Archer's best friend, with whom he shared an office, was the former athlete Adrian Metcalfe, and when Metcalfe was appointed the first head of sport at the newly established Channel 4 television station in 1982, Yvonne followed him there for the rest of her working life.

As the KMT prospered, on the whole (though Jimmie would never admit it), he at least finally achieved full charge of his own theatre when he negotiated a new lease on the Cranbrook for the Renegades alone and re-named it again as the Ilford Playhouse. And he could convince himself of his own doom-laden predictions in pointing out that the KMT only gave the theatre over to the amateurs for half the year. The pantomime there was always a professional show (in name at least), the rest of the programme filled by visiting professional companies and topped up with in-house shows such as a revival of *The Rocky Horror Show*, which went out on tour. So the profile of the KMT was really neither fish nor fowl, with a slightly downmarket regional theatre feel about it.

All the same, Ilford now had two theatres for the first time in living memory. In the short hiatus between the Cranbrook's closure and its re-opening as the Playhouse, the Renegades took two plays on tour to the Leas Pavilion, Folkestone. The new project went ahead with added gusto: the Ilford Playhouse sprang to life through the hard work of all the members and volunteers, led by Cooper, Yvonne and a redoubtable stage manager, Jane Hall – a teacher with a physics degree from Bristol University who had turned up one Saturday morning at the Little Theatre in the mid-1960s to paint sets and had stayed around, bustling backstage, ever since. The Renegades painted their own walls, hung their lights, furnished dressing rooms and snaffled some cinema seats from the rickety old Granada in West Ham that was being upgraded.

For several years, Cooper at last felt safe. It wouldn't last but, at the age of sixty, he could now take stock. In 1981, he summarised his daily routine:

breakfast, draft newsletter to members, pay bills, open mail . . . . work on play script inventing moves having decided where the doors, windows and fireplace are at . . . amend dialogue to suit actors I have . . . devise costume,

sound and lighting plots . . . decide on furniture, and the colour, to create
the right atmosphere . . . 6.30pm, Yvonne arrives to prepare an evening
meal . . . 7.30pm Monday, Wednesday and Friday, come the actors . . . same
pattern for 33 years! . . . weekends we clean, polish, tend garden at front of
Playhouse, repair scenery, refurbish theatre . . . check seats for loose screws;
after a comedy, there are quite a number . . . end day, write up diary, read
– especially Chandler and Garson Kanin – keep in touch with BBC World
Service, sleep around 3 am . . . in the precarious nature of theatre production
I feel I have left something, for around the world there are actors of both
sexes who once performed on stage with me, and carry forward my love of
theatre which I believe has been a saving grace since Aristotle. I hope to
play King Lear at eighty. So! 'What is to leave betimes?' Hope for Mankind.

He had at this point, he computed, put on 431 productions and given 1,824
performances. His words are strangely moving, for all the quaint eccentricity
implied, as in the old-fashioned, determined way of blocking out a play
before directing it, creating a world in which he is best able to cope with the
shortcomings of his colleagues. But as someone who carried the can for
every single department of the performance, he was in a way no different
from a genius like Hal Prince who, when asked by an actor what his
motivation was for moving, as instructed, at that particular moment down
stage right, replied: 'Because that's where the fucking light is!'

Jimmie created a world of theatre, often from fustian elements and a fast-
fading repertoire, which had about it an innate sense of integrity, a purpose
and a value. And his own failing physical resources were part of that quality,
too. Over the last ten years at the Playhouse, his memory started playing
tricks and his grip on his lines began to loosen. So, he devised a method of
tightening that grip which involved placing prompts around the sets he
designed to keep him going. The result was that you often saw a performance
that contained a most extraordinary ballet of opening desk drawers, peering
through windows or into coal scuttles, even shooting his cuffs or doffing his
cap to reveal (to him alone) the next line.

Once the line had been retrieved, there was no guarantee at all that Jimmie
would then re-start the play at exactly the same place he had left off or even
in the same scene. But whatever confusion ensued, it never showed in his
performance and he would glide around the stage and execute an elaborate
departure, stopping not a little short of waving and winking at the audience.
The audience, of course, loved this, rewarding him with a spontaneous round
of applause and muttering sympathetically among themselves in the interval
at the difficulty for someone of Cooper's vintage and experience of having to
work with such a crowd of carthorses, or indeed 'bunch of amateurs'.

Unfortunately, the church authorities were less interested in the spirituality
of theatre – let alone Cooper's graceful extrications in the name of art – than
in the material worth of their building and decided to sell out to a property
company, Swallow Developments Ltd, who had offices right next door. Prior

to the axe falling, and aware of the frailty of his tenure since about 1977, Jimmie had managed to secure the support of John Betjeman and a Grade II listing for the church (which is more than the church itself had done). The bad news from the London Congregational Church Union was followed by another hammer blow from Swallow themselves who terminated Cooper's tenancy and would oppose any application for its renewal on the grounds that they intended to reconstruct a substantial part of the premises as a leisure centre with squash courts.

Cooper was given an exit date in February 1981 having been defeated in court by Sir David Napley (representing Swallow) – Sir David, a prominent solicitor, included the Liberal Party leader Jeremy Thorpe and Princess Michael of Kent among his clients – who made a great point of saying, rather unpleasantly, how Cooper had 'spurned' the KMT out of pique and that the Grade II listing was essentially spurious because the windows and fittings that had secured the status could as easily be preserved elsewhere. In actual fact, it was the vaulted wooden ceiling that had been the main argument for the listing. But, in another twist, the Greater London Council's historic buildings committee rejected the conversion plans and Jimmie was still in business, even though Swallow retained ownership.

Amazingly, he struggled on for three more years before bringing down the final curtain with a music hall show called *Goodbye Gaieties* on 9 June 1984. But these were hard times. A newsletter he sent me in May 1982 had a most uncharacteristic, defeated kind of message scrawled in capital letters across the top: 'I press on but I'm not sure if I have the stomach for the fight. 500 productions in one lifetime seems enough. About time I retired from the hurly burly.' Like Peter Hall, but with no comparable remuneration or physical ease or public recognition beyond Ilford, he had done the state some service. His story was a tragedy of noble and admirable proportions.

The man who gave amateur theatre such a good name for so long died of stomach cancer on 8 March 1987 – within just five days of his doppelganger hero Danny Kaye's passing – less than three years after the closure of the Playhouse. He was seventy years old and had married Yvonne ten months earlier on a short break in Gibraltar. She's living still, on a small private estate in Woodford, Essex, alone but with good friends around, a sprightly and effervescent eighty-year-old. Her father, who built racing cars and died of a heart attack aged fifty-nine, never approved of Jimmie and would never have allowed her to become a professional actress – the same thing, in his eyes, as a fallen woman. The professional theatre's loss of this marvellous actress was Jimmie's – and the amateur stage's – glorious gain.

The centre of Ilford has changed inordinately since my time there, though the Town Hall still stands as proudly as ever and the Kenneth More Theatre nestles quietly beside it, in much the same way as the Octagon in Bolton sits more confidently alongside the sustained Victorian grandeur of the Bolton Library and the other great municipal buildings. I always had this notion, fostered by the Renegades, that a good and valuable theatre shone like a beacon in its community, was a focal point of activity and enthusiasm for a town and its citizens all pulling, more or less, in the same direction.

The notion was probably delusional to start with, but I think it informed the work of a company like the Renegades, and I found a gratifying echo of it in certain professional regional theatres I got to know in my subsequent life as a professional critic. And it was certainly fundamental – delusional or not – to the growth of amateur theatre in the country. Even the KMT stated, in its preliminary publicity, that this would be a theatre 'to stimulate the enthusiasm of all people, a source of vitality and enrichment for young and old in Redbridge . . . part of the redevelopment of Ilford town centre . . . and a focal point for community interests.'

But times change, as do cultures, and the demographics. The amateur theatre, no less than the professional theatre, is in retreat from this reality. The difference is that the amateur theatre is realistic and defiantly backs-to-the wall about the situation, without presuming to change that situation or cut suits with a different kind of cloth. When the KMT opened, it earmarked forty-three weeks each year for the amateurs. There were fifteen amateur drama companies in the borough of Redbridge. Now there are half a dozen, max. And their allocation of weeks is between just fifteen and twenty-two, bolstered by the continuing participation of the Ilford Operatic and Dramatic Society (no longer in the Town Hall), the venerable Wanstead Players and the Redbridge Theatre Company. The KMT's manager, Steven Day, a local lad who succeeded his mentor Vivyan Ellacott in 2010, then books the pantomime and small touring shows and comedians through personal contacts and variety booking agents.

Since the amateur groups themselves have fallen away over the past fifteen years, the audience, too, has gone into steep decline. 'In the old days,' says Day, 'you had to join the theatre's club just to get a ticket for the weekend, and even then it wasn't guaranteed. You don't have to do that anymore. What we can do here, technologically, and scenically, in presenting theatre has gone up and up . . . but the audiences simply haven't followed.'

The current facilities of the KMT are indeed amazing, certainly when compared to those of the Little and the Cranbrook/Playhouse, and probably even the old Hippodrome itself. There is a full fly tower (for hoisting and lowering scenery), a flat stage, a perfectly raked auditorium with untrammelled sight-lines and seating for 365, a good studio space with fifty seats (a prescient feature in the early 1970s as the fringe boomed in London), workshops, six well-appointed dressing rooms with showers and toilets, a splendid bar at the first level and an orchestra pit with room for over two dozen musicians.

The place has a professional staff of five or six – Day and his business manager, a box office manager and two technical staff plus a caretaker. Only the exterior looks a bit old-fashioned and shabby, but nobody worries too much about that sort of thing in Ilford, then or now. The KMT is owned by the London Borough of Redbridge and leased to the Redbridge Theatre Company for a peppercorn rent. The studio comes in handy for renting out to dance schools and tai-chi classes, as well as to chair-based exercise groups for the elderly and card-making hobbyists.

Why is the Kenneth More in Ilford? The actor himself had never set foot in the place until he came to the topping out ceremony in October 1973. It is possibly the case that once Maggie Smith – who really was born in Ilford – turned them down, and having decided not to upset too many interested parties by naming the theatre after their controversial local star and pioneer (James Cooper), the governors went fishing for a popular 'name' at a time when naming theatres for actors with no specific local attachment was all the rage: the Redgrave in Farnham, the Thorndike in Leatherhead, the Yvonne Arnaud in Guildford, the Adeline Genée in East Grinstead.

Kenneth More was born in Gerrard's Cross, Buckinghamshire, and had received a big boost to his fading popularity as a British film star with his appearance in the BBC Television serialisation of *The Forsyte Saga* in 1966. But if the council and governors were reluctant, understandably, to name the place for Jimmie, there were several other more obvious native, or local, contenders: the stylish comedienne Lynne Fontanne, for instance, from Woodford; or Anna Neagle from nearby Forest Gate; or film director Bryan Forbes from Stratford East; or popular film character actor Victor Maddern, he of the twisted gob and truculent manner, from Seven Kings; or the great RSC actor Ian Holm whose father ran the 'mental hospital' in Goodmayes; or even the genius jackanapes Ken Campbell from Gants Hill.

Still, the Kenneth More was an infinitely better moniker than the working title of the Redbridge Civic Theatre, and the governors confirmed that More had just the right kind of theatre image and actor image they wanted – 'someone with an image of warmth and solidity, not too avant-garde.' He certainly fitted that bill alright and he proved a diligent and much-liked patron, an active fundraiser who occasionally made unscheduled appearances to help out behind the bar. Here, he proved to be an unreliable barman, smashing bottles and glasses in high spirits before whisking the staff and actors away for dinner, though where on earth they all went in Ilford for 'posh nosh' remains a mystery. More's ten years of association ended when he died of Parkinson's disease in 1982. His widow, the actress Angela Douglas, now re-married to the National Theatre director Bill Bryden, gave the KMT all his memorabilia, which included theatre programmes, his CBE insignia and his Variety Club and BAFTA awards. They are – or at least were, until recently – well displayed, with an exhaustive and interesting biography, in the bar area at the back of the stalls.

Steven Day is at least as deep-dyed a local lad as was James Cooper, whom he never knew. He first set foot on the KMT stage aged ten in the choir of the Redbridge Music School. He studied at Chadwell Heath High, joined the Ilford Operatic for a revival of *Finian's Rainbow*, took his A-levels and went to Bognor Regis to work as a Red Coat in Butlin's holiday camp. He worked sporadically as a music director with such legendary stars of British comedy as Dora Bryan, Barry Cryer, Roy Hudd and Danny La Rue. He did a summer season with cuddly pianist Bobby Crush – last in a line of such post-Liberace keyboard crusaders as Winifred Atwell, Russ Conway and Mrs Mills – at which point he reckoned it was high time he got a proper job. He joined the Barking and Dagenham council as a visiting welfare officer ('Which I loved, because I love chatting to people'), moving on to work as an organiser for the Jack Petchey Foundation, a philanthropic trust set up by the millionaire, now knighted, East End entrepreneur, before settling into life at the KMT as musical director for seven years.

His position, always precarious, worsened seriously when Redbridge withdrew the theatre's lease in 2009, planning to knock down the KMT before the Olympic Games exploded along the road in West Ham in 2012, when they would build a replacement theatre on the other side of the Town Hall, extending into the car park. That never happened. Day struggled on. Cooper would have recognised in him a fellow theatrical animal with a survival instinct. In true Renegades spirit, Day boasts of roping in both (retired) parents to help out Front of House when he's short-staffed with volunteers. The hand rails running up the aisles of the warm brick and red-seated auditorium were 'done on the cheap' by his dad, too. In the studio, chairs and tables for the Friday night cabarets were supplied courtesy of the irascible Scottish restaurateur Gordon Ramsay, thanks to a business association with Day's husband.

This can-do outlook extends – or rather, did extend – to the KMT programme. Just as Cooper wheedled two plays out of Duncan Greenwood and fixed the *Twelve Angry Men* premiere, so Steven Day secured personal permissions from Broadway composer Maury Yeston to present *Nine*, an elegant and gorgeously outré version of Fellini's *8½*, by no means an obvious choice for an amateur theatre; and from Eric Idle for his comic oratorio *Not the Messiah* (based on the hilarious *Life of Brian* movie by Monty Python) as a fundraiser.

One of his more recent coups was the first non-professional production of *The Audience*, Peter Morgan's cunning 2015 play, which starred Helen Mirren, followed by Kristin Scott Thomas, in the West End. Day's neat, unfussy staging did not try and compete with the magical sleight-of-hand of Stephen Daldry's original – which cost a lot of money – but the standard of acting was fairly high. Day's business manager, Sally Woodfield, maintained a firm, glacial grip as the Queen at the informal weekly meetings between the monarch and her prime ministers, from a paternalistic Churchill through Harold Wilson and John Major (her two favourites, apparently) to Tony Blair (whom she disliked) and David Cameron.

This was an in-house, semi-professional production in so much as the actors, many of them 'resting' between jobs, had travel expenses reimbursed. An Ilford audience for *The Audience* does not discriminate anyway between amateur and professional, but there's no doubt this show was a cut above the average. Day had written to Morgan explaining the plight of the theatre and his ambition to produce new work – 'there are only so many times people are going to come and see Alan Ayckbourn or *Oklahoma!*' – and Morgan replied positively almost by return. The patrons were amused by the play, sedate in response, appreciative at the end. But only a third of the seats were occupied at the last performance on a Saturday night.

Within a year, in July 2018, came the hammer blow for what appeared to be a final nail in the Ilford theatre's coffin. Until then, the Redbridge Theatre Company received £160,000 a year from the council to operate the KMT. This was withdrawn and, within the next year, in March 2019, Day announced that it was now unfeasible for the RTC to run the venue. He cancelled all future shows during an indefinite hiatus while the Kenneth More's future is determined. No doubt the remaining amateur companies in the area will make other arrangements. But even as the council seemed to rubber stamp the end of live theatre in Ilford, Day achieved something even more remarkable than *The Audience* in one final hurrah: a fun-filled revival of Richard Bean's *One Man, Two Guvnors*, the hit re-working of Goldoni's *Servant of Two Masters* for the National in 2011.

The farcical dynamics were beautifully controlled, the roly-poly barrow-boy spiv brilliantly done by local comedian Josh Ward, and even the decrepit waiter who spends half his time being knocked down the stairs and battered with slammed doors found a way of invoking comparisons not all that unflattering with Tom Edden at the National. As with *The Audience*, this semi-professional effort exuded a sure sense of pace, and the modest scene changes were slickly executed. Not a sign of that fumbling around in the dark or fatal mishandling of props and scenery that you'd expect (or even half-hope for!) in a fully amateur production. And then, the final curtain. At the end of August 2019, Steven Day and the Redbridge Theatre Company left the building. The council's plans for the Kenneth More Theatre were unclear, its future as uncertain as that of the old Ilford Hippodrome immediately after the war . . .

The one and only time the Renegades played on the stage of the KMT was for Jimmie's memorial three years after they had been disbanded. Lila Myra and Leonard Charles, and one or two others, carried on acting and, in Len's case, directing, with companies who did appear in the new theatre. In his last letter to me, having sold his furniture and props from the Playhouse, packed away all his scripts (twenty boxfuls) and a straight run of the American magazine, *Theatre Arts*, dating from October 1941 to January 1963, Jimmie said he was 'impatient to get away, soak in the sun and feel the breakers washing away with a smoothing iron the sadness of selling up, and moving on.'

Vivyan Ellacott had kindly suggested the memorial in the theatre Jimmie had spent so much time and energy dispraising, a gesture that touched

Yvonne deeply. So she set about organising the evening in October 1987, all proceeds and other donations given in Jimmie's name to the intensive therapy unit at the local King George Hospital. Thus it was that on the KMT stage I finally bade farewell to the amateur theatre as a performer with a somewhat over-tempestuous and garish piano accompaniment to my brother Martin's inflamed rendition of an Edwardian dramatic monologue associated with the Henry Irving of the music halls, Bransby Williams, *The Pigtail of Li-Fang-Fu* ('They speak of a dead man's vengeance, they whisper a deed of hell, 'neath the Mosque of Mohammed Ali, and this is the thing they tell . . .'). I then entered calmer waters to accompany Liz Robertson singing her husband's lyrics from *My Fair Lady*.

Trumping us all was Ken Campbell, naturally, who rambled on wildly for about twenty minutes with his dog sat quietly by his feet on the stage. The Betty Finch Dancers, Liz's stage school – now the Linda Finch (Betty's daughter) Dancers – supplied a touch of the Young Generation television dance troupe that had once, and long ago, featured Linda's brother, Roger. Vivyan Ellacott and one of the KMT's leading lights, Loraine Porter, contributed a classy, you might even say 'professional', vaudevillian double-act. And Renegades past and present – including a magnificent-looking Roma de Roeper, a cadaverous Francis Dalvin, Angie, my fellow sinner from *Dark of the Moon*, Frank House and Jane Hall, Len Charles, Denise Sylvey and Roger Sansom – shuffled poignantly around the stage to the backing track of a Noël Coward medley ('The Stately Homes of England,' 'London Pride') and chipped in with affectionate reminiscences.

So, in the souvenir programme, did Basil Amps, his bulb in the *Ilford Recorder* just about still flickering:

> I remember one afternoon in the grim winter of 1947, a season of bitter cold when coal shortages brought frequent power cuts. I was in what was then the Savoy Cinema at Gants Hill. The screen went black. The manager appealed for entertainers. A young man responded – James Cooper. For almost an hour he kept the audience happy with a one-man show . . . Ilford has lost one of its most colourful and energetic characters whose resolve heightened the status of theatre in the town and whose talents gave pleasure to thousands.

The Ilford Playhouse has been converted – though not by Swallow, who migrated, or collapsed – into a set of luxury apartments which, the last time I looked, were selling very slowly. I rang a bell on the hoardings outside to arrange a visit to one of the show apartments but there was no answer. I left a message on the telephone number by the bell. No-one ever replied. The spirit of the Renegades had been sucked from the premises and James Cooper's memory erased. But not by those of us who had the pleasure of his challenging company and energetic vitality in those long gone days.

4

Modern Stirrings in Newcastle, Norwich and Halifax

The National Theatre story had its roots in amateur theatre. While the theatre of Arthur Bourchier extended into the West End, and groups like the Renegades based their work in a more familiar repertoire, the sharp end of the amateur theatre became more oppositional to the commercial theatre. We think of organised political theatre in Britain – always amateur – as originating in the 1930s, notably with the foundation of the Unity Theatre in London, which had links with the Left Book Club and the Communist Party and spawned other Unity Theatres around the country before the outbreak of war. But the roots went even deeper, and earlier, than those of Unity.

The People's Theatre of Newcastle

When it was launched in 1911, the People's Theatre of Newcastle – still one of our leading amateur companies, now settled in its fourth home in a converted cinema in the outlying Heaton district – was nothing less than an avowed branch of the British Socialist Party.

One of its four founding members was a footballing hero, Colin Veitch, captain of an Edwardian-era Newcastle United team that won the Football League Championship four times and the FA Cup in 1910. His prowess on the field was matched by his theatrical versatility as administrator, actor and musician (he composed a score for the annual pantomime). He was also politically tenacious as a trades unionist and co-founder of the Professional Footballers' Association.

The spiritual godfather of the People's was George Bernard Shaw, as he was for so many other amateur companies between the wars. 'If we are going to murder plays, let us – for glory's sake – murder the best!' was the call to arms of Colin's brother, Norman, as the two of them, and Norman's actress wife, Edith, set to work in the upstairs rooms of the British Socialist

Party, with a tiny stage and seating for just 100 people, on the corner of Leazes Park Road in the centre of the city. Although Shaw died in 1950, his second visit to the People's in 1936 was the occasion of his last speech from any stage: 'This being my last speech in the theatre,' he said, 'I like it to be this one'. He had long agreed to a special rate of royalty terms favourable to the People's in order, he said, to enable the building of a true repertory theatre.

This was the point. The amateur theatre of that time was more affiliated to the serious new writing theatre and club venues in London – what the producer Norman Marshall labelled 'The Other Theatre' in a famous book of that title – and the rest of Europe than to the comedies and musical shows of the West End. In addition to Shaw, John Galsworthy, Arnold Bennett and J. M. Synge, the People's authors over their first ten years included Ibsen, Chekhov, Hauptmann, as well as Molière and Shakespeare. The place embodied the intellectual idealism of the already vociferous campaign to found a National Theatre.

Meanwhile, the People's itself had moved in 1915 to less cramped new premises in the Royal Arcade, Pilgrim Street which – to give a specific example of how Victorian/Edwardian dignity has yielded to the march of time – is now the site of a roundabout and an office block. No plaque. Here there were productions of Shaw's *Pygmalion*, Molière's *Learned Women* and J. M. Synge's *Riders to the Sea* and *In the Shadow of the Glen*. Norman Veitch had met Shaw through a former People's stalwart turned professional actor, Hubert Humphries, in Birmingham and then invited him to Newcastle.

Shaw came to see *Man and Superman* in 1921, having recommended Humphries for the role of Jack Tanner. In the same play, Colin Veitch was praised by the author for his portrayal of Old Malone, the self-made wealthy American businessman of Irish peasant stock, Shaw's version of Lophakin in Chekhov's *The Cherry Orchard*. Shaw returned in the silver jubilee year of 1936 to see his *Candida*.

That production was in the People's third venue; they'd moved in 1930 to a disused chapel in Rye Hill, very near to the new theatre today of Newcastle University. Productions there included Shaw's *Saint Joan* and *Man of Destiny*; Harley Granville Barker's *The Madras House*, a 1910 masterpiece eventually produced by the National Theatre starring Paul Scofield in 1977; and a modern dress version of Shakespeare's perennially underrated early comedy *The Two Gentlemen of Verona*.

Rye Hill was the theatre also visited by J. B. Priestley in March 1933 on his extended jaunt around the country prior to publishing his beady-eyed travelogue, *English Journey*. Priestley attended rehearsals for *The Trojan Women*, and was astonished at the intensity and modern vernacular of the performance, concluding that the theatre itself deserved a word:

Its prices range from sixpence to a half-crown, and if you buy a serial ticket for five shillings you are admitted throughout the season for half-price. The productions that season included *Peer Gynt*, *Widowers' Houses*, *The Insect Play*, *Loyalties*, and *The Trojan Women*: good fare, solid tack, value for money.

To see a play like *Hobson's Choice*, Harold Brighouse's 1915 repertory warhorse, revived at today's People's is to discover it all over again, viewed in the company of an audience for whom the subject matter is still keenly appreciated. Henry Horatio Hobson, the shoe-shop owner, defines the suffragist's rights for women and his own daughter's spirited fight for independence as the consequence of insupportable 'uppishness,' as though political justice and human rights were a matter of etiquette only.

On my way to lunch in Newcastle city centre at one of the oldest private members clubs in the land, the Northern Counties Club (women members, welcome since 1999, have now provided the club's new chairperson), I had paused by the soaring pillar-like statue of Earl Grey, the Whig Prime Minister and primary architect of the 1832 Reform Act, whose government ratified the abolition of slavery. People's Theatre audiences are proud of these victories, but also know that these were battles in a still-continuing campaign and that *Hobson's Choice*, at the very least, commends vigilance in human rights and dignity.

The People's Theatre was known at first as the Clarion Dramatic Society, aligned with other socialist activity groups within the BSP such as the Clarion Vocal Union and the Clarion Cycling Club (which still exists). In the 1920s, persisting with Shaw, Ibsen and O'Neill, the theatre received 'bolstering' visits from Charles Trevelyan, Ramsay MacDonald's labour minister, and the legendary East End MP Manny Shinwell, a living link between the Fabians, Shavians and Harold Wilson's 1964 Labour government. The thread of socialist reforming zeal had not yet been compromised.

Chris Goulding, a teacher and People's Theatre member since 1979, has acted, stage-managed and lit countless productions, working in every department except wardrobe and the box office. He is now on the board, and notes, among the younger members, an increasing overlap between amateurs and professional fringe companies.

Even public money from the Arts Council has been – most unusually – involved, supplying a revenue grant in 1960 and contributing towards the recent £1.6 million refurbishment of the foyer, a light and attractive space hung with paintings, and the stunning new studio space on the ground floor, replacing the old one which was not sound-proofed against the 450-seater main auditorium. With this upgrade, they can now present plays simultaneously in both spaces.

Since the last war, the People's archival calendar is flecked with notable entries: the world premiere in 1949 of Sean O'Casey's *Cock-a-Doodle Dandy*, which the *Irish Times* was obliged to cross the water to review; one of the few public performances of Shaw's last ever play, *Buoyant Billions*, with a cast including Alan Browning, then a reporter on the local *Evening*

Chronicle, before he turned professional and married the legendary Pat Phoenix – Elsie Tanner in *Coronation Street*; the first Veitch memorial lecture, 'Theatre in the Community', delivered by the great director Tyrone Guthrie in 1951; and the 1955 launch of the public appeal to convert the old cinema attended by John Gielgud, Peggy Ashcroft, Moira Lister and George Devine.

This is, and always has been, no ordinary theatre. Thornton Wilder, American author of *Our Town*, said of it: 'I was deeply moved by the fact that over so many years the People's Theatre presented so many notable plays of the world. It is like having a living library in the town.' Dylan Thomas's *Under Milk Wood* and Harold Pinter's *The Birthday Party* were given very soon after their London premières, when both plays were still controversial.

The People's also mounted the British première of Arthur Miller's play about his marriage to Marilyn Monroe, *After the Fall*, in 1967. Such spark and daring meant that it became part of the RSC's main regional hub in the mid-1980s, the RSC's financial controller, Bill Wilkinson, being an old friend and member of the People's. The RSC's 1986 opening season in the Swan in Stratford-upon-Avon played here, led by Jeremy Irons and Imogen Stubbs, and the auditorium still contains the lighting rig installed by the RSC along the interior walls of the front stalls.

Shaw's *Pygmalion* was the centenary production in 2011. Television actor Kevin Whately, star of *Inspector Morse* and *Lewis*, is still actively supportive of his home town company. And brilliant stand-up comedian Ross Noble cut his teeth during some improvisational games with the youth theatre section, as well as in the main company. I asked Ross what the experience had meant to him:

> The People's Theatre is more than just an amdram group. It is very much the definition of a community. They have a proper working theatre so, as a kid, it felt like entering a world where creative things happened and creative people hung around. Meeting those people and doing things at the weekend which all week at school you would get mocked for was a total joy.

There you have it. We go from Shaw to Ross Noble. It's a paradigm of our theatre history. Confirmation, too, that a set-up like the People's represents even more than an important stepping stone for well-known professionals. It remains, and thrives, because of its sense of continuity at the heart of its community in a world of fragmentation, dislocation, tweets and soundbites. It's as necessary and important in the national culture as any more high-profile subsidised institution.

The Maddermarket Theatre, Norwich

Although the Maddermarket Theatre in the medieval hinterland of Norwich opened in 1921, the Guild of Norwich Players, the resident company, was formed in 1911, in a private drawing room with seats for seventy people, just as the People's was launched in its socialist eyrie in Newcastle. The room was that of the director Nugent Monck, a follower and colleague of William Poel, the founder of the Elizabethan Stage Society, which pursued an ideal of realism and Elizabethan methods, as an antidote to Victorian fustiness. This, you might say, is similar to Mark Rylance and his Shakespeare's Globe challenging the time-worn, academically-based methodology of the RSC.

Monck, a vicar's son renowned for his dynamism and sharp tongue, and a musician by training, had been invited from London to Norwich to produce some historical tableaux in 1909. He took a shine to the city and returned in 1911, aged thirty-three. The popularity of his drawing room dramas necessitated a move to a larger space in King Street owned by a brewery. He put on his plays there either side of the Great War.

The repertoire was as evangelical as at the People's. In the first ten years, it included Restoration comedy, Ibsen, Shaw, Strindberg, Pirandello, even Indian and Japanese Noh plays. Monck was a pioneer in the method of 'direct lighting' – what we'd now call 'white light', i.e, no colours or frills – integral to his scenic designs. This innovative approach, noted in the national reviews, was an acknowledged influence on the work of other important professional directors such as Barry Jackson at the Birmingham Rep (which Jackson founded, also in 1911) – he later took over the embryonic Royal Shakespeare Company in Stratford-upon-Avon – and Nigel Playfair at the Lyric, Hammersmith, in the 1920s.

Monck was on the look-out for an Elizabethan-style theatre and in 1921 discovered a derelict warehouse, formerly an eighteenth century Roman

FIGURE 4 *Maddermarket Theatre, in the medieval centre of Norwich, opened in 1921 under the direction of Nugent Monck who built the first Elizabethan thrust stage in the modern era and pioneered swift, uncluttered Shakespeare productions. (Photo: Mark Benfield.)*

Catholic chapel, which he bought for £1,700 and converted into a theatre in just six weeks – its domed and vaulted ceiling guaranteed a good acoustic – and fitted out with 220 seats. The church was on the site of an old medieval market where a scarlet dye known as 'madder' was sold during the wool trading era.

The Maddermarket Theatre, disarmingly intimate, was the first permanent recreation of an Elizabethan theatre in the country, complete with two wooden girders on the stage – comparable to the larger Corinthian pillars on the Shakespeare's Globe stage today – a tiring house, windows and oaken doors and carvings on the stage and a galleried second level with a wooden balustrade.

This footprint survives today. In spite of all the alterations over the years, the exterior of the oldest part of the building, with gabled portal and Tudor vertical wooden stripes on the frontage, remains the same. The stage was extended outwards in 1990 in a thrust and the gangways were re-aligned. This is basically, however, still Monck's theatre, and a 2017 revival of Jessica Swale's boisterous *Nell Gwynn*, originally premiered at Shakespeare's Globe in 2015, took full advantage of the architectural features, cleverly eliding period costume with modern dress (and bottles of mineral water) and by no means skimping on the roughhouse or the bawdy.

By 1933, Monck had staged all thirty-seven plays in the Shakespeare canon. Norman Marshall reckoned that, because of its flexibility and the intimacy of the atmosphere between actors and audience, the Maddermarket should be ranked as one of the few experimental theatres in England. He added that Monck's interpretation of a play was 'subtle, fastidious and exact' and that his productions – always speedy (*Twelfth Night* virtually uncut in under two hours), sometimes uneven – were never gabbled, scene following scene without pause. The crowd scenes in *Coriolanus* were the best Marshall had seen, he said, 'in any theatre'.

Monck had a peculiar rule of no curtain calls at the end of a performance, and no actors' names in the programme, and this applied right through to 1994, when audiences became intolerant of the feeling that they were watching a secret society. But in 1940 Bernard Shaw wrote to Monck: 'There is nothing in British theatrical history more extraordinary than your creation of the Maddermarket Theatre out of nothing, with no money and no municipal support . . .' (these words are still emblazoned on a plaque on the Maddermarket's outer wall).

Shaw also convinced Norman Marshall, who was a British Drama League adjudicator and a lecturer, as well as a seasoned professional, that 'the future of the drama is in the hands of the amateur' and that amateurs would 'provide an intelligent, enthusiastic and informed audience intolerant of slipshod acting, production and scenery . . . and not too bedazzled by stars irrespective of the merits of their performance'.

When Marshall declares in *The Other Theatre* that the growth of the amateur movement in the years between the wars was 'awe-inspiring', he had Monck's Maddermarket in the forefront of his argument. He applauded the breaking down of barriers between the amateur and professional theatre, as in the liaison firmly established in Soviet Russia, and argued that 'this should happen here, with more professional direction' in amateur drama.

The principle was never resoundingly established, but there have been many collaborations of professionals and amateurs, not least at the Maddermarket itself. Even today the place is managed by six full-time paid-up members of staff – general manager, artistic director, education officer, administrator, designer and costumes/wardrobe; the costumes are mostly made in-house; and the theatre runs a thriving costume hire business. Everyone else – actors and volunteer staff in the bars, front-of-house and backstage – is unpaid.

Monck was a churchwarden in the adjacent medieval marvel of St John Maddermarket. His ashes – he died in 1958 – are within. It is one of the great romantic stories associated with the Maddermarket that Will Kemp, Shakespeare's clown, completed his celebrated Morris-dancing jig from London to Norwich – the so-called 'nine daies wonder', which actually took him over three weeks – by jumping over the wall of the church. In 1952, Monck retired and gave over the theatre, its properties and its site to a newly formed theatre trust in exchange for a payment of £700 and a ground rent of £500 a year.

Monck was followed in rapid succession by three artistic directors, including the distinguished James Roose-Evans in 1954 (who later founded the Hampstead Theatre Club) before Ian Emmerson, an army education officer and a stage manager for Peter Hall at the Arts Theatre in London, steadied the ship in 1958 and ran the place for a further thirty-one years, the same time span as Monck's. 'No other theatre of amateur actors', said Hall, 'has such a big professional back-up'.

Emmerson's work rate was phenomenal. He directed nine of the ten plays each year and his programme, continuing in Monck's high-minded tradition, included Brecht, Beckett, John Arden, the French absurdist Arbuzov, Friedrich Dürrenmatt and Arnold Wesker (Wesker's best, and best known play, *Roots*, finally came home to Norfolk, where it was set) and took many leading roles himself, including Thomas More, Beckett's Hamm and Chekhov's Astrov.

From the outset, Monck's company was the Guild of Norwich Players, becoming the Maddermarket Theatre Company in 1997 and the Norwich Players again in 2011. Even though today's Norwich Players provide fewer productions than before – the theatre runs a mixed programme policy, with visiting professionals and other amateur groups – they still cling to a respectable selection of classics and top-of-the range comedy. Their productions are still box office.

Recent seasons have included Farquhar's far-from-easy masterpiece *The Beaux' Stratagem*; Ronald Harwood's *The Dresser* played back-to-back with its 'source' play *King Lear* (a production featuring a live video stream, multiple projections and a significant amount of pre-recording); Arthur Miller's *The Crucible*; Shakespeare's *Antony and Cleopatra*, Joe Orton's *What the Butler Saw* and Terence Rattigan's *The Deep Blue Sea*. Monck's memory and Ian Emmerson's continuation still marks the outlook and temper of the Maddermarket even though, since Emmerson's retirement in 1989, there have been several artistic directors, each lasting several years. It remains, palpably, a special place, something you sense the minute you cross the threshold.

The building itself has undergone significant changes since Emmerson took over. It survived the war-time bombing of Norwich in 1942 and, in 1953, the auditorium was finally extended, after a five-year planning period, to accommodate 300 seats and there was serious re-fitting of the warehouse, scene dock and front-of-house. The still-thriving youth theatre club was launched in 1963 and a 1964 development created the existing foyer and bar area, with new cloakrooms, a much larger wardrobe and a rehearsal room, doubling as a studio space.

More major work was completed, this time with new seating and air-conditioning, in time for the Norwich Festival of 2003, when the Maddermarket invited Simon Callow to direct the rarely seen medieval morality *Everyman* and play God, a double task he somehow managed to encompass. Callow had been on tour in Norwich, had called by the Maddermarket to take a look, got talking to one or two people and emerged on the street as their new patron. The *Everyman* was performed not on Monck's tiny stage, but in the fifteenth-century church of St Peter Mancroft, very near the Theatre Royal, and also on tour at the astonishing Hippodrome, Great Yarmouth – Britain's only surviving dedicated circus theatre.

Callow was confessedly astounded by the zest, concentration and seriousness of his amateur cast. There was an added bonus of some largely forgotten incidental music composed by Sibelius for the play and the participation of Harry Blech's renowned London Mozart Players as well as the local supernumeraries and small-part actors. A critic for *The Times* said: 'Callow himself played God, working up a right old vengeful tizzy from his lofty throne. But the bulk of the action was carried by the amateurs of the Maddermarket Theatre. There was nothing amateurish about their performances. The leads declaimed their dread-filled lines with compelling clarity.' Twelve years later, Rufus Norris began his regime as director of the National Theatre in succession to Nicholas Hytner with the very same play, excitingly staged, with Chiwetel Ejiofor as Everyman. God, in poet laureate Carol Ann Duffy's update, was a cleaning woman, a far cry from Callow's seigneurial divinity.

The Maddermarket, in its history and tradition, is at the core of the theatre ecology of Norwich, where the art deco Theatre Royal, magnificently refurbished in 2007, stands on the same site of the original 1758 theatre. The Norwich Puppet Theatre is housed in a nearby medieval church where it has prospered since 1979. And, in 1995, the attractively appointed

Norwich Playhouse opened in a former maltings, hosting comedy, music and kids' shows.

Simon Callow has done most jobs in a theatre, starting at university as an occasional dresser to visiting stars in Belfast, then manning the box office at the Old Vic under Olivier, before launching his pyrotechnical career of acting, directing, writing and generously supportive theatrical tub-thumping. In a fund-raising booklet for the Maddermarket, he wrote: 'The division between audience and actors has been very damaging, and the active involvement of citizens in this most natural form of expression has been taken for granted in every generation but the present. The Maddermarket is a beacon; lucky Norwich to have it in its midst.'

The Halifax Thespians

The Halifax Thespians in West Yorkshire were officially formed as a society at a meeting in the White Swan Hotel in September 1927 along the same sort of lines as the People's and the Maddermarket with 'an active interest in the more permanent and intelligent forms of dramatic art'. Halifax novelist Phyllis Bentley, a long-time admirer of the repertory companies in Sheffield and Birmingham, was seconded to the fledgling society and the meeting was inspirationally addressed by Alfred Wareing. Wareing was, at that time, running the Theatre Royal in Huddersfield, and was soon to become a pioneering director at the Glasgow Citizens and a staunch advocate of subsidy, the Arts Council and the dignity of dramatic art.

A young Wilfred Pickles, later a household name on BBC Radio's *Have a Go* (an early example in the burgeoning vogue for audience participation on the airwaves), was at this meeting, having made his acting debut as an extra in Henry Baynton's touring production of *Julius Caesar* at the Theatre Royal in the town, and was elected to the committee to draft a constitution for the society. The first activity of the Thespians was a series of play readings, starting with John Masefield's *The Tragedy of Nan*, in December 1927. Phyllis Bentley, who would be the president of the Thespians from 1945–49 and again from 1955–65, was beside herself: 'I shall never forget the thrill and excitement of that night. A rebellious, poetical, intellectual play read publicly in Halifax!'

For the next few years the company played in various venues, offering its first fully staged performance, J. M. Barrie's *Dear Brutus*, in the imposing Theatre Royal in March 1928 – four years before it was converted to a cinema, subsequently a bingo hall and then a nightclub, but standing sadly empty these past ten years – while short pieces were given at the old YMCA in Clare Road, one of Shakespearean extracts featuring Wilfred Pickles as Richard III.

At last, a home was found, courtesy of the Halifax Building Society – the Alexandra Hall in Commercial Street, very near the still operating Victoria Theatre of 1901. The new theatre opened in March 1931 with Czech playwright Karel Capek's idealistic *Adam the Creator* in which the hero tries to destroy the world and build a better one. The lead was taken by Wilfred Pickles's elder brother, Arthur, an architect and Liberal politician, later mayor, in the town.

Even more significantly, the *Observer*'s drama critic at the time, St John Ervine, attended the opening and declared himself an advocate of all such Little Theatres across Britain, citing Wareing's operation in Huddersfield and the new repertory theatres in Hull, Leeds and Liverpool. These serious new theatres, said St John Ervine, were made in the mould of the Abbey in Dublin, the Arts in Moscow and the Theatre Guild in New York, and no statement could express more clearly the status of amateur theatre in the cultural vanguard of the day.

Like most industrial towns around Britain at that time, Halifax was rich in theatre buildings, but the surge in popularity of cinema and the waning of the music hall meant that even the Frank Matcham masterpiece, the Grand, had fallen on hard times and was converted, like the Royal, into a cinema between 1925 and 1940. The Thespians were therefore, in effect, a quasi-professional repertory company throughout the 1930s, producing the plays of Shaw, Aldous Huxley, Pinero, J. B. Priestley, Clemence Dane and the Americans Susan Glaspell and Eugene O'Neill. When war broke out in 1939, the Alexandra Hall was requisitioned by the military and the Thespians moved into the Heath Grammar School (now the Crossley Heath Grammar School), where they stayed for eight years, with audiences increasing from 2,000 to an average of over 2,600 a week.

After the war, there was a renewed feeling that Halifax should have its own re-born amateur theatre, despite the commercial theatre collapsing all around. A disused Methodist chapel on King Cross Road was purchased – after a fund-raising campaign led by Arthur Pickles – for £2,500, with a target of £10,000 for conversion and equipment. The new Playhouse opened, after two or three years of volunteer gutting, rebuilding and architectural alteration, in September 1949, with *The Merry Wives of Windsor* in which Barrie Ingham, later a leading actor at the RSC and on television, played the lover-boy Fenton. The theatre is a Grade II listed building, with 240 seats and three alcoves with seating at the back of the auditorium, and a fine polished wooden box office, once the pay office at the town's renowned family business, Crossley Carpets

The Playhouse was officially opened by E. Martin Browne, the director of the British Drama League. The repertoire continued just as adventurously in King Cross Street and the coronation of Queen Elizabeth II in 1953 was celebrated in a cavalcade devised by Phyllis Bentley that included an extract from that first-ever English comedy, *Ralph Roister Doister* (1567). Barrie Ingham, at that time still working in the family furniture business in the

FIGURE 5 *The Halifax Thespians, formed in 1927, established their home in a converted Methodist chapel in 1949. The opening production,* The Merry Wives of Windsor, *featured the future RSC star Barrie Ingham. (Photo: Chris Baldock.)*

town, performed a speech from *Hamlet* and one of Bernard Shaw's prefaces to his own plays, and Arthur Pickles played Sir Peter Teazle in the screen scene from Sheridan's *The School for Scandal*.

Meanwhile, a professional weekly rep company, the Halifax Repertory Theatre Club, was launched at the Grand Theatre on North Bridge. But Matcham's building was in serious disrepair and the rep only struggled on for a couple of years. The president of the rep was Eric Portman, by now a movie star, son of a Halifax tailor who had caught the theatre bug watching touring shows at the Grand. Like Wilfred Pickles, he had made his professional debut at the Theatre Royal with Henry Baynton's company and had performed as an amateur with the Halifax Light Opera Society while working as a salesman for the department store Marshall and Snelgrove in Leeds.

As the crisis at the Grand deepened, with no investment forthcoming for essential repair work, Portman arranged a Sunday night fund-raiser in 1955 and brought his latest West End hit, Terence Rattigan's *Separate Tables*, with his co-star, Margaret Leighton, to Halifax. The Thespians chipped in with a scene from Priestley's *When We Are Married*. But in May 1956, the same month as John Osborne's landscape-altering new play *Look Back in Anger* opened at the Royal Court, the ceiling of the Grand collapsed overnight during the run of an Alan Melville play, *Simon and Laura*, starring Heather Canning and local favourite George Woolley.

Ironically, it was during the run of *Separate Tables* at the St James's Theatre in London (Portman and Margaret Leighton played a record-breaking 726 performances) that it became known that permission had been sought by a property speculator, and granted by the London County Council, to demolish the theatre and replace it with an office block. And this came to pass in 1957, despite a vigorous nationwide campaign led by Laurence Olivier and Vivien Leigh.

The Thespians offered to help out the now homeless, stricken repertory company, and shared facilities where they could, but the rep, almost immediately, disbanded and never appeared at the Playhouse. The Grand was demolished in 1959, leaving the amateurs alone to carry the burden of expectancy among locals who had been spoilt for choice in their theatre-going ever since the first theatre opened at Ward's End in 1790. The Playhouse prospered.

In April 1964, Phyllis Bentley arranged another pageant as part of the 400th anniversary celebrations of Shakespeare's birth. Again, *Hamlet* was on the bill, in extract form, and the programme reveals that four girl 'extras' included one Susan Hyman, then a young teenager who became my wife thirteen years later. Her father, Geoffrey, an orthopaedic surgeon, and his wife, Marie, had been friends of Phyllis Bentley's for some time. Indeed, that same pageant programme has a footnote announcing a forthcoming event for the play-reading circle of the Thespians on an afternoon in May: '*A Man for All Seasons* by Robert Bolt to be held at Acre Mead by kind permission of Mr G. Hyman.' Geoffrey Hyman succeeded Phyllis Bentley as president in 1966 and remained in post until his death in 1975.

In the first episode of the fourth series of the popular BBC TV series *Last Tango in Halifax*, broadcast in December 2016, the star of the show, Anne Reid as Celia Buttershaw, is stepping in to help out the local amateur company, the Halifax Players, as Madame Arcati in Noël Coward's *Blithe Spirit*. This is, of course, one of the nation's favourite war-time comedies in which the ghostly apparitions of dead loved ones was a source of comfort to audiences with family members who'd been called up and perhaps gone missing or worse.

It's only a matter of time before Reid's co-star, Derek Jacobi as her husband, Alan, is reluctantly roped in, too; at least Jacobi himself could plead amdram experience as a leading light in the ill-fated movie *A Bunch of Amateurs*. Another *Last Tango* regular, man-of-the-soil Paul Copley, asks if they can't write in a gardener for him to play, to which Jacobi plaintively replies, 'He's dead, the fellah that wrote it,' and he should know, having played in one of the all-time great Coward productions at the National Theatre, *Hay Fever* directed by Coward himself, in 1964.

By the time the performance comes round, Copley has taken over as Dr Bradman from an actor who's had a heart attack, but is deep in his cups before the show even starts and suffers a compound fracture in a bad fall.

So Jacobi has to 'go on,' script-in-hand, to give a studiously observed, arch 'amateur' performance, coming to the conclusion that, 'It's not my thing, I've realised, standing on a stage, people looking in.' 'Who d'you play next', Reid joshes him, 'King Lear?' 'Ooh no', says the actor who played an acclaimed Lear at the Donmar Warehouse in 2010, 'I don't know 'owt about drama.' But the idea of amateur dramatics being an endemic strain of activity in a provincial or rural community is an unshakeably true one in our popular culture.

The Halifax Players, according to *Last Tango*, performed in a Pentecostal church hall somewhere on Skircoat Road, quite a distance across town from the home of the real-life Halifax Thespians since 1946, the Playhouse on King Cross Street. There, the pseudo-professional pretentiousness alluded to in the television show was given full reign in a 2017 production of *Glorious!*, a 2005 play by Peter Quilter about the splendidly deluded New York socialite and diva Florence Foster Jenkins. After becoming a cult figure in the Manhattan salons of the 1930s, admired by the likes of Cole Porter, Enrico Caruso and Thomas Beecham, Florence allowed hubris to take over completely when she hired the Carnegie Hall and met with a critical response summed up by the *New York Sun*: 'She has a great voice; in fact, she can sing everything except notes.'

The Halifax performer in the role managed the illusion of delusion pretty well, without convincing us that she was only missing the notes because she chose to. It's like the old adage that in order to play the trumpet badly you have to be able, in the first instance, to play it well.

Still, this created an unusually exciting frisson of nearly achieved excellence falling down badly. Her great friend and pianist, Cosmé McMoon was played by an actor adept at pulling his face into expressions of disbelief for two hours-non-stop, while a couple of actors on the periphery served up risibly bad 'amdram acting' as, respectively, the Spanish maid and an irate music lover. The latter's attack on Florence's technique was delightfully marred by its own technically stuttering delivery. It is a nice coincidence that the role of St Clair Bayfield, an ageing actor and loyalist of the inner circle, was taken in the West End premiere, starring Maureen Lipman, by Barrie Ingham, who had appeared in the opening production of the new Halifax Playhouse in 1949.

Today's president of the Thespians, Leighton Hirst, a retired, professionally trained drama teacher, who also ran (usefully, for the theatre) a small buildings maintenance operation, has acted and designed at the Playhouse since 1985. He regrets that there is little crossover in the town's theatre activity, boosted these past thirty years by the lively Square Chapel Arts Centre offering a mixed programme of performance, dance, film and community work. It's also been kept buoyant by the excitingly renovated

Dean Clough Mills, once the home of Crossley Carpets, the biggest carpet factory in the world.

Dean Clough now buzzes with bars, restaurants and small businesses, as well as Northern Broadsides, founded by Barrie Rutter, who have toured the region, and the country, from this Halifax HQ since 1992. The Thespians have a closer connection, and indeed sponsorship, with J&C Jowell of nearby Sowerby Bridge, a business with the longest tradition of textile manufacturing in the entertainment industry, making theatre fabrics, curtains, drapes and stage machinery.

The catchment area for the audience is Halifax and that part of Huddersfield nearest to the town, but Hirst mixes a mood of get-up-and-go optimism with an undisguised acknowledgement of declining audiences and membership. That membership now stands at 330 (where once it was 1,000), and the single professional member of staff, the caretaker, works just two hours a day.

The theatre has received a major re-vamp in the foyer, though the wooden box office remains the focus. There are hopes of a lunchtime snack bar to improve the footfall on the door and to add another stream of income to the thriving theatre bar, installed at a time of financial crisis with the reluctant approval of Phyllis Bentley, much given to temperance in all things, including alcohol, and the other original trustees. Plays are now scheduled for just six performances, instead of – as until recently – ten across two weeks. The Thespians are in residence for thirty weeks each year, producing seven or eight plays with a fortnight of preparation on site.

The rest of the programme comprises visits from other amateur societies, small touring professional groups and – an important money-spinner – tribute bands on one-night stands. From an Eagles tribute concert, for instance, in 2016, the theatre made £800 in ticket sales plus bar takings, which were considerable. The bar itself is occasionally pressed into service for small, intimate shows, with a small raised stage and comfortable seating for fifty.

It is interesting that a society like the Halifax Thespians operates in an admirably democratic fashion with members being freely consulted on which of three proposals they would prefer in the new foyer. An audition-based system of casting has been replaced with a weekend workshop system, when directors can sit down and talk to members, run through a scene with them, and cast accordingly. At the same time, there is a rigid hierarchy of elected management. The president is in overall charge of a chairman, treasurer and secretary, a business manager, publicity manager and a casting committee with its own chairman, there is a management meeting every month and a directors' meeting every two months.

You get the impression that the Thespians will continue, almost defiantly, just the way they are, with the core repertoire and the best of new professionally performed plays as the rights become available, as well as running the popular stage-training courses for young people who want to come along. There is no thought of the sort of coercion, box-ticking or socio-cultural engineering that now governs the way the larger subsidised theatres and their chief funding body, the Arts Council, operate, mostly for the general good, but not always. In Halifax, as in most amateur theatre groups, you only have to do anything, or indeed watch anything, if you want to.

This may mean that the Playhouse itself will one day enter a period of serious decline, as we have seen at a theatre such as the Kenneth More in Ilford. But life in the theatre, as in any other stream of activity, is cyclical and having countered the onslaught of cinema and television, the challenges of adjustment facing the theatre, professional and amateur, are today more complex than ever. Amateur theatre, by its very definition, is where people who love the theatre put on plays they love, with love. And this, surely, is a virtual guarantee of survival.

5

London Pride of the Questors and the Tower

There was a time when fledgling theatre critics – as I was, on the *Financial Times*, in 1972 – were despatched with some regularity to the leading amateur theatres in the capital. The two that figured most significantly for me and my colleagues were the Questors in Ealing, which ran a New Plays Festival of some import in those days, and the Tower in Canonbury, Islington, which had its origins in the Educational Settlement movement of the Victorian era and which presented the first amateur performance of Harold Pinter's first professionally performed play, *The Birthday Party*, shortly after its professional failure in 1958. Pinter said of this production that it was the best there had been 'and, I am sure, the best there will be'.

Both theatres have a lot of laurels to sit on, but have continued to evolve, despite declining membership, over the course of their eighty-odd years of activity. The Tower was hatched as the Tavistock Little Theatre in 1932, the Questors one year later in Mattock Lane, Ealing, where they have camped ever since, opening their new adaptable theatre in 1964 on the site of a Victorian pile, Mattock Lodge, with a Catholic chapel attached that had served as their theatre in the interim. And both theatres are securely fixed in the interwar movement of amateur theatre alongside the new British and European theatres of the professional stage, the boundary lines blurred, visons shared, production standards often comparable.

Even today, you arrive at the Questors, hard by the pleasant greenery, cedar trees and fishpond of Walpole Park to discover scenes of animation and activity as uplifting as any in London. The place is bursting with students and junior dance classes – a student training programme was endemic to the place from early days – productions in the thrust 350-seater Judi Dench auditorium and the adjacent handsomely proportioned smaller Studio; a snack and coffee shop on the first floor next to the rehearsal rooms; the very amenable Grapevine bar built into the old Victorian lodge manned by volunteers; and actors and members discussing the set-building in the large workshop, the next round of auditions or just gossiping.

The New Plays Festival was set up by the Questors' founding member and guiding spirit, Alfred Emmet, in 1960, long before the fringe theatre as we now know it existed in Edinburgh or London. I saw the first of several festival plays, *Hans Kohlhaas*, in 1972. It was by James Saunders, whose beautiful and compassionate play *A Scent of Flowers* at the Duke of York's in 1964 had already made a deep impression on me, not least because of the presence in the cast of Jennifer Hilary and Ian McKellen, the latter making his London debut on the very stage where he would come full circle as King Lear in 2018.

Saunders was one of the Questors' most renowned house dramatists and *Hans Kohlhaas* was written after an extended period of improvisation and workshops with his actors and the director. It was a terrific Brechtian fable of a sixteenth-century horse-dealer who, after being double-crossed, took up cudgels against the system, led a peasants' revolt and was executed amid a series of blistering satirical scenes urging death to the lawyers and power to the people.

Thereafter, I kept an eye out, noting a lively first play by Michael Moriarty about the dead Christopher Marlowe returning to sort out the sexual and professional entanglements of Shakespeare with his Dark Lady and the Earl of Southampton; and an intelligent response to Chekhov, *Seagull Rising*, by A. E. Ellis which supplied scenes Chekhov 'had forgotten' to write and spiced up the dialogue somewhat – poor old Sorin, for instance, moaning about his bad health, declared that 'I couldn't get a cock-stand now if you presented me with the arse of Aphrodite.'

What all three plays had in common was a vitality of response to existing stories and historical/literary characters, underlining how rare it is to find that spark of true originality in playwriting. Alfred Emmet knew this but persisted in the belief that you put on new plays in the hope that some merit and value would ensue from imperfect material and that the promising or talented writer – as all three of these playwrights undoubtedly were – might hit the jackpot sometime soon. If that never happened, you'd at least have kept the new play juices running through the theatre and maintained a level of serious commitment.

Emmet also instilled a strain of self-criticism in the process. Productions were always accompanied by audience discussions during the run of a show and by in-house inquests after it, invariably kicked off by Emmet asking, 'This could have been better – how?' Not only was he running the first new theatre built in London for twenty years, and an architecturally unconventional one at that, he was pushing the boundaries, training young students, and attracting the support and admiration of the theatre profession. In 1951, Tyrone Guthrie and Christopher Fry lent active and vocal support, while George Devine, founder of the English Stage Company at the Royal Court, said, 'I consider its [the Questors'] continuance essential to the theatre life of this country'; and, in 1964, Peter Hall, hailed 'one of the most exciting laboratory theatres in the country'.

It had been a long, hard struggle getting to this point. The seeds for a new theatre group in West London were sown in a Soho restaurant in 1929 when seventeen young enthusiasts – including Emmet – who had acted separately and together in other amateur companies around Ealing, decided to form their own. The new Questors (no-one could think of a better name, says Emmet) performed a few productions at the Park Theatre in Hanwell (the first show cost £2, 19 shillings to put on) and achieved success with a triple bill at the British Drama League festival of 1931.

The company stalled financially during a season at St Martin's Hall in Acton, but was bailed out by a donation of £5. They set their sights on the disused Catholic Church in Mattock Lane, sharing it with Ealing boy scouts and working throughout the summer of 1933 on building and equipping the stage, installing lighting and hanging curtains – at a cost of £75. In October 1933, the Questors Theatre officially opened in the Iron Church, or Tin Hut as it became known, with speeches from the stage and a lighting demonstration by Frederick Bentham, the great guru of modern stage lighting. The first production, two months later, was an American play which prompted one critic to say, this was 'undoubtedly the most experimental work done by a London society in recent months, if not years'.

The Questors' landlady, an unpredictable eccentric, Miss Ann Webb, who had inherited Mattock Lodge and its gardens from the priest she had cared for in his declining years, was something of an obstacle to progress, but she amused the company by sending out, often and surreptitiously, for six penny's-worth of hard liquor from the pub at the end of Mattock Lane (it's still there) and walking about in the garden at night with candles. She didn't think all that much of the repertoire of modern English authors and European classics and wasn't remotely impressed by three Rodney Ackland pre-West End premieres in the 1940s, including *Dark River*. Nor did she care for the inaugural conference of the Little Theatre Guild being held on her patch, nor by the fact that between 1945 and 1950 the company presented seven new plays as well as masterworks by Ibsen, Chekhov, Pirandello and Ostrovsky. Then, in 1951, she died.

Immediately, Emmet and his colleagues purchased the whole site, including the lodge, for £8,500, the scouts having moved out, and pushed on with their fundraising to build a new theatre. Throughout the 1950s, money was raised through variety bills, donated performances by professional visitors such as Bernard Miles (film actor and founder of the Mermaid Theatre in Puddle Dock) and Harry Locke (a character actor in British movies over three decades), talent contests with celebrities as judges à la *Strictly Come Dancing* or *The X Factor*, garden parties on the lawns and the supportive participation of Sybil Thorndike and Michael Redgrave, the latter taking on the Questors' presidency in 1958.

The Tin Hut held a capacity of 183 and played to an average audience of 150, with membership climbing (people paid for the privilege) to a couple of thousand and the lodge's accommodation divided into six bedsits let out to members. (One of the longest-serving tenants was Michael Green, author of *The Art of Coarse Acting*.) The 25th anniversary season comprised contemporary plays, ranging from Bernard Shaw and Robertson Davies to several unknowns (the newly formed student group, Young Questors, put on Lorca's *Blood Wedding*) and the building of two new rooms, the Shaw and the Stanislavsky (later, the Studio).

The fundraising continued slowly until a crucial turning point in 1959, when Alfred Emmet learned that the People's in Newcastle had been awarded a grant of £10,000 by the local council on Tyneside. So, he applied for a similar amount from Ealing council and secured £7,250, a quarter of the balance of the overall sum required, on a knife-edge vote witnessed by anxious Questors dotted around the public gallery in the council chamber. The Calouste Gulbenkian Foundation came through with £3,000 and, by June 1961, the new theatre fund stood at £46,709.

The contract was ordered with the building company, Taylor Woodrow. But costs had risen way beyond the original estimate and a further £30,000 was now needed before the construction could begin. The Questors' bank allowed an overdraft on the mortgage of £23,000 and Taylor Woodrow were instructed to proceed with a detailed new estimate and plans. Another charitable donation delivered £5,000, but the members still had to raise £10,000 by the end of the 1961/2 season. This they did – just about – when the final appeals from the stage on the last night of the season's final production, a new play by the poet Dannie Abse, hit the target.

As the Tin Hut was demolished and the building work progressed, all productions were staged in the Stanislavsky Room. One of them, in 1964, was the first one-act version of Tom Stoppard's *Rosencrantz and Guildenstern Are Dead* – then a one-act *jeu d'esprit* titled *Guildenstern and Rosencrantz*, itself a stream-lining of a more complicated Shakespearean burlesque, written in verse, *Rosencrantz and Guildenstern Meet King Lear*. It was directed by the future distinguished RSC playwright Peter Whelan, who had played a virtuoso solo performance of Beckett's *Krapp's Last Tape* two seasons previously, so he was readily au fait with the absurdist philosophical vein in Stoppard's writing.

The company had fallen in love with the Stanislavsky Room as an intimate performance space after Emmet showed the way with his 1960 revival of Tennessee Williams's *The Glass Menagerie*. The studio theatre was a brand new concept, forced upon amateur theatres in constrained circumstances, but inspired, too, by the intimate theatres of Max Reinhardt and August Strindberg on the continent fifty years earlier. The London fringe of attic and cellar was still ten years away; even the club theatres of the 1930s and 1940s were mostly housed in rudimentary versions of the traditional proscenium arch theatres.

Unsurprisingly, therefore, the Stanislavsky (not re-named the Studio until 1974) became a mecca for the ambitious and talented tyro directors Emmet encouraged within the ranks. One of these was Alan Clarke, a young theatre and television director who had been working in Canada and returned to England to pick up his career in television here. He would later make such blistering, controversial films about the youth sub-culture as *Scum* (1979), *Made in Britain* (1982) and *The Firm* (1989). The distinctive characteristic of these films, apart from their content, was the brilliance of the acting. Clarke learned how to direct actors, he always said, at the Questors, and developed as a director in all ways in his work there, in the Stanislavsky, which included Peter Whelan's Beckett solo hunched over his tape-recorder; O'Neill's *Long Day's Journey Into Night*; new plays by James Saunders and Barry Bermange; outrageous versions of *Macbeth* and Euripides' *Hecuba*; and – surely the first in amateur theatre – an all-male version of Genet's *The Maids* in 1967.

The foundation stone of the new theatre was laid by Michael Redgrave in July 1963, to the accompaniment of greetings from amateur and professional theatres alike, and a personal message from Laurence Olivier. The building was completed in early 1964 with an accumulated debt of £20,000 – still a large figure in those days – and opened with a production by Emmet of Ibsen's *Brand* – no-one could now doubt the seriousness of the Questors' intentions – attended, rather sportingly, one suspects, by the Queen Mother.

Even though Stephen Joseph had initiated in-the-round theatres in Scarborough and Stoke-on-Trent in 1955 and 1962, architect Norman Branson's design was a more flexible version of this idea, allowing for a

FIGURE 6 *The Queen Mother meets the cast of Ibsen's* Brand *at the new Questors in Ealing, west London, after she had performed the opening ceremony in April 1964. (Copyright Photograph: Middlesex County Times and West Middlesex Gazette, courtesy of the Questors.)*

proscenium-style end-stage option if required, as well as the distinctive thrust stage, which supplied two playing areas between which the action could alternate, aiding the flow of the play and the ease of the relationship between actor and audience. This arrangement still applies today, with 'vomitariums' around the playing area allowing actors to enter and exit the stage by a wide variety of routes.

Nothing like it had been seen in Britain. The Elizabethan-style thrust stage at Stratford, Ontario, which opened, pillared and porticoed, in 1957, was the closest, larger-scale, comparison, while Stratford's offspring, so to speak, the 1962 Chichester Festival Theatre, lost its way by forfeiting an intimate sense of scale and creating huge problems – and huge distances – between actor and audience. And today, most new theatres favour the thrust stage principle – the RSC so much so that both their new main houses in Stratford-upon-Avon, the RST and the Swan, are thrust stages, with The Other Place offering an experimental studio option down the road.

Between the opening of the new Questors and 1989, its twenty-fifth anniversary, over half the plays presented were by non-British authors. There were thirty-four productions of Shakespeare, ten each of Saunders and Pinter, nine of Ibsen, eight of Ayckbourn and seventeen of writers from the US, including seven of Tennessee Williams (seven, too, by Chekhov and Brecht). Dannie Abse and David Mowat continued to feature prominently in the new plays list, alongside Saunders and others who may not have made a comparable impact. New plays generally began to find their way more easily to the ever-expanding fringe, as well as the committed new-play theatres beyond the Royal Court such as Hampstead, the Soho Poly, the Open Space, the Bush, and the Tricycle.

As well as an international vision, there was also a sharp focus on the local community. Ties within it were forged with other amateur companies and, crucially, schools in the area. Chief among these was Latymer Upper, in Hammersmith, then a direct-grant grammar school with a paramount interest in music and drama for its pupils, many of whom were state school children paid for by the local authority.

One such was Tony Barber. He was hopeless, he says, at all he did after he left school. He started out as an accountant and ended up as a salesman in exports for an American company, but his life was transformed by the Questors in 1957. His old English master, Wilfred Sharp, who directed all the plays at Latymer (a few generations later, Alan Rickman was a pupil and protégé of his) telephoned Barber – he was one of several masters associated with the Questors – and asked if he'd like to be in *Henry V* in the Tin Hut. Barber leapt at the invitation and played the five-line role of the Duke of Bedford. The head of maths at Latymer was the Duke of Exeter. Barber then joined the student group and trained in voice and movement with professional teachers and in acting, Stanislavsky-style, in Alfred Emmet's classes, which also involved a fair dollop of theory. In the following season he appeared in *The Voice of Shem* – edited passages of James Joyce's *Finnegan's Wake* – directed by one of Questors' historically renowned directors, Colette King, who was at that time head of drama at St Mary's College, Twickenham.

Barber's future wife was in that company, too, but they didn't get together until the 1961/2 season, the last in the Tin Hut, when they appeared in Turgenev's *A Month in the Country*, this time in the Stanislavsky Room. Barber was the dashing young tutor with whom his employer's even younger ward (played by Barber's future wife) falls helplessly in love, naturally. It is not uncommon for relationships to be made (and just as often broken) in the world of amateur theatre, but Mr and Mrs Barber have raised a family and sustained a marriage throughout a lifelong association with the Questors.

Barber, now in his ninth decade, has been treasurer (when he did the company's accounts himself), closely involved with the Grapevine Club (formed in 1958 as much for social drinking reasons as for financial revenue) and duty manager. As an actor he has appeared in more than eighty productions, his dark hair turning snowy white, bowing out with small roles in *The Master Builder* in 2015 and, three years later, a kindly old parish priest in a stark, choric staging of Colm Tóibín's short story *A Priest in the Family* on a typically adventurous Questors' double bill with another notable short Irish text, Brian Friel's version of Chekhov's *The Bear*.

That early pioneering streak of new plays in the Questors' history diminished of necessity, as the fringe expanded, though from the mid-1970s they were quick to reverse the process and bring in to The Studio such landmark plays as E. A. Whitehead's *The Foursome*, Stephen Lowe's *Glass Houses*, Barrie Keefe's *Gotcha!* and even Caryl Churchill's supremely challenging *Light Shining in Buckinghamshire*. Like many other amateur companies, they learned how to secure rights to such plays as well as to the most recent West End hits.

Michael Green published *The Art of Coarse Acting* in 1964, too, so the Questors took care to ensure that the book was not mistaken for a manifesto for the new building. The idea of staging a coarse theatre show – slapstick rejoicing in the time-honoured crudities of some amdram – dates from 1970 when Emmet suggested a coarse acting competition as part of the activities on one particular Open Day. The second competition, in 1972, attracted visiting teams from elsewhere, including one from the RSC, with Anthony Pedley and Roger Rees enacting the murder of Julius Caesar as performed in amdram, with Caesar (Rees) blowing his top, trying to stab Brutus (Pedley) before pursuing him, while spurting blood in all directions, round the auditorium and through an exit door.

That same event featured a surreal Agatha Christie spoof, *Streuth* – the title was an amalgamation of an exclamatory declaration of disbelief ('God's truth' contracting to 'strewth') and the title of Anthony Shaffer's famous thriller *Sleuth* – which began twice, had no conclusion and entangled, fatally, all the characters in their own lines. The Questors took their Coarse Acting Show to the Edinburgh fringe in 1977, offering both *Streuth* and a D. H. Lawrence parody, *A Collier's Tuesday Tea*, in which the kitchen table collapsed at tea-time as a premonition of a more serious disaster at the pit; the tea-time miners couldn't leave the table to fend for itself, so they all went off to the pit carrying the table with them. A sell-out Edinburgh fringe visit from the Questors in 1979 included *Henry the Tenth, Part Seven* and *The Cherry Sisters* sort-of-by Chekhov. Brian Rix invited this show to the Shaftesbury Theatre in the West End for a three-month season, paving the way, no doubt, for *The Play That Goes Wrong* forty years later.

Another first in this period was a visit to the cliff-side Minack Theatre at Porthcurno, Cornwall, with Racine's great tragedy *Phaedra*, the first of the Questors' biennial visits, which continue (though not biennially) to this day. As indeed do the training and education programmes, though not with the intensity of the school visits they sustained in the 1970s, when Questabout was the largest Theatre-in-Education team in England. In addition, the Questors has always been involved, since its formation in 1952, with the International Amateur Theatre Association (IATA) and Emmet organised the first of six IATA festivals in Mattock Lane in 1969, inviting groups from Italy, Moravia, France, Poland, Dublin, the United States and Romania. They participate in the IATA to this day, proud of the fact that they can claim to be the largest independent community theatre in Europe. And in 1996 the theatre received a grant of £667,500 from the National Lottery towards a much-needed comprehensive refurbishment programme.

How and why did all this happen? The story of the Questors is as extraordinary as any in British theatre. Alfred Emmet, one of nature's born networkers and communicators, despite being rather reserved, was a director of the Columbo Commercial Company, which imported tea and rubber from Ceylon and Sri Lanka between the wars. At some point in this career, fascinated by theatre, he read Stanislavsky's *My Life in Art*, and that was it. His successor, and son, David Emmet, an Oxford law graduate, was trained (by his father) on a Questors' course and started to direct at the theatre, edit the members' magazine and take classes. Ten years ago, at the request of his students, he began writing reviews, which he circulates in-house, of every show he sees in the West End, four or five a week, more than the majority of professional critics. 'I see everything except musicals and solo shows' and then he punctures his own high-flown seriousness by telling me that he is about to direct *Daisy Pulls It Off*, a trite but delightful send-up of the Angela Brazil novels, 'because I absolutely love it'.

This overlap of seriousness and triviality is a constant theme in amateur theatre whereas the professionals traditionally keep more severe separations. Emmet clarifies that there is no dynastic thread in the administration. Even if there were, it would end soon, for he has no children and his sister has long since moved away from the theatre – though he remains a member of the board of trustees and the company secretary, director of studies for the training course, casting adviser and chairman of the auditioning panel. At the moment, you have to audition to audition at the Questors. Emmet is adamant – 'It's quality control; I strongly resist going to open auditions' – but not everyone at the theatre agrees with him about this.

What they are all agreed about is the increased importance of hiring and letting their premises – the theatre now has a contract with the University of West London taking all three rehearsal rooms, and lets those rooms to television and professional theatre companies, too. They also uniformly recognise the significance in the growth of the youth theatre, both socially and economically. For the Christmas shows, there are three rotating groups of young people on the stage, so all their parents, relatives and godparents buy tickets, which helps beef up the box office inordinately. In addition to that, there are usually fourteen classes underway every Saturday, each with twenty young people in it, each using every available room, nook and cranny in the place, creating what is undoubtedly the biggest youth theatre of its type in the country. The dwindling general membership – about 1,200 now – means that membership fees, once the largest source of income, produce far less revenue than either the Grapevine bar or the youth theatre classes.

Youth theatre groups are open to all young people between the ages of six and eighteen, and many of them progress to the theatre's Young Studio and a more intense foundation course in acting. As in all the best young theatre the idea is not to train, or even encourage, people to become professional actors, but to give them a good experience, a degree of opportunity and a chance to build confidence and express themselves. This can result in professional success stories, but not every day. Henry Lewis of *The Play That Goes Wrong* fame attests to his time in the youth theatre wing of the Questors as a time when he learned a lot, with a chance 'to get involved in things and try new things out'. And Michael Rosen, the poet, former children's laureate and author of *We're Going On A Bear Hunt*, now a hugely popular children's play, who was a member of Young Questors from 1958–62, has never forgotten the experience: 'I've used those workshops, rehearsals and productions over and over again throughout my life, whether as a performer, public speaker, broadcaster, workshop leader, performance poet or university teacher . . . It was a way of experimenting with the "self" and from that I know I developed a curiosity and a confidence.'

That experience now extends into participating in one of the most exciting initiatives of the National Theatre, the Connections programme of

ten short plays written by practising playwrights, and performed all over
Britain by school and youth theatre companies before a production of each
play is selected for a performance at the National itself in a festival week. In
2018, Young Questors performed *The Changing Room*, a striking, lyrical
piece of sloganeering, antiphonal theatre by Chris Bush for a large ensemble
of young people on the cusp of adulthood, about to take a metaphorical
plunge in a swimming pool.

Young Questors were part of a West London satellite group playing for a
few days in May at west London's Bush Theatre, home of new writing –
other groups included Acton High School and the White City Youth Theatre
– and not least of the pleasures was seeing each group support their peers by
staying on to watch the other play with whom they shared the bill. And it
was clear that maybe a handful of those Young Questors on stage might be
featuring at the Questors proper and beyond in the coming years.

All the same, one area of crisis the Questors shares with many other
amateur theatres is the lack of people on the production side. There is no
shortage of willing actors and directors – although, as in the work place at
large, there is a new surge towards casual employment – but people are not
committing so often to a place or a project over a long period of time, which
means that stage managers, set builders, even designers, are increasingly
hard to find. Because there are fewer volunteers coming in to build the
biggest show of the year, the pantomime, that set was outsourced a few
years ago at a cost of £15,000, an expense that could be absorbed in the box
office takings of at least £45,000 for the annual festive event. But the
experiment wasn't satisfactory, and the panto build returned in-house.

Other areas of expenditure are necessary because of what David Emmet
calls 'an encroaching professionalism': many of the jobs they once did
themselves, such as plumbing and electrical work, they now have to pay for.
The requirements of the new licensing act in 2004 are increasingly hard to
fulfil, says Emmet, which means they might well soon be paying for duty
managers front-of-house. The knock-on effect of that licensing act was to
eliminate the point of being a members-only theatre as the Questors was
obliged to comply with all the requirements asked of any public theatre. So
the members' club became a public theatre in 2005.

> It's good, in a sense, that we no longer have just that captive, committed
> audience, but a much wider one, which in turn means that we have had
> to become far more commercial in our programming. We can no longer
> do an Ibsen in the Judi Dench, for instance – it simply won't sell. We still
> do Shakespeare in the larger space, but Ibsen and probably Chekhov will
> have to be produced in the Studio in future.

This hard-headed approach is shared by Jo Matthews, who has served as
actor, stage manager, director and sometime chair of the board of trustees.
Her daytime occupation is Trusts and Foundations Associate at Shakespeare's

Globe, but her commitments are intensifying by the week as her work as a Questors rep at the Little Theatre Guild has propelled her to the vice-chairmanship of the organisation with the top job a routine matter of course in the near future.

There is no way you can look at her CV and think of her involvement in amateur theatre as a side-line, or a hobby. It's as much a part of her life as her Globe work, her family or her assiduous theatre going. The first production she directed for the Questors – and the Questors, uniquely, allows 100 hours rehearsal for each play, that is four nights a week plus Sundays for six to eight weeks – was Shelagh Stephenson's *A Memory of Water*, a favourite on the amdram circuit, and a sharp and funny piece about three daughters picking over the life and clothes' cupboard of their lately deceased mother.

Matthews trained at Manchester Polytechnic School of Theatre, where her contemporaries included Julie Walters, Matthew Kelly and Bernard Hill, before moving to Germany with husband and children where she taught English. In a life crowded with incident she has been a café manageress and events organiser for the yachting crowd at Cowes on the Isle of Wight, personal assistant to the owner of a big London estate agents and television project co-ordinator for ITV's Year of Promise in 1999. This experience led to her appointment at the Globe under Mark Rylance, where she reports to the development director.

There are similarities with the Questors. Both theatres are the creation of dominating visionaries – Sam Wanamaker and Alfred Emmet – and in both there are dynastic consequences: Wanamaker has three daughters, two of them (not actress Zoë) with a non-executive interest in the place, while David Emmet maintains his father's strict ideas of quality control. Matthews is close to both Andrea Bath, the full-time paid chief executive, and another Questors ex-chair, Anne Gilmour, who is UK representative at the International Amateur Theatre Association, IATA, which Alfred Emmet helped establish.

The whole question of the professional/amateur divide was profoundly re-defined for Jo by one single remark at a recent conference made by the representative of the Plaza Theatre in Romsey, Hampshire: 'I am running a professional venue.' By which he meant that the venue itself is subject to the same legislation, health and safety requirements, and so on, as applies to any professional theatre, whether or not the actors are being paid. The Plaza is perhaps entitled anyway to think of itself as quasi-professional as it has one of the largest seating capacities in the Little Theatre Guild, seating 231 customers in its main auditorium and forty-five in the studio.

Despite all the mounting problems, Matthews reckons the Questors is well set to continue successfully as long as it a) keeps up its momentum, b) copes with the laborious new data protection legislation, which is defeating some smaller theatres, and c) maintains its phenomenal activity as a training and youth theatre centre. 'The cosy social club side of it all is unrealistic financially,' she says, pointing out the complete change from the 1940s and 1950s when ticket sales were the chief source of income and membership fees close behind. Today, income from ticket sales is still at the top, but only just: people are hiring the venue for £3,000 a time, the income from the training classes has multiplied, and membership is down.

One of the nightmares for Matthews is the matter of rights. Although more and more plays are being released to amateurs almost as soon as they have completed their initial runs, there remains the problem of getting rights for an Arthur Miller, say, if there is a major professional production in the offing. Producers are often concerned (absurdly, perhaps) that a performance of the play in a remote amateur theatre venue will damage its own commercial prospects in the West End. Time is the factor here, as most amateur companies have to plan their schedules up to eighteen months in advance. This is an issue Matthews and the LTG are determined to try and sort out.

Alfred Emmet was rather against musicals and pantomimes – the first ever Questors panto was in 1980 – though he did rubber-stamp productions of *The Threepenny Opera* and the two bright beacons of pre-Lionel Bart and Lloyd Webber musical theatre, *Salad Days* and *The Boy Friend*. His most relaxed idea of a Christmas show was either *Charley's Aunt* ('I'm Charley's aunt from Brazil – where the nuts come from') or a Victorian melodrama. So he might be slightly aghast today at the pantomime fixture on the schedule and the plethora of musicals in the eighty-seat Studio.

All the same, a recent Studio revival of *Sweet Charity* drilled right down to the cynical, hard-hearted centre of a report from the front line in the sex-worker game and managed the not inconsiderable feat of evoking the grime and melancholy of the musical's origins in Fellini's *Nights of Calabria* movie while revelling in the sheer knock-'em-dead splendour of numbers like 'Big Spender' and 'Rhythm of Life' as immortalised by Sammy Davis Jr. And an even more difficult piece, *A Little Night Music*, caught exactly that sweet mordancy in a show described by its first director, Hal Prince, as 'whipped cream with knives' and utterly confounded my confident expectation of it being beyond them. The show was notably well dressed and played, without too much strain, in a traverse arrangement, Stephen Sondheim's waltz score of gossamer and gluten eked out sensitively on a trio of keyboards, cello and flute/clarinet.

In the Playhouse itself, recent productions of classics such as *Twelfth Night* and Wycherley's *The Country Wife* – one of the most delightfully filthy plays ever written, which may have kept it on the main stage instead of being consigned, with Ibsen, to the Studio – have not wilted unduly in comparison with professional interpretations. The first was presented as Viola's dream, arriving on a foreign shore as a refugee with a suitcase; she hadn't really been ship-wrecked and hadn't lost her twin brother at all.

Perhaps the Belfast-accented Malvolio was trying too hard in his yellow tartan kilt and deerstalker, and perhaps the Olivia was a bit too squeaky, though definitely capable and original in her reading. But Feste had some very good songs, and Antonio delivered the avuncular line to Sebastian about checking out his lodgings before anything else from the bed they were suddenly sharing – very cool, very modish, very RSC.

The Country Wife was a fairly fussy, old-fashioned production, but it was intelligently cut and played with a brisk friskiness as befits the story-line of a so-called 'eunuch', Horner, being entrusted with married ladies by their husbands because of his apparent innocuousness, lured by promises of sharing his pieces of china, nudge-nudge. The costumes were serviceable 'Restoration' and Sparkish the fop was played most foppishly. The three strands of the plot were well defined and the simple set comprised two standing doorways and three upstage musicians who filled in the small roles. I enjoyed, not too guiltily, one of them opening a door and standing by it with an open cupped hand, as if waiting to catch a raindrop, or a drip from the ceiling, thus earning the show a Coarse Theatre bonus point.

The Country Wife opened in early 2017 in the same week as *The White Devil* in the new Sam Wanamaker at Shakespeare's Globe and coincided with two broadsides about the classics from David Hare and Michael Billington. Hare derided 'the cult of Ivo van Hove' and other European directors 'infecting' the way the British theatre now does the core repertoire, while Billington accused the National Theatre, as it announced a new season, of 'a scandalous dereliction of duty' when it came to the classics. Increasingly, you feel that you might have to clock in to the amateur theatre to see a half-way decent production of a great play at all, let alone one that's not been conceptually mucked about with. There was a time when *The White Devil* and *The Country Wife* turned up regularly in the regional repertory theatres. Not any more, not even in their small studio spaces. You are far more likely to find such plays, and others like them, at the Questors. The amateur theatre might well be returning to its pre-eminent position in the 1930s of custodian of the core classical and European repertoires.

And in fifty years' time that repertoire will probably include several plays by Alan Ayckbourn, whom the Questors have always done fairly well. Their revival of one of Ayckbourn's best black-edged comedies, *Seasons Greetings*, in the Judi Dench, was funny and well cast. In its blend of comedy and tragedy, high farce and low desperation, merriment and disaster, over three days of Christmas, it is often described as Ayckbourn's most Chekhovian play; does that mean, in fifty years' time, it will be produced in the Studio? One hopes not. There was an added irony, too, in an amateur production as good as this when Uncle Bernard rehearsed his dismal puppet play about the three pigs (following the previous year's never-ending Ali Baba with long intervals between the appearance of each of the forty thieves) to the accompaniment of ribald commentary from the others and explains his bizarre dedication to the puppet cause with 'I do it purely for love. I could never accept money for it.'

Peter Whelan, like James Saunders, was a fine dramatist who might have slipped through the net but for the Questors. Like Saunders, he never lost his devotion to the place. He died in 2014, but his last play, *Sleepers in the Fields*, written in 2009, remained unperformed until January 2018 when John Davey directed it in the Judi Dench auditorium. The play is rich in the qualities of decency, ambiguity and suppleness of argument that characterised all Whelan's plays. As in most of them, you never really know what is going to happen next, mainly because the playwright surprises you with characters who don't conform to type. Michael Billington said that Davey's production was 'alive to every nuance of this deliberately unromantic drama' and was 'exceptionally well acted'.

In many ways, the production was a statement of core values, commitment and continuity: Davey himself has directed at the Questors for over forty years; Robin Ingram, who played a war-time refugee from Bratislava, was tutored by Alfred Emmet before training at the Guildhall School and appearing in three Peter Whelan plays at the Questors prior to this one; while Claudia Carroll, who played a central, pivotal character, trained at Questors and has worked there as a Youth Theatre teacher. Everything about the place reinforces the impression – formed by its professional supporters right at the start – that the Questors is a microcosm of our national theatre activity, and an irreplaceable phenomenon of our theatre ecology.

Second looks and second chances in amdram: An interlude

Something else the regional theatre used to do far more often than it does now is take a second look at plays by major dramatists that didn't find box office favour in the West End. Ayckbourn's *Damsels in Distress* trilogy of 2001, performed in rotation on different nights by the author's Scarborough company in London, received mixed reviews. It fell into that category of Ayckbourn drama where, as opposed to the sure-fire success story of a play like *Seasons Greetings*, an audience is not quite sure whether theatrical oomph matches the indisputable craft on display.

The problem in the West End was complicated, too, by the confusion arising from the fact that patrons who were keen to see a new Ayckbourn play were less keen on seeing three of them on different nights and then not being sure, if they saw just one, that they would pick the best of them. Result: commercial failure. As the box office slumped, the London producers attempted remedial action by dropping two of the plays in the week and playing the whole trilogy only on Saturdays. This led to a serious stand-off between Ayckbourn and his quintet of producers – one of whom, Michael Codron, had been associated with many Ayckbourn West End hits over the years – and a declaration by the playwright that he no longer wanted anything to do with the West End (he has of course had two or three productions on Shaftesbury Avenue since the spat).

So it was interesting to discover that the little Archway Theatre in Horley, Surrey, had presented the triple bill, very successfully, several years after the West End disaster. It's difficult to see how: the three unrelated plays are admittedly all set in the same London Docklands riverside apartment, but the Archway stage, housed inside one of the ten railway arches the company has occupied since 1952, is seriously tiny. Still, there are only seven actors in the cast, and the Archway collaborated with two other amateur companies – the Lewes Little in East Sussex and the Oast Theatre, Tonbridge (located inside an old Kentish oast house) – and shared the spoils of the play as it went out on tour to each other's home base. The Lewes company has also presented one of Ayckbourn's least known, most haunting and, you might even say, upsetting plays, *Woman in Mind* in which the housewife of the title imagines, in a psychological reverie out on the lawn, an alternative family to that which she's lumbered with indoors.

These undertakings completely belie the popular misconception that amateur theatre is some sort of cosy artistic cocoon devised primarily for the benefit of those taking part. The second half of that definition is arguably sometimes the whole point – but I've increasingly found myself turning to amateurs to see second productions of new plays. And the rights are more readily available today than they were ten years ago. Take the phenomenon of Jez Butterworth's *Jerusalem*, one of the really outstanding plays of the century so far, not least because of Mark Rylance's outsize performance as Johnny 'Rooster' Byron, the alcoholic, homeless traveller defying the authorities and a nanny state clean-up campaign in the heart of the Wiltshire woodlands.

The play struck a deep atavistic chord in audiences rediscovering something moving, true and mysterious in their ideas of a larger sort of inclusive patriotism than the one prescribed by the Brexit campaign. This outspoken, raunchy and radical roller-coaster of a state-of-the-nation play has become the darling of amdram all over the country, with the performance rights being released to amateurs from Bromley to Newcastle, from Bath to Solihull and Leamington Spa, with one new Johnny Byron apparently basing his performance of what he called 'a pirate punk Puck' on Joe Strummer of the Clash. The director of the Leamington Spa production, 77-year-old Gordon Vallins, described the play as 'a wild journey through ancient and modern England, from weathered standing stones to William Blake, to losing one's youth, to dope and booze, to Trivial Pursuit and gnomes in a wheelbarrow – it appeals to the rebellious side of all of us'.

We really have moved on in the theatre very quickly in the past fifty years, especially in new writing – there are no more citadels of taste, decorum or morality for the theatre to breach and the amateur theatre can be instrumental in cementing this progress as it becomes far less easily perceived as a branch of the Women's Institute and National Trust than a supplementary outpost on a new frontier. That is certainly one way of winning back younger audiences and re-wiring what is incessantly, and annoyingly, now termed the national 'conversation'.

These thoughts were first prompted when I turned up one evening to see a revival at the Tower Theatre of Lee Hall's outrageous *Cooking with Elvis*, a 1999 play premiered at the professional Live Theatre in Newcastle and presented soon after on the Edinburgh fringe, and then in the West End, starring the comedian Frank Skinner as a butt-naked, slow-witted cake-maker in the blackest of all possible comedies by the author of *Billy Elliot* and the *War Horse* movie. Amateur companies would not have countenanced doing such a play several decades ago, but as tastes and norms of acceptability changed with Beckett, Pinter and Joe Orton, so the amateur theatre has followed suit. And with increasing rapidity. In this seventy-fifth anniversary season at the Tower in 2017, the programme also included revivals of Debbie Isitt's *The Woman Who Cooked Her Husband* and Bryony Lavery's *Frozen*, both significant and hard-hitting contemporary plays that are regularly revived on the amateur circuit.

Tower Theatre

Cooking with Elvis was produced by the Tower in the little Teatro Technis in Camden Town, one of three north London fringe venues they have occupied since losing their home base in Canonbury, Islington, in 2003. It really is astonishing that they have survived in the intervening period and are now, at last, ensconced in a new permanent home in a fine octagonal Victorian Gothic building in Stoke Newington, north London, which has been used in the past as a Methodist chapel, a synagogue and a women-only gymnasium.

Could we look forward, therefore, to an opening season of *The Mystery Plays* (with Wesleyan hymns), *Fiddler on the Roof* and *Lysistrata*? Such a programme would perfectly demonstrate the range and seriousness of the Tower tradition since its earliest days in Tavistock Place, Bloomsbury, when, in 1921, a 'dramatic art' centre was incorporated as part of the Mary Ward Educational Settlement (Mary Ward was a socially conscious Victorian novelist). The large hall there had already been used by the innovative Shakespearean William Poel – the man who discovered Edith Evans – for his Shakespearean rehearsals, and by the St Pancras People's Theatre, which included such important budding actors as Maurice Evans (the first 'uncut' Hamlet on the modern American stage in 1938) and Jessica Tandy, before they joined forces with the new professional People's Theatre of Nancy Price at the Little Theatre in Adam Street off the Strand. To this day, the Tower, as it is known, is registered as the Tavistock Repertory Company on account of its first location.

The Tavistock Little Theatre opened in 1932 with a double bill of a fourteenth-century French farce and a nineteenth-century Spanish comedy, followed by plays of Noël Coward, St John Ervine, Gogol, Karel Čapek, and *A Midsummer Night's Dream* with music by Michael Tippett, who was taking a class at the Settlement. The constituency of the company, according to one of its earliest members and historian, Frank Smith, was ambitious amateurs such as Alec Clunes, on his way to Croydon Rep and the Old Vic; working women, some in acting schools, some in part-time teaching; and, prominent among the men, a type of 'professional amateur', who devoted all of his spare time to the cause. Smith himself, who became one of the leading actors and directors with the company, also helped out at the Arts Theatre when Clunes transformed it during the 1940s into the most successful club theatre London had ever seen, with a membership of 25,000 and premieres of plays by Christopher Fry, Peter Ustinov and John Whiting.

The Tavistock Rep itself was very much part of this climate of seriousness and new work, touring to other Educational Settlements in South Wales, before war broke out, with Shaw's *Arms and the Man* (Shaw reduced his royalty fee to a minimum and also sent a donation), André Obey's *Noah* and J. B. Priestley's *déjà vu* drama *I Have Been Here Before*. And, after the war, the company played at the open air theatre in Torquay. The current Tower Theatre continues this tradition, with less educational zeal, perhaps, in touring to the Minack in Cornwall, or the Jardin Shakespeare in the Bois de Boulogne in Paris. The extent to which the amateur theatre in the 1930s and 1940s was stitched into the cultural fabric of the nation is clear from the links the Tavistock Rep had, for instance, with the left-wing Unity Theatre (whose first life member was H. G. Wells and whose general council included Stafford Cripps, Tyrone Guthrie, Sean O'Casey and Paul Robeson) and the Open Air Theatre, Regent's Park, both set-ups also dating from the early 1930s.

The forward momentum continued when the Tavistock Little Theatre became increasingly unavailable, and indeed too small, for the company, and they took a fifteen-year lease, renewable every five years thereafter, on the Tower in Canonbury in 1952. The Tower was a copy of a sixteenth-century church in Kent belonging to the estate of the Marquis of Northampton. It had been home, at various times, to Thomas Cromwell, Sir Francis Bacon and Oliver Goldsmith. The estate trustees leased to the Tavistock at £600 a year on condition that they undertook all the repairs necessary and left the floor of the auditorium completely flat, with seating that could be stacked and stowed away.

The place had panelled walls, beautiful furniture, one of the oldest wooden staircases in Britain and a lovely garden. In all, an oasis of enchantment in what was, in those days, a fairly insalubrious area still. After an appeal to raise funds and garner donations from the likes of Edith Evans, Gracie Fields, Thornton Wilder and Compton Mackenzie, the new Tower opened in February 1953 with a version of the Don Juan story, *Man Into Action*, by André Obey, and the simple policy statement of 'plays of quality at prices which all can afford' supported with a season of Lorca, Shakespeare, Ibsen and James Bridie.

As at the Questors, the roster of classic revivals in the 1950s is amazing – Gogol, Tennessee Williams (film director Ken Loach directed *Summer and Smoke* with a visiting Oxford University group in 1957), Somerset Maugham, Jean-Paul Sartre and Oliver Goldsmith, who had lived in the Tower for two years. The overlap with the professional theatre was reinforced in the mid-1950s when John Fernald, the principal at RADA and a friend of the Tower, sent along three of his outstanding students – Siân Phillips, to appear in *The Just* by Albert Camus; Tom Courtenay in Andrew Rosenthal's *Third Person*, an American comedy about a deep attachment between two men, one of them conventionally married; and Joanna Dunham in Turgenev's *A Month in the Country*.

And then the first London revival of Pinter's *The Birthday Party* in May 1959 in which David Jones, then working at the BBC and later to become an RSC associate director and indeed a very fine director of Pinter (he directed the movie of *Betrayal*), played McCann. After hitting a brick wall when he asked Pinter where McCann had come from before he turned up in the boarding house, Jones was forced, he told Michael Billington, Pinter's biographer, to face, and then accept, the idea that plays were more interesting if people were as mysterious or unexplained as they were in real life.

Jones directed Beckett's *Endgame* and Ghelderode's *Pantagleize* at the Tower before moving on to his distinguished career, notable for his brilliant RSC productions of Gorky. In the 1959/60 season, no less than ten of the sixteen plays presented received coverage in the national Press. One of them, Euripides' *The Bacchae*, went up to the Edinburgh Festival, where Kenneth Tynan proclaimed in the Observer that it was 'the best and strongest show on the fringe – indeed on the whole theatrical wing of the festival,' adding that the chorus of Maenads were 'magnificently drilled' in David Thompson's production.

The Tower's reputation was now secure, and further consolidated in the 1960s when Richard Baker, the celebrated BBC television newsreader, who had been with the company for many years, played Fancourt Babberley in *Charley's Aunt* and Sara Randall, an actors' agent and later artistic director of the Tower, played the lead in the British premiere of Williams's *The Milk Train Doesn't Stop Here Any More* ('a resplendent monstre sacré' said Irving Wardle in *The Times*). The repertoire in that season of 1968/9 – Edward Bond's *Saved*, Brian Friel's *Philadelphia Here I Come*, Ionesco's *Exit the King* and Christopher Fry's *Venus Observed* – was comparable to any professional theatre's in the land, including the National's. After a gala to celebrate the funding of major improvements in the auditorium and on the stage, they produced Congreve's *Love in a Bottle* and the British premiere of Arrabal's sexually explicit and poetic *Car Cemetery*.

By the time I turned up as a reviewer in the early 1970s, the gorgeous, welcoming little theatre was no longer a cultural oasis in a run-down area, but a surprise feature of a rising property market and a fully incorporated symbol of middle-class improvement and gentrification. It still maintained its very high production standards and I remember the pleasure of discovering that two of our leading young designers of that time – William Dudley and Sue Plummer – had cut their teeth working there. Dudley, who would go on to work at the Royal Court and the National Theatre, was a local lad on his way to art school and had stumbled across the Tower through contacts made on his Saturday job in the renowned nearby Canonbury Bookshop. Regular visitors to the place – which comprised an art shop, as well as a bookshop – included playwright Joe Orton and his lover (and future murderer) Kenneth Halliwell, while the actor and songwriter Anthony Newley lived in a flat on the top floor. Dudley found himself painting sets and then building them at the Tower while progressing through St Martin's and the Slade art school.

His first design, in 1966, had been for Machiavelli's *Mandragora*, and he and Sue Plummer, who came to the Tower already qualified as a graphic artist, and was en route to designing for the Half Moon, Hampstead Theatre and the National, worked together feverishly and continued that relationship, often designing sets and costumes between them, into their subsequent professional careers. The Tower still retains this palpable sense of belonging to the theatre world at large, not least because in devising its own constitution of committees, directors and chairmen, it has always believed in having an artistic director as the final arbiter of policy and plays. The model had been found in such London creative powerhouses of the 1930s as the Gate Theatre at Charing Cross run by Norman Marshall, the Mercury of Ashley Dukes in Notting Hill and the Old Vic and Sadler's Wells of Lilian Baylis on either side of the river.

The artistic director of the Tower at the time of writing is Martin Mulgrew, a prosecuting barrister from Newcastle, specialising in manslaughter and murder cases, most of which, he says, he wins. He recognises 'absolutely' the element of performance link between court room and theatre and confirms that he retains total control of the choice of plays for each season. Like so many accomplished amateurs, he didn't want the insecurity of the professional acting life, training instead, after taking his law degree, with the now disbanded Poor School in King's Cross, London, and then joining the Tower, where he has acted and directed for many years. He is not at all happy about the lack of diversity in the company – 'we are almost totally white' – and has no less than four assistants looking into ways of broadening the appeal to newer, and younger, audiences, not to mention members.

The sense of belonging that the Tower inculcates in its members has waned in the years since losing Canonbury in an unfortunate accident in

2003. The seventh Marquis, whose interests included Freemasonry and ancient forms of mysticism, always wanted his rent on time but the solicitor in the company charged with posting off the cheque that year missed the post and the lease was promptly withdrawn. The building is currently used as a Masonic research centre.

Whereas Mulgrew has looked on the bright side of being peripatetic, Jean Carr, a retired educational psychologist and experienced director at the Tower, notes that the younger people who join don't have the same 'yearning to belong' as she did – 'they all belong to lots of other things as well!' Jean recalls loving the strict discipline of the place, the doing of all sorts of odd jobs – making some doors was her first task thirty-odd years ago – and someone cooking roast dinner in the Tower every Sunday. Not only is she interested in the range of talents used in the process of making theatre, she believes that 'acting is often about escaping from oneself to find one's role, literally, in life'.

Such a philosophy is shared by many, I'd even say the majority, of professional actors. Though not, perhaps, by the actor Simon Williams, whose amusingly disdainful tirade against the amateur theatre, already quoted in the introduction to this book, contains the following:

> It is a little galling when theatres that struggle to cover their overheads with a professional company have the House Full boards out when the local am-drams put on a show. Imagine a group of unpaid locals in, say, medicine or banking, rocking up to suggest that the doctors or bankers take a week's unpaid leave from their hospital or bank because, 'We always fancied having a go.' You can see why we lesser-spotted thespians get our codpieces in a twist.

If Williams had seen a Tower lunchtime performance of one of Alan Bennett's television *Talking Heads* monologues by Ian Recordon, a long-standing Tower member, he might have revised his opinions. The piece in question was *A Chip in the Sugar* in which a middle-aged mother's boy (first played by Bennett himself, which added to Recordon's problems), a repressed homosexual, intervenes in the courtship of widowed 'Mam', with whom he still lives, by an old flame with suspect views and another life.

Recordon missed barely a lilt or a nuance in this delicately written short piece, which burns all the same with a peculiar brand of suburban ferocity. And he did so without any hint of the fine-grained superciliousness Bennett himself imparts so gracefully in his performances. The heart, and the fear, of loneliness was the point.

Shared values, shared purpose, these define the best amateur theatre companies and indeed best fringe theatre groups, and are less commonly found in the more mercenary and fragmented world of professional theatre, where the making of careers and money leads actors into all variety of bargains – some good, some less so, as Simon Williams himself would attest

– in the consuming maw of the entertainment media. The work of a company like the Tower, at its best, can stand in pristine and refreshing relief alongside the professional theatre world. I believe this appeal often transcends the work that is less good, and sometimes even downright bad, and gives it another sort of validity, and vitality, in the enthusiasm and technical innocence of the production standards.

This was certainly the case with Jean Carr's production (one she co-directed with another Tower stalwart, John Morton, also a psychology maven, with a PhD from Reading University) of *Much Ado About Nothing*, which played at the Bridewell in May 2017 before touring to the Jardin Shakespeare in Paris. *Much Ado*, to start with, is a fiendishly difficult comedy to pull off, and Jean at least made a move in the right direction by setting it in Regency/Jane Austen period costume – the play demands a conclusive decision about its period and setting; successful recent professional interpretations have commandeered *Downton Abbey* in the First World War and *Dad's Army* in the Second – with Beatrice channelling Gwyneth Paltrow as Austen's calculating heroine Emma in her rush to the wrong conclusion all the time and, as she calms down, the emergence of a sympathetic humanity at work.

But there was a classic amdram miscalculation in the design, which substituted fussy standing scenery and trite furnishings for the outdoor 'gulling' scenes, which need speed and lightness. Benedick, though, was handsome and fairly dashing, while a lovely little actor, the Tower old-timer Peter Novis, played a finical, defeated Verges alongside John Chapman's confidently booming Dogberry. I followed the production to Paris in the hope of seeing improvement in the comedy scenes with Dogberry's raggle-taggle watch, which were hampered with crude physicality and some really disastrous, unfunny 'business' with a knob falling off Dogberry's cane. But in the serene boskiness of the Jardin Shakespeare, even though John Chapman had been succeeded as Dogberry by the actor also playing Don John (surely a first in the all-time annals of doubling-up), there was that damned knob again, still coming away from its loading bay to an audience reaction of deafening silence, even in French.

Overall, though, the audience at a schools matinée in the Jardin were beside themselves. They had obviously studied the play, and followed the text carefully without resorting all that often to the summarising sub-titles projected at the side of the stage. The performance was interrupted by a spectacular thunderstorm and the audience was sweet, especially the crowd of convent school girls discussing the play, and Benedict's obvious attributes, with their religiously attired teacher. Theatre, for me, is as much about the outing as about the show. And I liked seeing the play in sharp relief to its interpretation, as though reading a score in 3-D while a scratch orchestra fails to deliver the music aurally. I found myself warming, for no good reason, to Leonato's stock repertoire of grinning amiability and semaphored gestures. Antonio made a good fist, too, of his great rasping speech of anger about Claudio's false allegation against his beloved Hero.

I even relished the moment when Jean Carr came up to me before the show started and said that she was hoping to turn the Jardin into a 'mini-Glyndebourne'. Good luck with that. For the theatre, created in 1857, and re-named the Jardin Shakespeare in 1953, is a slightly sad and run-down location. The hedges and the planting are not of an exactly Kew Gardens, or even Regent's Park, standard. There is a stone pit along the front of the acting area, a lovely permanent grotto, and a tunnel running off to the side, all providing a good variety of entrances and exits fully exploited by the Tower, who have been coming here for two decades. This setting, with its indigenous, innate scenery, was a vast improvement on the glum banality of the Bridewell at Ludgate Circus, and made you think that, yes, all Shakespeare that had been written for the open air theatre was infinitely better in the open air, even 400 years later.

Now, in their new home in Stoke Newington, the Tower can restore the one key element they have been lacking these past fifteen years or so since losing their home in Canonbury: the social and community side. Each production, admits one of their longest serving directors and board members, David Taylor, has of late been an entity unto itself, cocooned from the company at large. The new premises has a resplendent new bar and social area in addition to the flexible theatre space (with seating for approximately a hundred). On the top level, three rehearsal rooms, an office, a set-building area, props and costume stores, and even a basement, formerly housing a swimming pool with sauna cubicles (legacy of the women's gym days), which is now converted into storage and more reading and rehearsal space. The octagonal structure is the key to the attractiveness of the new auditorium, which rises magnificently into the timber roof of the building.

The renovation has gained the advisory support, too, of William Dudley. He recalls turning up to meet the company when they first looked round their new home and, although he didn't know any of them, he was touched by their high spirits, enthusiasm and, above all, sense of fun. Nice people, he thought, just as they were when he joined and found his life suddenly transformed. Just as the Questors studied the form and looked to the future while building their new home in 1964, so the Tower has been fortunate in securing the advice and *pro bono* input of their own practitioner who has worked in every kind of theatre space – the adaptable courtyard of the Dorfman and the challenging Olivier at the NT, the Royal Court and international opera houses in the post-proscenium theatre age.

Towards the end of 2018, the new theatre opened with *Henry V*. I loved the provisional, deliberately makeshift tenor of the production – 'O for a Muse of fire, that would ascend/The brightest heaven of invention,/A kingdom for a stage, princes to act/And monarchs to behold the swelling scene!' – as Penny Tuerk's tough and importunate Chorus beseeched us to piece out their imperfections with our thoughts. And then she took her place at an all-too-visible stage management table, among the cues and props, as the play proceeded with spirit, candour and invention. As Jaques says in *As You Like It*, 'And one man in his time plays many parts.' Penny was also the governor of Harfleur and a French soldier. Another actress was the Duke of both Gloucester and Orleans as well as Captain MacMorris. And a debutant actor took on the Dauphin, Lord Scroop and Queen Isabel. This was a flexible, engaging production with a young heroic actor at its centre as the king. This was his second Tower production, the programme informed us, 'having appeared in the title part of Frankenstein earlier this year'. That's the spirit. A new dawn at one of our leading amateur companies seemed emblematic of exciting times ahead.

Both theatres, the Questors and the Tower, clearly, are not merely amateur sideshows to the main event of British theatre, but plugged into the energising activity of forward momentum and artistic innovation. They are, and always have been, as much a part of the national theatre as the National Theatre itself. And as if to underline that point, in April 2019, the Questors presented a revival of Mike Bartlett's challenging *King Charles III*, first seen at the Almeida starring the late Tim Pigott-Smith in 2014. The lead was taken by Ian Recordon, switching horses from the Tower, and finding a more broken, defeated figure in the monarch-in-waiting than did his illustrious predecessor in the role, egged on to fatal nemesis by two performances by Claudia Carroll and James Burgess as Kate and William that had 'professional' stamped all over them. We may not have had, in this production, the ghost of Diana in person, but we certainly had the Macbeths of Windsor Castle, as Bartlett's satirical conceit defines them, in full satanic glory.

6

Three Non-Professionals in Profile: Robert Pennant Jones, Penny Tuerk and Michael Godley

It is high time to get close up and personal with some exemplary stalwarts of the amdram scene, veterans who have lived full professional lives as well as, on the whole, fulfilling non-professional careers on the stage. Two of our trio – Michael Godley and Robert Pennant Jones – have indeed flirted with the professional stage and carry with them a partial history of their respective post-war university days at Oxford and Cambridge. Here, a great tranche of our national theatre has originated, or been nurtured, in the Oxford University Dramatic Society (the OUDS) and the Marlowe Society.

Although the first drama degree was offered at Bristol University in 1947, where Glynne Wickham headed the theatre studies department, the most influential nexus of theatrical advancement, rooted in the classical tradition, and in Shakespeare, was a two-pronged evolutionary process through the twentieth century at Oxford and Cambridge. Oxford student theatre produced two key directors in the early days of the English Stage Company at the Royal Court – friends from the same region of West Yorkshire, Tony Richardson (who directed John Osborne's *Look Back in Anger*) and William Gaskill (who championed John Arden, Ann Jellicoe and Edward Bond), as well as arguably Britain's greatest critic since Shaw, Kenneth Tynan.

Cambridge was the cradle of the Royal Shakespeare Company. Peter Hall, alongside the academic John Barton, led the light blue domination of the theatrical directocracy in the latter half of the twentieth century when, having founded the RSC in 1961, he succeeded Laurence Olivier as artistic director of the National in 1973. Hall was followed by three successive Cantabrigians – Richard Eyre, Trevor Nunn (who had succeeded Hall at the RSC) and Nicholas Hytner.

The key figure in this history, with an indissoluble link to both the Cambridge undergraduate theatre and the amateur theatre at large, is Ian McKellen.

McKellen is arguably the pre-eminent classical actor of his generation. He is patron of his home-town amateur theatre, where he trod the boards as a schoolboy – the Bolton Little Theatre – and was, for ten years, a notably active patron of the Little Theatre Guild, even as he achieved international fame in two major Hollywood film franchises, *Lord of the Rings* and *X-Men*.

Robert Pennant Jones

Robert Pennant Jones was a contemporary of McKellen and a friend since the day they were both interviewed for a place at St Catharine's College in 1957. They both joined all the student theatre societies, both won – and forfeited, due to their theatrical activities – Exhibitions to read English, and both ended up taking lower second class degrees. Pennant Jones appeared in just nine student productions whereas McKellen took part – and major roles – in no less than twenty-six.

Pennant Jones's audition piece at his college interview was by James Shirley, the Caroline dramatist who was one of the most significant alumni of St Catharine's. Sixty years later, he went with McKellen to see a London fringe revival of Shirley's *The Cardinal*. Throughout his amateur acting career with the Tower Theatre, McKellen has been a constant friend, dropping in on Pennant Jones's highly regarded King Lear in 2015 ('Well', said McKellen to Pennant Jones's wife, after the performance, 'he need never act again') in between playing the role himself, twice.

McKellen was a grammar school boy, whereas Pennant Jones had sniffed the smell of the greasepaint at Bradfield College, where he played both Antigone and Oedipus at Colonus in Greek (though he was not a Greek scholar) as well as Cassius in *Julius Caesar*. At that time, Pennant Jones believed he was the best actor in the world. He did his National Service and went up to Cambridge where he found his ambition of global pre-eminence at first challenged, then seriously undermined, not only by McKellen, but by the budding talents of Derek Jacobi, Clive Swift, Corin Redgrave, Miriam Margolyes and Terrence Hardiman, not to mention a bunch of budding directors who would find notable success later on – John Tydeman, Waris Hussein, Richard Marquand, Richard Cottrell and a mop-haired Trevor Nunn. Pennant Jones realised that this lot were, even then, totally committed to careers in the theatre and the arts. Although he claims to have upstaged Jacobi's Prince Hal while playing the Sheriff in *Henry IV, Part One* (in which McKellen was a widely noted and decrepit Justice Shallow, tutored in 'old man' acting by John Barton), he eventually realised, too, that, as none of his nine roles were major ones, he'd better think again.

So he became head of British Petroleum (BP) in Britain instead. While working his way through lower managerial ranks, he was lured by a friend to the Tower Theatre in Canonbury, just a few stops on the underground from his London city office in Moorgate. Rehearsing in the evenings and on

FIGURE 7 *Robert Pennant Jones, centre, as John Cadmus in John Whiting's* Marching Song, *directed for the Tower by Penny Tuerk in December 2014. (Photo: David Sprecher.)*

Sundays was compatible with his work as a junior manager without travel obligations. He took about twenty roles and directed, among others, Marlowe's *Tamburlaine* in 1964 (the first since Donald Wolfit's at the Old Vic in 1952); Beckett's *Waiting for Godot* – which led to an invitation to meet Beckett in Paris – and John Osborne's *The Entertainer*. 'There wasn't a play I didn't want to do; there wasn't a part I didn't want to play', Pennant Jones tells me in his house in a quiet square in Borough, south London, the living room dominated by a huge mural painting depicting scenes from all thirty-seven of Shakespeare's plays.

The painting was a retirement present to himself in 1994 at the age of fifty-six. Over the previous sixteen years, away from the Tower, he became a senior executive at BP with several overseas postings. But he kept in touch, arranging sponsorship, for instance, for the Tower's annual visit to perform in the Jardin Shakespeare in the Bois de Boulogne in Paris and, on retiring, promptly returned to the Tower to play Hugh, the hedge-school teacher and classicist in Brian Friel's *Translations*; Captain Shotover in Shaw's *Heartbreak House* ('because I admired Scofield in the role so much'); the old professor in Chekhov's *Uncle Vanya* ('I'd admired Max Adrian in that role'); Pozzo in his second 'go' at *Waiting for Godot*; Prospero in *The Tempest*; and Lear.

'I've never regretted not acting professionally', he says, though he did acquire an Equity card by working at a little theatre in Wisbech, Cambridge, when it was run by another university friend and contemporary, the actor Michael Burrell. He played the murdered Duncan in a production for schools of *Macbeth*, but when he returned later in the performance as the doctor in the sleep-walking scene, a boy in the front row piped up, 'I thought that old bugger was dead!'

This was one of only three professional assignments for which he accepted payment. The other two, on which he certainly deserved to earn a little corn, were the real-life mass murderer Harold Shipman for a docu-drama on Japanese television (his mug-shot in *Spotlight*, the casting directory told him, rather disconcertingly, had done the trick) and, on a five-city tour to India, directing the Broadway comedy *Butterflies Are Free*.

In 2009, the designer William Dudley, one of the Tower's most distinguished alumni, asked Pennant Jones to put together a show celebrating the genius of Christopher Marlowe to raise funds for the newly discovered remains of the Rose Theatre just round the corner from the thriving Globe. Pennant Jones produced a short 'virtual reality' film of great Marlovian speeches projected onto the stage area, shown on the hour, every hour, and delivered by, among others, Judi Dench, Alan Rickman, Harriet Walter, Antony Sher, Ian McKellen and Derek Jacobi.

This academic and practical activity re-boots the whole notion of the enthusiastic amateur, for Pennant Jones is as dedicated to the craft of theatre and its literature as any vaunted professional. He formed a small film production company where he has performed dramatic monologues such as Robert Browning's deeply affecting 'My Last Duchess' – he suddenly breaks off in our conversation to recite it, then notes that Ian McKellen had included the piece, partly at his suggestion, in a fundraising solo show for the Park Theatre in north London in the summer of 2017 – and a four-voice version of T. S. Eliot's *The Four Quartets*.

He made a series of short programmes for the BBC Radio World Service about fathers and daughters in Shakespeare, and his catalogue for the large Shakespeare painting is a mine of fresh, practical criticism of the plays – the famous stage direction in *The Winter's Tale*, 'Exit pursued by a bear,' when Antigonus deposits the infant Perdita on the barbarous shore, having been instructed by her father, Leontes, to dispose of her altogether, gets him going: 'The stage direction is often cited as the most ridiculous in Shakespeare. That's nonsense. It's one of the most pregnant and moving moments in the entire canon. It has a crucial point: old age sacrifices itself for youth. The incident is the turning point of *The Winter's Tale*; a seed is planted that will flourish next spring.'

Most members of the Tower muck in with backstage work, front-of-house duties, painting scenery and so on, but not Pennant Jones. You do not, in his book, have to be a wilting violet or a jack-of-all-trades to be a good company member: 'I don't do tickets or serve behind the bar. I'm an actor, a director, and a friend.' In his one stint as Tower's artistic director, for the 1965/6 season, he presented a season of West Indian plays followed by a visit of the Negro Theatre Workshop, one of Britain's first Afro-Caribbean companies, founded in 1963, and then a three-play season of tragic revenge plays performed in repertory by the one company – the *Agamemnon* of Aeschylus, Tourneur's *The Revenger's Tragedy* and Arthur Miller's *A View from the Bridge*.

Such a programme at least matched, in ambition and seriousness, most other work in the regional, let alone London, theatre of that time. He concedes that an element of cultural high-mindedness has gone from the company, but not completely. 'I used to say that we are the theatre that does the second production of any West End show that deserves a revival. But you don't see us doing things like *The Libation Bearers* so much these days. The Tower audience is not so much a classical audience now, but it is still a very *good* audience.'

The Tower was peripatetic for fifteen years in all. If he were to be invited (he wasn't) to direct the opening production in their new Stoke Newington, north London, home in 2018, he would have loved to direct the play in which he made his Tower debut back in 1962 – the stark Elizabethan docudrama *Arden of Feversham*. 'I am amazed the Tower has survived the loss of its home base in Canonbury, where the bar was the social hub of the company. I really thought it would wither, dissolve and disappear. But it has survived, and the stalwarts have kept it going in the most amazing way. And now it's back in business on its own new turf. I take my hat off to us.'

Penny Tuerk

One of those stalwarts was Penny Tuerk, who died unexpectedly in early 2019 after suffering a stroke. She was chairman of the Tower for two seasons in the early 1980s, served as artistic director for three years, played many leading roles with a signature toughness and incisive articulation and directed *Curiouser and Curiouser*, her own adaptation of Lewis Carroll's two *Alice* books, in 2007.

Unlike Robert Pennant Jones, she did more than her fair share of 'mucking in'. She manned the box office, ran sound and lighting cues, and provided the sur-titled summaries in French for the Jardin Shakespeare performances in Paris. And she directed thirty productions for the company, ranging across Shakespeare, Osborne and Henry James to an award-winning *Once in a Lifetime* and Amelia Bullmore's witty student piece *Di and Viv and Rose*.

She met her husband, Laurence Tuerk, a retired sound engineer at the BBC, when they both worked on a 1975 Tower production of *Oh, What a Lovely War*. He was, and still is, one of the Tower's most experienced and dependable technicians and stage managers. Penny herself, a graduate of York University, worked at the BBC World Service as an arts producer (I was a regular contributor on her arts programme, *Meridien*, in the 1970s) then as head of presentation at the World Service, rising eventually to be head of planning and controller of the World Service network.

FIGURE 8 *Penny Tuerk, centre, as Margrethe Bohr in the Tower Theatre Company's production of Michael Frayn's* Copenhagen, *performed at the Bridewell Theatre in May 2006. (Photo: Ian Cole.)*

She always wanted to act, and did so at York, but was discouraged by parental pressure – even though her mother had trained as an actress and her father hailed from a line of music hall performers, one of whom, Syd Walker, a star of BBC Radio's 1930s comedy show *Band Waggon* alongside Arthur Askey and Richard Murdoch, kept three families on the go. Show business, even the serious theatre, was not quite the middle-class 'done thing' until very recently, and even less so for women. So Penny was one of many propelled into the more respectable establishment maw of the BBC administration.

But even as a schoolgirl and a member of the National Youth Theatre during the holidays, NYT contemporaries such as Helen Mirren, Barrie Rutter and Timothy Dalton, she admitted, exuded a more focused, driven purpose to their work, just as Pennant Jones perceived among his Cambridge motley crew. But Tuerk was also aware of an outside perception of 'amateur' in the theatre very different from the idea of an amateur in, say, music or the visual arts, where levels of competence and interpretation are less open to dispute.

At a basic level, anyone can get up on a stage and play Hamlet. It's rarer, and more difficult, to play a Beethoven concerto or paint a portrait, however badly. Even Bernard Shaw, she reminded me, differentiated between the sort of amateur actor who sees theatre, like frocks, as a desirable dressing in life and the sort who is interested in the work itself. She belonged in Shaw's second category.

And this interest was channelled when she joined the BBC as a studio manager. After a brief spell with the BBC's own Ariel Players ('to get to know people'), she settled at the Tower, which operated on an altogether more serious and organised level. She always felt she was suited to play Portia and did so, but only in the second half of the play, when the actress she'd directed in the role in 1999 developed a migraine in the interval of the Paris tour in the Jardin Shakespeare.

The integrity of her life in amdram, and her Lewis Carroll connection, had further validation in the fact that her great grandfather, Dr Charles Daniel, was a nineteenth-century tutor, and later provost, at Worcester College, Oxford, and was a friend of Charles Dodgson (aka Lewis Carroll). He published a 'garland' of poems for his daughter Rachel, Penny's grandmother, on her first birthday in 1881. The contributors included Robert Bridge, W. E. Henley and Dodgson himself. Dr Daniel's wife Emily, a keen supporter of amateur theatre, pestered Dodgson in June 1895 into allowing them to present *Alice in Wonderland* in the beautiful lakeside gardens of Worcester College – the first ever open-air OUDS production. It was to be directed by the shooting star of the OUDS, Nigel Playfair, a renowned actor manager at the Lyric, Hammersmith, in the 1920s.

Rachel played the title role. Dodgson/Carroll – ever given to eccentric, secretive behaviour – chose to witness the rehearsals from the shrubbery, like some oversized woodland imp. Nigel Playfair was told by the vice-chancellor of the university that no tickets could be sold on the door as the production had not been officially rubber-stamped. So, instead, the audience, who were allowed in free, paid to get out at the end – a suitably *Alice*-like topsy-turvy arrangement.

Penny Tuerk, who spent nearly fifty years with the Tower – one of the rehearsal rooms in the new premises at Stoke Newington has been named in her memory – was convinced that losing Canonbury 'woke us all up' and that, with everything revolving around the bar, they'd all become a 'bit too cosy'. In Canonbury, they had the luxury of a six-day 'get-in' whereas in the recent rotation of performances in three London fringe venues – Teatro Technis in Camden Town, the Bridewell Institute near Ludgate Circus and above the Gatehouse pub in Highgate – they had a more difficult get-in and technical rehearsal over two days only. 'This certainly tightened up our approach in getting a show on.' Membership is not exclusive nowadays, many personnel working with other leading London amateur groups such as the Kensington Drama Company, Sedos or the Questors. But Tuerk was a one-company loyalist, a tower of strength and a Tower legend.

Michael Godley

Michael Godley, who went up to Oxford immediately after the Second World War (he was a pilot in the Fleet Air Arm) had as luminous an array of theatrical contemporaries as Robert Pennant Jones at Cambridge, only a few generations earlier. He was a star juvenile turn among the likes of John Schlesinger, Sandy Wilson, Tony Richardson, Kenneth Tynan, Robert Hardy, William Gaskill and Shirley Williams (the future Labour Party politician and co-founder of the Social Democratic Party). He decided to turn professional on graduating despite everyone urging him not to. He nearly went to Stratford-upon-Avon to carry a spear with his friend Robert Hardy, but decided instead to join the newly established West of England Theatre Company in three-weekly rep 'to learn my craft', as he expressed it.

In his home city of Sheffield, Godley's father, a Christian Science healer, knew and had helped (though didn't heal) the critic Harold Hobson, a wheelchair-bound quadriplegic. And now Hobson, who in 1947 had succeeded James Agate as critic on the Sunday Times, put Godley in touch with the West End producer Henry Sherek, who produced the plays of T. S. Eliot, directed by E. Martin Browne. Sherek thought of casting Godley as Peter Quilpe in *The Cocktail Party*, as Donald Houston was dropping out of the New York-bound cast to take up a film role. The series of disappointments in Godley's short-lived professional career began with Sherek changing his mind and offering him understudy and a minor role in the last act. And then changing it again and dropping him altogether.

After minor roles in rep at Windsor, Leatherhead and Guildford, he queued up to audition for a 1950 West End play, *Cry Liberty*, by Esther McCracken (grandmother of actress Imogen Stubbs), which he describes as a dismal comedy about trying to get planning permission for a hen coop in the garden. He was hired, at £15 a week – the national average wage was £8 a week – as an assistant stage manager and understudy with one short speech in the role of a removal man.

Suddenly, he thought he'd arrived and could afford to marry Heather Couper, his girlfriend and fellow student thespian at Oxford. While on its pre-West End tour, the play opened to a rapturous ovation in Newcastle, the playwright's home town, it then attracted pitiful audiences in Glasgow and Manchester before limping into the Vaudeville on the Strand and closing after six weeks. Still, he married Heather anyway in 1950; she'd spent a couple of years flying round the world as one of BOAC's first long-haul air stewardesses.

Godley then participated in two notable classical productions: *Hamlet* for the 1951 Festival of Britain, starring and directed by Alec Guinness, with Tynan as that infamous Player King (see Chapter 3) and Wolfit's *Tamburlaine* at the Old Vic in the following year. The first, in which Godley played Barnardo ('Who's there?') and Fortinbras, had a technically disastrous first night, with all the lighting cues out of sync and Michael Gough's Laertes receiving a huge laugh on learning that his 'sister's drowned' (because she couldn't see where she was going, was the gist of the audience reaction). In the second, as a walk-on and understudy to Leo McKern's defeated emperor Bajazeth, Godley played that imprisoned enemy at the second performance because, at the first, McKern had over-done the bashing-his-brains-out-against-his-own-cage bit and contracted an almighty migraine. McKern – 'the bastard' – returned immediately the following night.

Godley took the hint. Now aged twenty-eight, and keen to start a family with Heather, he joined a graduate training scheme as a handbag buyer for the John Lewis Partnership and, after a few years of that, took a job in Derby with the sales department in the Rolls Royce aero-engine division. After eighteen months, he returned to London with Heather and two small daughters, taking a big flat on the river in Twickenham which necessitated also taking in lodgers to help pay the rent. With a lively-looking CV, he determined to become an export sales manager with an engineering firm in Uxbridge. In 1970, after thirteen years in that role, he was made redundant and re-settled into what he calls 'a nice job' as the London region director of the National Federation of Building Trades Employers (NFBTE).

During this period and beyond, he continued to act in amateur theatre each summer with a company that was 'my lifeline, my soul's saviour'. This was at Stockwells, the home and garden of the magnificently eccentric heiress Paulise de Bush, near the village of Aston Upthorpe in the shadow of the Berkshire Downs. Every summer she staged Shakespeare on her estate of restored cottages and sylvan landscape, pulling in favours from professional acquaintances she'd made while appearing (briefly) as Charmian to Cathleen Nesbitt's Cleopatra by invitation for the OUDS at the New Theatre, Oxford, in 1921. There, aged twenty-one, Paulise had fallen in love with the stage manager, Herbert Lugg, whose father had played Claudius to Henry Irving's Hamlet at the Lyceum. They married and established Stockwells in the style of the country house private theatricals of the eighteenth and nineteenth centuries – the neighbouring village of North Aston had been home to three generations of the Bowles family who had converted a barn on their estate for theatricals in 1776.

Paulise's family owned a chemicals company which they sold on to the American Dow Chemical conglomerate and, with a huge trust in her name, she became ever more theatrically proactive as time went by, often hiring and paying professional directors and funding elaborate scaffolded sets and seating on the greensward. She put up the actors – the Godley family camped in the cottages every August for twenty-odd years – while also supervising an historical and theatrical costume collection, which is now managed by the National Trust at Killerton House in Devon.

One of Paulise's friends was the Oxford don Nevill Coghill, who fostered many a theatrical career in his love of the theatre and his special advocacy of Shakespeare and Chaucer. He was a friend, and indeed mentor, of the young Richard Burton. In the summer of 1946 Paulise asked Coghill to send her 'a nice young man who could act' and he sent her Michael Godley. Godley played Demetrius to Paulise's much older Hermia in *A Midsummer Night's Dream*, always the most popular outdoor Shakespeare play, and he re-joined her after the Old Vic *Tamburlaine* in 1952, playing Hamlet, with Paulise as

Gertrude, and with William Russell – another Oxford contemporary who would have a far more successful professional career – as his Horatio.

Less appropriately, Michael was Benedick to Paulise's Beatrice – 'You have to realise', he says, 'that while Paulise was besotted with the theatre, she wasn't a very good actress and was, for good measure, very plain and nervous, not half as exotic as her own life story, and her name, might have implied'. Michael also played at Stockwells opposite visiting professionals: as Petruchio in *The Taming of the Shrew* with Maroussia Frank, wife of the RSC star Ian Richardson, as Katherina; and as Florizel in *The Tempest* with Prunella Scales – 'she was then at the Old Vic drama school; her mother was an opera singer, and she already knew everyone, including John Gielgud' – as Perdita.

Scales's husband, Timothy West, was also a visiting director at Stockwells. As indeed was Leslie French, the most famous Puck of the 1930s, who visited a Guildford drama school with Paulise in order to cast Puck and the four young lovers in a 1970 production of *A Midsummer Night's Dream* at Stockwells. (Other Stockwells student alumni down the years include Alan Bates, who played Romeo while at RADA, and Siân Phillips, a regal Olivia in *Twelfth Night*.)

At Guildford, French alighted on my brother, Martin, as Puck, who, virtually naked, put a girdle round the earth by diving into a hedge while a tracking arc spotlight swooped up into the sky giving the impression that he had launched himself into the atmosphere. Oberon and Titania moved across the water in a punt for 'through the house give glimmering light,' an effect that encapsulated the pictorial production style. In the same year, Peter Brook's legendary white-box gymnasium version of the same play for the RSC emphasised how far the professional theatre had moved on from these charming, Mendelssohn-drenched shenanigans of open-air country-house Shakespeare.

But for Godley, 'bliss was it in that dawn to be alive' forever. His daughters, Julia and Georgina, were pretty young fairies, one later becoming an actress and drama teacher, the other a well-known fashion designer on graduating from the Brighton College of Art. Heather, however, of whom, Michael says, Paulise was terminally jealous, was rarely cast in major roles at Stockwells and, like so many good amateur actors, combined a busy after-hours career at the Teddington Theatre Club and the Questors with 'real life' as a history teacher.

When Paulise died in 1975, she left enough money for Stockwells to be taken over as a registered charity by the nearby Blewbury Players, who built their own amphitheatre twenty miles away – the Garden Theatre in Orchard Dene. They continued operating as an amateur company all year round with plays and cabaret in either the village hall or the church. The original idea had been for Michael and fellow actor Robin Sewell, who worked for the Bush family firm, to run Stockwells, but – with a heavy sigh, Michael concedes that such catastrophes 'always happen to me' – Dow Chemical had made a big investment error which deprived Paulise, posthumously, of her share value. So Stockwells was sold off by Paulise's daughter Mary and the properties sold on, modernised and overrun by stables. This truly was the end of an era.

Godley went on to play Falstaff in *The Merry Wives of Windsor* for the Blewbury Players, but his heart wasn't in it and he withdrew from the summer idyll completely, following Heather to Teddington and the Questors in the 1970s. His professional life at the NFBTE became complicated when he fell in love with his PA and embarked on a long-running affair with her. She covered for him in the office when busy with rehearsals and gradually his theatrical itch returned to such an extent that in, 1984, he acquired an agent and sought professional employment after a hiatus of thirty years.

His salary at work had been adversely affected by the financial crisis of the 1970s. It was, in effect, about half of what he might have expected after thirteen years on the treadmill. Still, Heather was furious at his determination to re-conquer the West End and he promised her that he would not allow his income to fall beneath £800 a month. Nor did it, until he stopped altogether, aged eighty, in 2005, though he took an awful lot of supplementary DIY jobs, wall-papering and decorating to make up the short-fall, not to mention the occasional television advert and voice-over work.

But the old glory of the professional stage proved as elusive as it was in the beginning. He appeared in low-grade new work in fringe theatres and was recalled twice for a take-over role in the West End hit musical *Me and My Girl* starring Robert Lindsay and Emma Thompson. He didn't get the role. But, still sprightly in his late sixties, he spent six happy months at the Royal Exchange in Manchester playing a major in a Falklands War play, and a supporting character in Ben Jonson's masterful comedy *The Alchemist*.

At the end of the 1980s, he *did* reappear on the West End stage – with Rowan Atkinson and Derek Jacobi. Atkinson led the cast in Ronald Eyre's production of *The Sneeze*, a collection of eight short stories and plays by Chekhov, adapted by Michael Frayn for the producer Michael Codron at the Aldwych in 1988. In one of them, *Swan Song*, Godley was a sort of theatre rat, a prompter emerging from the dust covers, as Timothy West, playing an old-style 'laddie' actor, was caught backstage after a benefit matinée to be confronted by death in the darkness of an empty theatre. The Jacobi production at the Old Vic in 1990, directed by Sam Mendes, was Jean-Paul Sartre's *Kean*, with Godley as a Danish ambassador whose wife becomes an object of the hell-raising actor Edmund Kean's (Jacobi) attentions. He was back once more in the famous old theatre on the Waterloo Road. He'd arrived, after a fashion, all over again.

And then, of course, another catastrophe. His luck was out big-time when his agent went bust with accumulated debts in 1996. Michael got half of what he was owed, which was admittedly not all that much. Still, ever resilient in defiance of all the odds, he thinks he's been blessed, enjoyed every production 'since I came back' and remains forever grateful to Paulise de

Bush. 'My enthusiasm for theatre, which started at school, has never dimmed. I have no regrets whatsoever.'

These lives of Robert Pennant Jones, Penny Tuerk and Michael Godley, lived in the nimbus of amateur theatre while working full-time in industry and the BBC, seem to me to be rich and rewarding. Tuerk and Godley juggled their parallel lives with the prospect of a soft landing in regular employment and secure domesticity, while Pennant Jones is a rare beast, a leading actor manqué who, having been frightened off by the competition at Cambridge, came into his kingdom at the Tower anyway, without bartering too many of his dreams for material comfort and the status of good citizenry.

7

All Aboard for the National Theatre

Geoffrey Whitworth, Crayford, Kent

In 1983, on the centenary of Geoffrey Whitworth's birth, a commemorative tribute on BBC Radio 4 included a quotation from George Bernard Shaw: 'Who is this man named Whitworth? What is he? He is not a great actor. So far as I know he has never acted in a play. If he has written any plays, I have not seen them. And yet, wherever I go, I hear the name: Geoffrey Whitworth. He is one of the most important people in the theatre today.'

Indeed he was, and in my estimation, remains so, however forgotten his name or unread his writings. For Whitworth, in whose name and memory stands one of the most successful and impressive amateur theatres in the south of England, was a lecturer for the Workers' Educational Association, founder of the British Drama League and a prime mover in the campaign for a National Theatre.

In 1931, he became an active secretary for that campaign, which had secured the influential support of not only Bernard Shaw, but also Harley Granville Barker, Winston Churchill and the actor-manager Herbert Beerbohm Tree. The impetus behind a National Theatre was Whitworth's and the British Drama League's parallel promotion of professional and amateur theatre in the country at a time when almost every town was acquiring a cinema.

And Whitworth's fire had been lit by a chance visit to Crayford in Kent in 1918 to deliver a lecture to the town's branch of the Workers' Educational Association in what was then known as the Rodney Hut (so named for Lieutenant William Rodney of the Rifle Brigade, killed in action), now the site of the theatre that bears his name. The audience comprised workers in the Vickers munitions factory, along with other arms workers in Kent, at Erith and Dartford, ironically implicated as dealers in death while immersed in a life-enhancing project of literature, drama and education.

After delivering his talk, Whitworth was invited by the workers to stay on for a reading of two short plays by Stanley Houghton – one of the prominent Manchester school of playwrights at that time – and was so moved by this experience that he envisaged a National Theatre, right there and then, on the spot:

> With books in their hands, and with a minimum of action, they did not much more than speak the words of the play, pointing them with a few gestures. And yet, through the sincerity and reality of the interpretative intention, the characters came to life upon that stage, and, as I sat and watched and listened, I felt that I was understanding the fundamental quality of dramatic art in a way I had never understood it before.

Fifty-odd years later, the actor Michael Gambon, a heroic figure in the history of both the National and the RSC, but especially the National, was himself a member of the theatre as a Vickers apprentice engineer after studying at Crayford Secondary School, though he split his loyalties by set-building and then acting, too, at the Erith Playhouse in nearby Bexley. While still working at Vickers he moved on to moonlight as a set-builder, then actor, at the Unity Theatre in north London. He is now the Geoffrey Whitworth Theatre's president.

Whitworth died in 1951, two months after the Queen Mother laid the National Theatre's foundation stone on the South Bank (the new NT opened a mere twenty-five years later, in 1976). The original hut in Crayford gave way to the present building, home of the so-called New Theatre Group – an off-shoot, in 1948, of the Dartford Amateur Operatic and Dramatic Society – when Sybil Thorndike opened the new Geoffrey Whitworth Theatre in 1959 with the resounding cry: 'An amateur is one who loves the theatre, who performs because he is dedicated to it not merely earning a living. All of us who really care for the theatre are amateurs.' In that one sentence she defined the ineradicable connection between amateurs and professionals. In the end, it all comes down to an engagement with the medium and a spur for communication.

Riding the crest of a wave when the Little Theatre Guild was formed in 1946, the New Theatre Group's impetus in breaking away from the Dartford Amateur Operatic and Dramatic Society was a desire to concentrate on serious new and classical plays. Fourteen original members each contributed the princely sum of one pound and the embryonic GWT was conceived and born. The bust of Whitworth in the foyer has an accompanying plaque noting the inspiration that brought 'intelligent recreation and pleasure to millions of people all over the world', quoting from Shelley's spiritual manifesto, the lyric 'Hymn to Intellectual Beauty': 'For love, and beauty, and delight/ There is no death nor change; their might/ Exceeds our organs, which endure/ No light, being themselves obscure.'

The Whitworth has long been the only theatre in Crayford. Two years before it opened, the town's one professional theatre, the 1,000-seater Princesses, built right on the river by Vickers for the entertainment of their employees was demolished and replaced by a block of shops and flats. A builder was employed at the Whitworth to put in the walls and foundations, and everything else was done by volunteers.

There followed, throughout the 1960s, a repertoire that embraced Pinter, Thornton Wilder, Albee, Orton and Tennessee Williams, and the earliest stage performances of Diana Quick – as Juliet and as Princess Katharine in *Henry V* – before she went on to further burgeoning glory with the Erith Theatre Guild (in *The Boy Friend*), while still a pupil at Dartford Grammar School. Her parents had met while performing in *The Pirates of Penzance* with the local operatic society, but they developed a lifelong commitment to the GWT. Her father, a dentist, worked as a stage manager at the Whitworth while his wife, a hairdresser, helped out with costumes and coffees.

Family connections and overlaps run through the history of amateur theatre, especially this one, which serves a wide area of Kent including Dartford, Tonbridge and Bexleyheath. The nearest professional outfits are at Bromley – a town which also has a phenomenal number of amateur theatres, as it happens – and Greenwich. But they are, these days, receiving houses, not producing theatres, and the GWT has the highest standards, and the best facilities, for many miles around. So the social fabric of a theatre like the Whitworth, on and off stage, is rich and varied, even if basically white, middle-class, professional and aspirational. And such participants, on stage and out front – and I sense this perhaps more keenly at the Whitworth than at any other amateur theatre I've visited – are the bedrock audience of the professional stage in the capital.

Whitworth stalwart Ross Holland, whose mother was a GWT member, has an elder brother who runs a company that helps visualise West End shows for blind people. And because of his mother's involvement, Ross, like Diana Quick, came along to audition, as a young teenager; he was cast as Ronnie Winslow in Rattigan's play. When I visit the theatre to see another Rattigan play, *Cause Célèbre*, he is quietly bustling around the place and talks of his time at the GWT with all the keenness and enthusiasm of someone who's just joined, not spent his life here acting, directing, designing and building sets, even arranging the sound and the lighting. He clearly could have worked in the professional theatre. He opted instead for a life of financial security as a business analyst in the shipping industry while following his dream at the GWT for over forty years.

Another old-timer, Maurice Tripp, a retired shopkeeper in Sidcup, has been a trustee at the theatre for ten years, specialising in the company accounts, insurance and maintenance, as well as general policy. This is something much more than a mere hobby for such people. And yet, what precious, unsullied enthusiasm they succeed in retaining. Tripp tells me that the lines that haunt him down his life are those of Noël Coward in his stage-struck poem 'The Boy Actor': 'I never cared who scored the goal/ Or which side won the silver cup/ I never learned to bat or bowl/ But I heard the curtain going up.'

One of the New Theatre Group's founding members in 1948 – the fateful gathering was at a certain Arthur Simpson's house at 32 Bean Road, Bexleyheath – John Measures, was a barrister, and is remembered as most often seen talking in the bar with another John, who was a taxi driver. As well as teachers, lawyers and solicitors, the membership today includes a caterer, a supermarket employee, several journalists, market porters and a tattoo artist.

And a fully engaged professional theatrical in Vivien Goodwin, a long-standing acting and backstage member who is a former managing director of the play publishing and performing rights company Samuel French. She is currently the first ever managing director of Rodgers and Hammerstein Theatricals Europe (RHT). The fact that she hails from California and trained in the drama department of the University of California, Santa Barbara, means she has come full circle with her native culture. She has brought her experience in licensing and performing rights at Samuel French to bear on the control and worldwide dissemination of musical theatre,

FIGURE 9 *Vivien Goodwin as Blanche du Bois in Tennessee Williams's* A Streetcar Named Desire *at the Geoffrey Whitworth Theatre in October 2016. (Photo: Robert Piwko.)*

alongside her predecessor in the post, Bert Fink, the former New York theatre press agent, who has moved sideways to do a similar job for Cameron Mackintosh's Music Theatre International.

Goodwin was MD during the last phase of Samuel French's tenure as a bookshop in Fitzroy Square. That shop always had a special place in my life as, in the mid-1960s, my brother and I would often visit its then premises in Southampton Street, just off the Strand, to thumb through play scripts and, as many visitors did, chat about the state of the theatre world and the West End with the always well-informed and helpful staff. But the passing trade was diminishing in Fitzroy Square and the company eventually retreated to an office and online existence before re-opening a scaled-down bookshop in the circle bar at the Royal Court in 2018. By then Goodwin was at RHT and whizzing round the world, seeing the Rodgers and Hammerstein revivals, and the other musicals she looks after, as well as liaising with Ted Chapin, her company's president in New York, while keeping her hand in, when time allows, at the Whitworth.

On RHT business in Moscow recently, she caught up with the boyfriend she accompanied back to Britain after they met on campus in California. Jonathan Salway, who now runs an English-speaking theatre company in Moscow, was on an exchange course from Hull University, and she returned with him to Hull where she fell in with Hull Truck, the professional new work company founded by Mike Bradwell in 1971. From 1984, the artistic director was playwright John Godber (author of the amdram staple *Bouncers*), and Vivien joined a woman's group run by his wife, Jane Thornton. Jonathan's quest for work took him down south, and Vivien followed him, taking secretarial jobs while Jonathan chased professional employment. Their relationship foundered, but not before Jonathan introduced Vivien to the Whitworth, where he had become a member during their life together in Woolwich and Dartford in south London. Leafing through a free magazine, Vivien saw a small ad placed by 'a leading theatrical publisher' seeking a secretary. She knew it could only be Samuel French, applied for the job and was appointed by the then managing director – whose best friend happened to be an actress at the GWT.

Vivien has acted there since 1987, sometimes taking two or three roles a year, sometimes one, or sometimes none for a year or more. Like many GWT members, she helps out in the bar (drinking as well as serving, she is quick to point out!), sometimes stage-managing, and even helping to build the set. She met and married her first husband, Alan Goodwin, in the company and also her second, Andy Briggs. In 1998 she played Cordelia in *King Lear* with Alan as Kent and Andy as Edgar, the first humiliated in the stocks, the second stripped half naked while feigning madness on the heath.

Her roles have included Schiller's *Mary Stuart*, Christopher Hampton's virtuous, but susceptible, Madame de Tourvel in *Les Liaisons Dangereuses* (six months after giving birth to her daughter), Shakespeare's Juliet, and Roxane in *Cyrano de Bergerac*. Her favourite role, though, is Blanche

DuBois in *A Streetcar Named Desire*, which she's played twice: 'Once, in 1991, when I was too young and once, in 2016, when I was, perhaps, too old!' As a keen student of acting, she is conscious of other interpretations of the role and the differences she found in it herself on each occasion: 'It is such a gift of a role, but I wasn't experienced enough in life, and the world, first time around. Second time, I got her so much more.' Does that mean she brings herself totally into every role?

> Yes. Some actors are technically capable of faking it, but I'm not. I'm an emotional person. I looked at Gillian Anderson both onstage and in the live screening when she played Blanche at the Young Vic. She was brilliant because she managed to convey so many things. The delicacy and detail of her work on film she managed somehow to enhance on stage. And then I saw the live screening of Maxine Peake's performance for the Royal Exchange in Manchester. In her own way, she did exactly the same, although she is much broader in the role and comes across as much more of a stage actress on the screen. I wasn't going to compare myself with either of them in some kind of 'Blanche-off', but the experience of watching them didn't make me feel unhappy with what I did, the second time around at least.

One of the best loved of the GWT family was an extraordinary character actor, Fred Ridgeway, who played in two seasons in Crayford in the 1990s before turning professional in his mid-forties and starring as a cockney criminal in Richard Bean's *One Man Two Guvnors* alongside James Corden at the National and on Broadway, completing that run just ten weeks before he died of motor neurone disease in November 2012. Although Ridgeway had been encouraged to join the National Youth Theatre while at school in south east London, he began a meteoric career in finance at the age of eighteen, becoming an associate director of the Exco gas company and working on Wall Street in New York, where he fed his passion for theatre by taking classes at the Actors' Playhouse in Greenwich Village.

Returning to England, and living a luxury lifestyle in Chislehurst, Kent, with his wife and children, he plunged into amateur dramatics, first with the South London Theatre in Norwood and then with the GWT, where he played roles he had studied at first hand in the performances of his idol, Dustin Hoffman: Willy Loman in Arthur Miller's *Death of a Salesman* and Shylock in *The Merchant of Venice*. In 1996 he turned professional and within two years was playing Joe Orton's dodgy police inspector, Truscott of the Yard, in *Loot* in the West End. There was something ferrety and innately, absurdly comic, about his appearance in this role. You couldn't help remembering, as you watched this remarkable performance, that another late-starter in the professional theatre, Leonard Rossiter, who had spent six years in amateur theatre in Liverpool while working as an insurance clerk, had also triumphed on stage as Truscott, in 1984. He died of a heart attack in his dressing room between the acts aged just fifty-seven.

Ridgeway played in two other Richard Bean plays before *One Man Two Guvnors* – as a chirpy philosopher in *England People Very Nice*, and as a psychopathic IRA killer in *The Big Fellah*. 'I can see him now', said Bean at the time of his death, 'staring out into the stalls, unblinking, monosyllabic, and totally believable'. Like Rossiter, and indeed Michael Gambon, Ridgeway had an ingrained, unsentimental streak running through his fibre like a steel filament. And there was nothing obvious or showy about him offstage, either: a salt-of-the-earth sort of a bloke in direct contrast to the popular notion of an actor, amateur or professional, as a self-glorifying poseur.

I doubt, though, if he could ever have outfaced 'the great Gambon' (as Ralph Richardson dubbed him) in the self-effacement stakes. There's an awful lot more, physically, for Gambon to self-efface with. Gambon's the exact opposite of Ian McKellen as a public spokesman for the theatre – taciturn, not voluble – just as he's the opposite of McKellen as an actor: carthorse and champion filly was his own comparison for the two of them in the career stakes. Gambon is a pretty relaxed patron, too, though he has been known to turn up on a GWT first night and buy his round at the bar afterwards. The Whitworth works best as this kind of community theatre. Apart from another cadre of ageing set builders, there is a team of lady volunteers known as 'the scrubbers' who come in once a month to clean up inside.

I taxed Ross Holland about this problem of ageing and renewal in the amateur theatre:

> The constant cry is – the audience is so old; and it still is, but they can't be the same old people! The oldies are constantly renewing themselves: the new audience tends to be the young people when they've become old … but we do have a lot of younger people, too, on social media, and having a Young Company helps.

At its core, the company renews itself through its members. That membership stands at 1,700, 150 of whom are actively involved. And 30 per cent of each season – ten productions running from October through July – is pre-sold before they even start.

The irony now is that the GWT, lodged on an originally working-class estate of employees at the long-gone Vickers factory, is less of a local community theatre than it would like. The severe-looking pebble-dash two-storey houses of the former Vickers estate do not exactly pour forth participants, or even audience, into the Whitworth. Indeed, one of the Whitworth's regular actors, the BBC news announcer Justine Greene, flatly declares that the good people who live thereabouts

> don't like us driving up 'their' road … and if they think we're not there rehearsing, they will deliberately move their cars from their driveways into the road merely in order to make it difficult for us to get in and out. We just have to try and explain to them that the theatre was there before

they were and that there are lots of worse things they could have in their street; we're not exactly rowdy!

Greene moved from London to Kent fifteen years ago, settling in Greenhithe, a village near Dartford. She discovered the GWT by phoning up then turning up. She had grown up in Coventry and had been dancing since the age of six, acting since ten. She joined the Belgrade Youth Theatre in Coventry as a teenager and then took a drama degree at Loughborough University, writing for the university newspaper and representing the university kick-boxing team (where the dance training came in handy). Seeing how tough it was for people she knew entering the professional theatre, her faith was shaken in making it her own career. So she took a post-graduate degree in broadcast journalism at Portsmouth University.

A start in commercial radio in the Midlands led to presentation work with BBC TV in Wales and London, and her work as a newsreader for BBC Radio 2 and 6, as well as a Sunday morning slot as an anchor/presenter on BBC Coventry and Warwickshire. Acting at the GWT is therefore part of a varied schedule of work – along with all the news reading, she teaches, judges dance competitions, and is the 'radio voice' on BBC TV's long-running soap *EastEnders* – in which the distinguishing labels of professional and amateur seem to be completely obliterated. She is an example, no less remarkable for being by no means unique, of a totally dedicated performer. The GWT is not an add-on, but an essential part of the stream of her life and her friendships. She has no children and says the company was a bulwark when her marriage broke up.

On stage, Greene has that priceless quality of being 'alive' in the moment, something Geoffrey Whitworth himself would have recognised while also appreciating the repertoire of plays in which she has appeared over the years: not just the contemporary work of John Mortimer, Ronald Harwood, Stephen Poliakoff and Martin McDonagh, but also the classic texts of J. B. Priestley, Arthur Miller, Tennessee Williams and Shakespeare. In a fairly experimental production of *The Tempest* – part of the RSC's Open Stages project, which filmed the production for their archive, along with the thirty-six other plays as performed by three dozen amateur companies – she played the goddess Iris in a pair of three-foot wings and devised a dance routine based on the seven strands of brocade in Tai Chi.

Crescent, Birmingham

The Tempest production at the GWT was, for good or bad, many degrees of separation from the sort of Shakespeare you would have expected to see in an amateur theatre twenty, or even ten, years ago. Stock amdram Shakespeare would invariably involve a perilous arrangement of rostra, a balsa wood arch or two, black drapes, a dodgy soundtrack and costumes made of curtain material.

Another sign of the changing times was a daring, imaginative *Macbeth* at the Crescent in Birmingham, one of the most renowned of all British amateur theatres, whose founder member and first chairman, Norman Leaker, took the theatre into the newly formed Little Theatre Guild in 1946. The production could be looked at in two ways: as a fairly competent 'school play' with a couple of masters (i.e. senior members) helping out; or an adventurous synthesis of random ideas about *Macbeth*, which could well stimulate the discussions of the schoolchildren who mostly comprised the show's audiences.

Macbeth himself was played by a professionally trained drama teacher. The witches (two girls, one boy) were accompanied by child-like doppelgangers and made up to resemble mythological Japanese ghosts, or spirits. Lennox and Ross were both girls, black Hecate a scary transvestite and the general choice of weapons sticks, not swords. Lady Macduff had six children, each of them executed offstage with a single bullet shot. You could have easily imagined you were watching the RSC. The Brummie Porter, though, was a bit of a disaster, failing to find any comedy at all in his badly edited prose scene and resorting to a 'knock, knock' (who's there?) routine which wasn't funny, either.

Comedy in the earliest days of the Crescent meant French romantic froth or Shavian thrust and parry, more than it did Shakespeare, though *A Midsummer Night's Dream* does, inevitably, feature in the early annals. These date back to 1924, when the Municipal Players, as the company was first called – they were all employees, a fraction of the total 25,000, of the Corporation of Birmingham – started putting on plays in their own canteen after they struck a chord with a successful Christmas revue.

A performance of Edmond de Rostand's *Les Romanesques* (source, eventually, of the long-running off-Broadway musical *The Fantasticks*) at the YMCA in 1925 donated all proceeds to the Lord Mayor's Unemployment Distress Relief Fund. The company thrived at the heart of the city centre in the Birmingham Council House. In addition to productions in the canteen and, from 1926, in the Midland Institute, they offered play readings, study groups, playwriting competitions and a summer school of acting under the direction of W. G. Fay, co-founder with Yeats and Lady Gregory of the Abbey Theatre in Dublin.

The Municipal Players were hailed as the largest and most progressive amateur dramatic society in the city (there were many). By 1930 they had produced forty plays, acquired 370 members and gained considerable profits towards building their own theatre. As reported in an edition of the *Birmingham Despatch* in November 1930, Sybil Thorndike made a speech in the city declaring that the theatre in Britain was passing through a queer time and needed to pull up its socks, but that the biggest sign of revival 'lies in the steady growth, all over the country, of amateur dramatic societies'. The company was applauded in the following month by the critic St John Ervine for producing plays 'not known to the commercial managers'. Norman Leaker, who worked in the town clerk's department, won the playwriting competition with a piece about a European earthquake which fortuitously ended a war.

The accumulating argument for a municipal and civic theatre – i.e. a municipally established and civically supported amateur theatre – was the same as the argument for a National Theatre. And, at last, the company found a disused property, Baskerville Hall, a mere stone's throw from Victoria Square and very near the site of the modern Birmingham Rep and the amazing new library, which they 'rolled into' two adjacent Georgian houses in the Crescent, off Cambridge Street, hence the new name. The long hall, with a narrow stage, had a high vaulted ceiling, seating for 200, a working pit and a scene dock under the stage.

At the opening ceremony in April 1932, the Lord Mayor congratulated the Municipal Players on performing 'hopeless plays' (plays that could not be done in the commercial theatre); the opening season comprised Rostand's *The Romantics* once again, Shaw's *Caesar and Cleopatra* and Harley Granville Barker's *The Voysey Inheritance*. The Crescent was thus seen as the first 'legitimate' theatre in Birmingham since Barry Jackson built the Birmingham Rep in Station Street in 1913, the first purpose-built repertory theatre in the world.

The Crescent's reputation was maintained and its participants expanded to include members not employed by the council, until war broke out in 1939 and the theatre closed in line with government restrictions. But when those restrictions were relaxed in 1940, the theatre decided to help the war effort by temporarily renaming itself the Garrison Theatre, dedicated to the entertainment of the troops and auxiliaries. A programme of revues, comedies and thrillers extended to the end of the war and, in 1946, the Crescent reclaimed its artistic decorum and joined the nascent Little Theatre Guild. The significance of the Crescent, and the amateur theatre at large, was confirmed when, on the twenty-fifth anniversary in 1949, Shaw sent a message to the jubilee dinner quoting Wagner: 'Music, he said, is kept alive on the cottage piano of the amateur; same thing in the theatre.'

Over the next decade, the site of the theatre was expanded to include a rehearsal theatre and the professionally run Crescent Theatre Training School. Plans were made to double the size of the auditorium and productions were travelling far and wide on tour when suddenly the council gave the theatre notice to quit, offering them a site in Cumberland Street, not too far away, just off Broad Street, and an interest-free loan of £30,000 as part of the civic centre redevelopment programme in which the theatre they had fitted out themselves with gas heating and electric lighting systems was to be demolished.

Work started on the new Crescent in 1962 and a limited company was formed to run it. The design, based on the train turntables at nearby Tysley

Station, was entirely radical, intended to set drama free from the picture stage convention by placing half the audience on a revolving platform. So, when it opened in October 1964 at a total cost of £100,000 and exactly six months after the Questors' unprecedented adaptable Elizabethan stage in Ealing, west London, Britain possessed two revolutionary and visionary playhouses, neither of them in the commercial sector, both raised and run by amateurs. Unlike the Questors, however, the Crescent could not afford to maintain its training school. The money ran out, too, for the proposed top storey.

Still, the building was a great success and the architect, Graham Winteringham, was promptly commissioned to design the new Birmingham Rep which would open in 1971 on Broad Street in the area later reconfigured as Centenary Square, with the concert hall to its left and the library to its right. The number of productions at the Crescent increased, the policy was relaxed to include more musicals, the new studio was a boon to members seeking further opportunities and experience, the theatre was let out for hire to other companies, and a youth theatre was formed. All these developments still apply in great part to the Crescent of the early twenty-first century.

One of the Crescent's leading lights and jack-of-all-trades in Cumberland Street was Ken Hill, the future playwright and protégé of Joan Littlewood in her last period at Theatre Workshop, Stratford East. In the first few years in Cumberland Street (1965–69), Hill swept the Crescent stage, directed plays by Jean Anouilh, William Inge and Tennessee Williams, lit *The Birthday Party*, designed and built the set for *Troilus and Cressida*, wrote a revue, acted in Shaw's *You Never Can Tell*, Willis Hall and Keith Waterhouse's *Billy Liar* and *The Clouds* by Aristophanes, and stage-managed *Thark* by Ben Travers. His partner during this non-stop period, and mother of his two sons, was Janet Grant, also an acting member of the company. What took Ken from Birmingham to east London was 'the bright lights of Stratford East; and many other women', according to Grant and said without rancour.

In fact, Hill had been working as an investigative journalist at ATV and a report he made on local government corruption in the Midlands – ironic, given the origins of the Crescent in the Municipal Workers – caused an uproar. This brought him to the attention of Littlewood, who had just returned to Stratford for her last hurrah and wanted a similar sort of thing – a satire on local authorities. The result was Hill's *Forward Up Your End* in 1970, followed by a stream of jaunty, rough-house musical shows – *Gentlemen Prefer Anything*, *The Count of Monte Cristo*, *The Hunchback of Notre Dame* and *The Invisible Man* – that helped Stratford East survive a tricky transitional period after Littlewood's departure in 1976.

Hill succeeded Littlewood as artistic director for a couple of years and in the early 1980s wrote his *Phantom of the Opera* (with operatic insets) that prompted Andrew Lloyd Webber to first consider producing Hill's show in the West End (he never did) then go one better and write his own musical version. Hill died young, aged 57, in 1995, but his original *Phantom* is still widely performed. Meanwhile, Janet Grant took up teaching in Solihull and now appears regularly, and directs, with the Oldbury Rep in the middle of the Black Country. The standards are not as high as at the Crescent, she says, but the theatre is a thriving small community venue, playing six or seven shows a year in its 173-seater main auditorium and another six or seven in the fifty-seater studio.

As in many leading amateur theatres during the 1960s, the Crescent's programme of plays – regardless of how well or badly they might have been done – put the bill of fare at most professional regional theatres to shame. Between January and September 1969, for instance, you could see not only *Thark* and *The Clouds*, but also Peter Weiss's *The Marat/Sade*, Ionesco's *Rhinoceros*, Christopher Fry's *The Lady's Not for Burning* and Wilde's *The Importance of Being Earnest*.

The coming of the new Rep, though, together with the general decline in audience numbers all over the country, meant that by the end of the 1970s, the Crescent was struggling, showing box office losses in 1978 and 1979 for the first time in its history, even with attendances of around the 60 per cent mark. The annual turnover was £34,000; the assets remained healthy, in excess of £250,000.

The company started raising money for an extension, but by the end of the 1980s they were caught up for the second time in the council's development plans, this time in Brindley Place. Their ground lease was disposed to the developers who claimed that the architecture of the theatre did not fit in with their proposed 'prestigious' scheme for shops, offices and restaurants. Eventually, Brindley Place – so named for James Brindley, the engineer of the Birmingham canal – agreed to finance a new Crescent building nearby on a canal-side site fronting onto Sheepcote Street, on the edge of Ladywood, once dubbed the poorest area in the UK, but these days showing signs of renewal.

The foundation stone for the third Crescent Theatre was laid in December 1997 by Clare Short, then the Labour MP for Birmingham Ladywood (and first cousin of the Canadian actor and Broadway star Martin Short), a National Lottery award of £500,000 having been secured to add to the £3 million from the Brindley Place developers towards the overall estimated cost of £4 million. The Crescent chairman Ron Barber, who had appeared in the opening 1964 production in Cumberland Street and directed the last one there (*Design for Living*) in 1998, invited the actress Celia Imrie to cut the opening ceremony ribbon in October 1998 for the first performance, Wilde's *An Ideal Husband*.

The new venue, designed by Terry Farrell and John Chatwin, compact and comfortable, boasted a fine end-stage auditorium seating 300, a small, high, flexible black box studio (named for Ron Barber), a full-size fly tower, a scene dock, an excellent stage with generous wing space, two big dressing rooms with showers, property stores and a light-filled wardrobe with sewing room looking out over the canal. The most recent appeal – to raise a modest £15,000 – is to replace the main house stage after two decades of wear and tear.

The theatre is blooming, sort of, but it does have professional competition from both the Rep and the Hippodrome on its doorstep. In 2007, it was playing to half-full audiences, but the last few years have seen a marked upturn and the current chairman (only the fifth since Norman Leaker), Andrew Lowrie, a canny Scot who works in sales and marketing in the construction industry and is a musical theatre maven, is looking further down the line all the time. The Crescent has proved adept at adapting itself, losing all practical connections to the local council – 'with all the local government cuts, we're simply not on their radar anymore', says Lowrie – along with the 'improving' ideals, come to that, of the Municipal Players, about ten years ago.

Lowrie sees the role of the Crescent as much more of an 'arts in the community' project these days, with thirty young people in the Youth Theatre, links with the Ladywood youth groups that bring disadvantaged kids into the building and onto the stage, as well as with the University of Central Birmingham and the Royal Birmingham Conservatoire. On the recent hike in property prices in the Ladywood area, he says this is all part of the influx into the city of the HS2 rail project and the building of a 'super hospital' in nearby Smethwick. 'Forty per cent of people in this area are under the age of twenty-five. It's a very young city and we are gearing ourselves up for that.' The Crescent – which has the strongest commercial arm of all the LTG members, hosting BBC TV's *Strictly Come Dancing* spin-off shows, the all-male stripper dance troupe the Chippendales and other amateur groups' musical shows – still puts on four main house shows a year of its own, and eleven in the studio.

The night I turned up for that new production of *Macbeth*, a young man serving behind the bar asks a customer, as he hands over a pint, 'Are you coming along to see my willy next week?' I learned later that the barman was the theatre's youth leader and about to play Willie Mossop in a forthcoming revival of *Hobson's Choice*. Anyone joining the Crescent to act on the stage is told in no uncertain terms by Lowrie that, if they want the theatre to survive, they must all work together – and that means backstage, on props and behind the bar. 'Hopefully we've got everyone to feel pride in this theatre. We have to remember how Norman Leaker and his colleagues grafted with their hands. And the LTG, thanks to Leaker, started in this city and first spread through the Midlands. Whatever happens, there will always be an amateur theatre here.'

Running parallel to the story of the Crescent's second new home, and eliding with its third in Brindley Place, is that of Roma de Roeper, leading lady of James Cooper's Renegades in Ilford, whom we left as she yielded her status in both Cooper's theatrical and personal life to her convent school protégée Yvonne Haesendonck (see Chapter 3). Andrew Lowrie acted with Roma in *Nicholas Nickleby* and remembers her fondly, as does everyone; there's a plaque bearing her name outside one of the two rehearsal rooms in the new theatre. She had auditioned for the Crescent in Cumberland Street in 1978 and was asked to play a scene from *Hay Fever* with another auditioning hopeful, Michael Barry – she as Judith Bliss, he as Simon, her son. Barry would become a close friend for the rest of her life. Indeed, he described their relationship as almost exactly the same as they were required to play at the audition.

Roma, hailing from a family of Dutch jewellers, spent her first five years in Paris and fetched up in East Ham when her father started working for Ilford Film. The gung-ho side of her nature, and there was one, was no doubt accounted for by the fact that her Uncle Bruno was a flying ace nicknamed 'The Red Baron' (after the German fighter pilot von Richthofen). Even before entering the Ursuline High School in Ilford, she won prizes for elocution and 'lyrical verse speaking' in East London music festivals and, as a teenager, took gold and silver medals as a licentiate of LAMDA before training as a teacher.

On the rebound from James Cooper, and on leaving the Renegades, she met and married Ted Skiffington, a divorced teacher and educationalist, and moved with him to Rubery, a village ten miles from Birmingham, taking a job as a teacher at Bourneville Technical College. Her elderly mother came to live with her, too, and the stress of this, juggling her care duties with her commitment to Ted, while also cutting down on her teaching, drove her to the bottle, says Michael Barry. But she entered a clinic and then tried her luck at the Crescent.

Barry was a dancer who had toured with John Hanson in Ivor Novello's *Glamorous Night* and done panto in St Helen's – so, no arguing with *his* credentials – but he'd also trained as a teacher. These days, he teaches at the Birmingham Conservatoire and works as a movement director at the Royal Opera House, Covent Garden. When he joined the Crescent, with Roma, he found the work there far more challenging than his adventures in professional theatre. In between Roma's appearances at the Crescent – Barry particularly admired her portrayals of the mother in Hugh Whitemore's *Stevie*, Big Momma in *Cat on a Hot Tin Roof* and Miss Prism in *The Importance of Being Earnest* – there were two spectacular fallings off the wagon. But she pulled herself together, big-time, by working as a counsellor for Alcoholics Anonymous and graduating from administrative work and production assistant at the Crescent to directing many admired productions of her own.

Ted Skiffington died, says Barry, the morning after she opened a love letter to him from someone else. She said nothing to him but discovered later that the affair had been going on for some time. There was nothing safe or undramatic about Roma de Roeper. With her energy and passion, dark beauty, sharp tongue and ever present gang of good-looking younger gay men, including Michael Barry, her 'special' one, I think of her now as the Coral Browne of the amateur theatre. She was eventually immobilised by rheumatoid arthritis and an experiment with her medication resulted in methotrexate poisoning, lung damage and inflammatory heart disease.

She remained devoted to the Crescent, but her real joy, says Barry, had been the Renegades and particularly her beloved Jimmie. Yvonne, who had married Jimmie shortly before he died in 1987, visited Roma on her final lap. The situation, and their conversation, should have been recorded by a playwright and written up as a mark 2 version of David Hare's *Breath of Life*, in which Judi Dench and Maggie Smith as wife and lover of the same dead man met unexpectedly to contest each other's memories of him.

Perhaps, in some ways, the play had already been written. In Ilford, in 1959, the three of them had appeared in the Renegades' revival of Tennessee Williams's *A Streetcar Named Desire*. Roma was the heavy-drinking seducer Blanche DuBois; James Cooper, the bestially attractive Stanley Kowalski; and Yvonne, his comparatively supine wife, and Blanche's younger sister, Stella. Roma died in February 2013, aged ninety-three. Yvonne, still attractive, alert and petite in her eighties, lives alone in Woodford, Essex, guardian of the memory, and archive, of James Cooper, while Michael Barry tends Roma's sacred flame.

Little Theatres in Bolton and Doncaster . . .

Digging ever deeper into the soil that bore the foundations of our contemporary theatre, we return north. Bolton was once at the heart of the cotton weaving and textile industry, Doncaster a centre of the railway and locomotive business. Both large towns have been reeling for years from the post Industrial Revolution collapse, economic downturn and social misery. But both have feisty amateur theatres and resilient soccer teams, though it is over sixty years since one of them (Bolton Wanderers) won the FA Cup at Wembley. So resonant is this famous incident in Bolton's history that the cup-winning silk shirt and boots of the club's star player in the 1950s, Nat Lofthouse, remain on prominent display in the city's Central Library.

Bolton's most famous theatre son is Ian McKellen – although he was born in Burnley and moved with his family to Bolton after a short time in Wigan, where he saw his older sister, Jean, a teacher and life-long amateur theatre actor and director, play Bottom in Shakespeare's *A Midsummer Night's Dream* at the all-girls Wigan High School. He remains patron of the Bolton Little in Hanover Street, near the old market, where he first trod the boards aged fourteen, as a schoolboy recruited by one of his teachers who was in the company. The play, in 1952, was *Spring 1600* by Emlyn Williams in which a runaway girl, Ann, disguised as a boy, arrives in London to meet

William Shakespeare and become the first actress on the British stage (shades of *Shakespeare in Love*). McKellen played Ann's page.

While at Bolton School, where he became head boy, he was further encouraged at the Hopefield Miniature Theatre, a converted Edwardian house with an auditorium for fifty people. It was here, in 1953, that he played one of his very few drag roles – Millie, a Bolton mill girl who cheats her way to the final of a beauty contest in a play by Leonard Roe – and also Malvolio in the letter scene from *Twelfth Night*. In the following year, as a member of the Bolton Youth Theatre, he appeared for one night only at the Little in a play called *Paradise Perplexed*, followed by a demon and a pierrot in two other forgotten pieces before he signed off, in 1958, during his final term at school, and en route to Cambridge, as Sebastian in *Twelfth Night* wearing a green floppy hat and standing a good foot taller than his identical twin, Viola.

McKellen never trained as an actor except in the non-stop variety of his experience as an amateur. His senior English master at school, Frank Greene, had been a great encouragement to him, and performing in the main hall, which required, he said, 'Experimenting with being audible above the constant squeal of eight hundred bottoms shifting about on eight hundred rush-bottomed chairs', proved Mr Greene right when he said: 'If you can't be heard, you can't act onstage.'

His ambition took flight the moment he arrived at Cambridge, but his confidence had wavered slightly on the school's annual summer camp to Stratford-upon-Avon, where he slept in a canvas tent on the river bank and punted with his pals downstream from Tiddington to see the Shakespearean performances of Laurence Olivier, Vivien Leigh, Charles Laughton, Edith Evans, John Gielgud and Paul Robeson: 'I was convinced that the divinity of Peggy Ashcroft's Imogen [in *Cymbeline*], for example, bore no relation to my own flat-footed amateur acting and started in my teens to think I might train as a chef or a journalist.' He soon grew out of that.

The Bolton Little Theatre, or BLT – the acronym long pre-dates its appropriation by the high street coffee shop chains to denote a sandwich of bacon, lettuce and tomato – which has occupied the same building, on the site of a graveyard, a former foundry and glass factory next to the Hanover Street gas works since 1934, was also the setting for the first play ever seen by the illustrious former theatre critic of *The Times*, Irving Wardle. And this was hardly surprising, as Irving's father, John Wardle, had started the place.

What is more surprising is that the play, in 1937 (Irving was seven or eight), was *Fifinella*, a children's play by the film and theatre mogul Basil Dean which, apart from being the future critic's first play, was also his first taste of 'how the theatre works': a formal opening by the palace gates, he recalled in a memoir published in the short-lived magazine *Intelligent Life* in 2012, was 'interrupted' by three children – they were plants – declaring it was all a load of rubbish and barging their way onto the stage: 'Although I couldn't have explained this at the time', he wrote, 'I understood that as soon as the dramatic pretence begins, it generates a force field that becomes as tangible as barbed wire if anyone tries to walk through it.'

Wardle senior had been a touring actor in Manchester and Ireland, working a bit with the legendary Ben Iden Payne who ran the Gaiety in Manchester, Britain's first repertory company, for its founding director, the tea heiress Annie Horniman, and hoping to become a playwright along the lines of the Manchester School at the Gaiety.

But his plays had been brusquely rejected by Horniman and he had to remain satisfied with small roles, such as Strato and Pindarus, in Lewis Casson's 1913 production of *Julius Caesar*. At least, as an aide to suicide, he got to kill off the two lead characters (Brutus and Cassius) – good training for the drama critic he later became. On being demobbed in 1918, he took a degree in French at Manchester University, worked briefly as a schoolteacher and settled into what Irving describes as 'a humdrum job on the *Bolton Evening News* – which left him free in the evenings to get on with the acting'.

So, while he ended up, miserably, as librarian and theatre reviewer on the *Evening News*, he made up for lost time by playing the big roles he never had the chance to appropriate in rep with the textile designer and playwright Frank Sladen-Smith's Unnamed Society (of amateurs) in Manchester's Little Theatre, a scruffy warehouse in Salford. The Unnamed launched the careers of later actors such as Doris Speed (unforgettable as Annie Walker, the acidic landlady of the Rovers Return in *Coronation Street*) and Lithuanian immigrant Larry Skikne, aka Laurence Harvey (who won an Oscar for his performance in Jack Clayton's game-changing movie *Room at the Top*), while Wardle senior graduated to the leading roles he craved in Ben Jonson, Goethe and Eugene O'Neill.

His first wife, Irving's mother, Nellie Partington, a renowned Bolton pianist, died soon after giving birth to Irving in 1929 and his father almost instantly remarried. Irving's stepmother was a vivid and ambitious young actress, Norma Wilson, who had hurried back 'up north' after suffering humiliation in London. On graduating from the Royal Academy of Music, she had been cast in a West End play, *The Eight Bells*, as the only girl, a stowaway, on a ship full of men. Half-way through rehearsals, the director replaced her with his girlfriend. Still, she brought some of the West End with her, Irving recalls: she called everyone 'Darling'. Until, that is, one crusty old neighbour told her straight that his name wasn't Darling, Mrs Wardle, but Mr Scholes.

The Wardles and a few like-minded colleagues thought of starting their own Little Theatre in Bolton and kicked off, in 1931, with an experimental season in the Co-operative Hall. Their first play was *Mr Prohack* by Arnold Bennett and Edward Knoblock. Then came two more seasons in the hired hall of plays by Shaw, Elmer Rice, J. M. Barrie, Tolstoy and James Bridie until, in 1934, a kindly disposed landlord, James Wigglesworth, allowed them the run of the derelict premises in Hanover Street that has remained their home ever since. The BLT members dug out the embankments of cinders on which tiered benches had stood during the last incarnation of the place as a boxing hall and did the interior plastering and raking of the auditorium floor while builders took care of the extensions for wing space, dressing rooms and the foyer.

Before he died, Wigglesworth put the house in legal order, transferring the building to a board of trustees with the stipulation that there was to be 'free use of the premises as long as the theatre exists'. The poet Tom Sefton, who had lost one of his hands in the war, was another co-founder of the BLT. During a Christmas-time game of hide-and-seek at the theatre he climbed to the flies in pitch darkness and was found dead on the stage when the lights came up.

On his way to study at Oxford and the Royal College of Music in London, Irving continued his BLT association as the villainous Oliver in *As You Like It*. John played the old menial Adam. 'In the role of my father, Adam could humiliate me; while in the role of Oliver, I could address him as an old dog.' This filial antipathy had been exacerbated by Irving's irritation at being hauled up for spending time between scenes tangled in the straw of a rustic wheelbarrow with the flirtatious girl playing Celia: 'There came a night when Adam came in search of [the wheelbarrow] and executed a surprise reversal from his Shakespearean to his parental role. "Stop making such a fool of yourself", he hissed before trundling the wheelbarrow onto the adjoining farmyard scene to take it out on some blameless hollyhock.'

John and Norma were prominent respectively as actor and director in these early years, but Norma was furious that John enlisted yet again when the Second World War started up, her loudest complaint 'that by joining in the invasion of Italy, he had thrown away his only chance of escaping the local newspaper and getting a job on the *Manchester Guardian* while the young men were away'. Irving thinks his father joined up partly out of patriotism but possibly, too, to have an extended break from Norma. While he was away, the BLT was requisitioned as a food store and packed to the roof with sugar.

As normal life resumed on civvy street, John and Norma found jobs at the BBC in Manchester. One of their acquaintances there was a documentary maker who, it was said, did a bit of theatre on the side. She – Joan Littlewood – often stayed at the Wardle household. Another milestone in the making of a critic came when Irving went along with his parents to see an early Theatre Workshop performance, *Johnny Noble*, at the Miners' Hall. Written by Littlewood's then husband, Ewan MacColl, it made an indelible impression on him in its imaginative use of minimal means: music, lights, a cast of six and a piece of rope conjured the heroic fable of a merchant convoy under attack from German U-boats.

There was always one Shakespeare per season at the BLT (until the late 1970s, anyway) and the programme for the 1940s and 1950s is quite remarkable, mixing English comedy from Shaw to Peter Ustinov with fine, not always popular, contemporary playwrights – Charles Morgan (Irving's predecessor as *Times* theatre critic), Denis Cannan, John Whiting – and European classics.

The membership took itself very seriously, but they could see the funny side, too. A short play by G. K. Chesterton, *Magic*, in the 1955–56 season, paired with a Thornton Wilder rarity, threw up a spectacular mishap when the actor due to deliver a pile of correspondence on a tray forgot the salver as he crossed the stage behind the set in the dark and entered with the brave line, 'I'm awfully sorry, your Grace, I meant to bring some letters for you to sign . . .' thus allowing 'his Grace' to get quickly back on track with his next line, 'Never mind about that, Hastings, I've got something interesting to tell you.'

Instead, his Grace, responding to the improvisation, exploded into a new line of his own, 'Forgot them? Well, go and get them, and be damned quick about it!' The actor returned, behind the set, to the other side, bumbling around in the dark and bumping into other actors awaiting their cue, causing general havoc as he went. He retrieved the tray, crash-bang-walloped his way back to the other side again and entered, gasping, 'Here are the letters, your Grace . . . .' To which his Grace blithely replied, 'Never mind about that, Hastings, I've got something interesting to tell you . . .'

In the same season, Norma directed *Hamlet* with John playing the Ghost. On the opening night, he appeared on the ramparts and in his rich deep voice bade Hamlet, 'Mark me . . .' followed by a slightly over-long pause and the all-too-audible prompt piping up with '. . . my hour is almost come, when I to sulphurous and tormenting flames must render up myself.' Those flames were further fanned by Norma when he came off and she was fired up even more when, in the closet scene, the Ghost stepped out of a grey felt slipper and left it on the podium just as Hamlet said to Gertrude, 'Do you see nothing there?'

This production further cemented its place in BLT folklore when the dead hero was carried from the stage not, as Norma had planned, to the accompaniment of a mournful passage of Sibelius, but – in those far-off days before push-button technology in sound and lighting – to the catchy strains of 'Tea for Two'. This was the final straw, and Norma flew round to the sound box and assaulted the hapless technician, a volunteer schoolboy, for which transgression she was banned from Hanover Street for three months.

She was back in favour three years later when she directed the second amateur production (hard on the heels of the Tower's) of Harold Pinter's *The Birthday Party*. And this was almost wholly due to the intervention of her stepson. Irving had started his career in London as a sub-editor on the *Times Educational Supplement* – before moving on to deputise for Kenneth Tynan on *The Observer* in 1959. He took over the reins as the *Times* critic in 1963 and was flexing his muscles on the intellectual theatre magazine *Encore* and in a London column for the *Bolton Evening News*.

Under his by-line on the *News* of 'Sancho' he rounded up London shows, and in June 1958, reported on the brief sojourn of the critically reviled Pinter premiere at the Lyric, Hammersmith. Pausing only to remark wisely that Harold Hobson's lone voice of approval in the *Sunday Times* seemed more deadly than any other critic's attack, he calmly proceeded to analyse the acting and the meaning of the play, commending its theatrical energy and passages of obscurely menacing rhetoric played as cadenzas of gibberish sustained by an almost operatically vocal delivery.

While Pinter said (at Hobson's memorial service) that without that *Sunday Times* review he might have stopped writing plays altogether, he was equally glad of Irving's response and happily went up to Bolton to sit in on Norma's rehearsals in the autumn of 1959. He commended the production, as he had commended the one at the Tower a few months earlier.

Irving says that he doesn't know what Pinter really thought about it, but was convinced on one front: 'There was no question of his impact on the girls in the company (one of whom gate-crashed his carriage all the way back to Euston), and on Norma herself, who fell for him as a solid gold specimen of "the best". As Pinter put it to me after recovering from this northern adventure, 'She really put on her dark glasses for me.'

Irving, in the wake of Tynan, was now set to bear witness to the most exciting period in the post-war British theatre, specifically the consolidation of the radical changes in new writing and staging at the Royal Court, the RSC and the National, as well as the first furious flourishing of the fringe. And there's no question that his unrivalled authority as a critic, and one who really knew his stuff, from the mid-1960s to 1989 on *The Times*, was partially rooted in his experience in and around the BLT. I remember his stepmother turning up with him on Press nights at the Royal Exchange, Manchester, in the 1980s. We all loved seeing her while Irving skulked silently to one side, but she was, unwittingly, a key instrument in his critical development.

'My personal bias', he confessed in his *Scenes from a Life* memoir,

was all for ensemble – thanks partly to my own cold war with my queenly stepmother, a star-worshipping elocutor with loud opinions and orchestral vowels which she turned up to full volume in roles like Oscar Wilde's Gwendolen, causing me to cringe and close my eyes. Then, to my disbelief, she was cast in a radio series about customers gossiping in a barber's shop, and her false West End voice gave way to the rasp of an authentic Bolton woman. If only, like her acquaintance Doris Speed, she had found a berth in *Coronation Street* on ITV, we might have become friends. Or perhaps not: like many people, she wanted to be admired for what was classy and difficult, and disdained what she could do naturally.

Another distinguished alumnus of the BLT was Eric Bentley, the great critic, scholar and translator, who enthusiastically attended productions in the earliest seasons as a teenager (he was born in 1916) before graduating at Oxford and going to Yale in 1938. He's been in America ever since, teaching at Columbia University and writing in *The New Republic*, as well as publishing countless books, many of them about Brecht, whom he met in Santa Monica in 1942. The symbiotic relationship and friendship between this critic and this playwright – Brecht in exile needed a champion in the US, Bentley needed status as a scholar – was described in a play written by Charles Marowitz in 2006, *Silent Partners*, and later performed in its UK premiere at the BLT in a 2009 production by Michael Shipley.

Irving admired this production for the amount of feeling the actors put into the play, noting (in a privately circulated review), the theatricality of Marowitz's invention of a Satanic fantasy in which a Faustian pact between playwright and acolyte is floated as a possibility. But, as Michael Billington observed in his *Guardian* review when *Silent Partners* was produced on the London fringe in 2013, the dependency of the two men on each other was sullied, in the end, by their political differences. Bentley was a classic liberal; Brecht a hard-line Marxist.

Michael Shipley had first joined the company in 1948 as a cheeky urchin from Bolton School – the same school where Irving Wardle had played Hamlet aged eighteen and where, as McKellen has reminded him, he (Shipley) gave the future star his first stage kiss in a production of Robert Greene's Elizabethan comedy *Friar Bacon and Friar Bungay*. Shipley caught the BLT bug as a twelve-year-old in Thackeray's *The Rose and the Ring* and as a page to Paris in *Romeo and Juliet*. Shipley, who's been the company's chairman and secretary over the years and an important cog in the LTG wheel, read law as a scholar of Trinity Hall, Cambridge, before returning to his home town as a family lawyer and carrying on, so to speak, at the BLT.

He is a great expert on the indigenous Manchester School of Harold Brighouse, Stanley Houghton and Allan Monkhouse, who aimed to present the human comedy of Lancashire in a way, and with a success, that had no 'new writing' equal at the repertory theatres in, say, Birmingham, Bristol or Glasgow. Several of these writers' plays – notably Brighouse's *Hobson's Choice*, Houghton's *Hindle Wakes* and Monkhouse's *Mary Broome* – have been kept alive, and acknowledged as being of lasting value in amateur productions, as well as in the professional repertoire, not least thanks to the BLT.

I'm slightly exaggerating in the case of *Mary Broome*, which was in fact lost to the professional stage for a century before a revelatory revival in 2011 at the little Orange Tree in Richmond, Surrey. Here, the critics and public discovered, was a truly compelling drama, with serpentine plot twists and subtle arguments, about a mis-matched young couple – Len, a poised aesthete and writer in a trade where 'the better you are, the less you make', has 'taken advantage of' Mary, a housemaid in Len's middle-class Manchester family. They make a decent fist of their relationship, resisting censorious fury at home and living in penury before, inevitably, parting.

Michael Shipley has been at the heart of the company's foreign tours in Europe and America – a revival of Emlyn Williams's *The Corn is Green* was played in a corn field in Minneapolis, Brian Friel's *Dancing at Lughnasa* visited Lodi, California – and he personally supervised, from 1974 to 1992, the annual early summer presentation of a play in the great medieval hall at Smithills, a fine manor house set in 2,000 acres of land on the edge of the West Pennine Moors, where Shakespeare might well have performed with Lord Essex's players when they visited in 1594.

He also extended the festival to include music, poetry and a gala supper each Saturday in order to give the occasion 'a touch of Glyndebourne'. The tradition faded when the council decided to charge for the use of the hall – the substantial profits had often rescued the theatre's finances for a season – and this also marked the end of many years of subsidy from the council, which used to come in the form of direct revenue grants.

A jubilee appeal with a target of £100,000 was launched in 1984, with plans for a major refurbishment and the creation of a second studio space, the Forge, within the main auditorium which was, in the re-build, sliced in two – or rather two thirds and one third. There were technical requirements from the 1982 licence inspection behind this move to carve out a smaller theatre – the licence was extended only from play to play while work urgently required on electrics, fire prevention, toilets and the roof was undertaken. It was also necessary to reduce the seating capacity from 270 in the main house to a combined 220 in both houses. In addition, like everywhere else, it was becoming harder to attract an audience for serious plays.

On a few occasions, the BLT was kept afloat by raucously popular revivals of John Godber's *Bouncers* and *Shakers*, a pair of nightclub knees-ups with venomous attitude that brought in a fresh, younger audience. Michael Shipley says that the effort to prepare the new building, clear the place up, decorate and re-carpet the foyer was so intense that when they eventually re-opened at the end of 1988, the sense of stake-holding among the membership was redoubled and pride in the theatre reinvigorated.

The Forge opened in 1989 with Houghton's *Hindle Wakes* and a determination, still prevalent, that the studio should not syphon off all the serious and experimental work from the main stage, but complement the overall policy of seriousness tempered with, hopefully, popular appeal. Still, the BLT teetered on the edge of bankruptcy in 1993, before recovering to achieve a drastic backstage refurbishment in 1996 with the help of a

National Lottery endowment of £100,000. They celebrated with another UK premiere, this time of another playwright much admired by Michael Shipley, Romulus Linney, father of actress Laura Linney, whose eighty-five dramas (he died in 2011) have been performed nationwide in the US by professionals and amateurs alike, but rarely in Britain.

The play was *Holy Ghosts*, dating from 1971 but with a strong pedigree of professional productions behind it. It features a sort of ecstatic revivalist and choric element that lends itself to large cast ensemble groups more easily found on the amateur stage, perhaps, not unlike the appeal of *Dark of the Moon*. Linney often dug down into the Southern Appalachian culture of his upbringing and in *Holy Ghosts* the Pentecostal Church, with its sect of snake-handlers offering refuge to a woman on the run from her marriage. She finds salvation, and a future new partner, in the charismatic reverend Obadiah. By the middle of the first act, the whole cast of fifteen characters is on stage and stays there until the end of the play, which proceeds with hymns, prayers, sermons and declarations of faith, moving inexorably to the climactic seizing of the snakes, each character struck by a vision of God and his own salvation. The live snakes of the script were done with mime and sound effects.

One can imagine the overpowering close contact effect the play might have had in the Forge studio, though such a piece would surely belong most appropriately on the main stage. But the audience might not have followed it there. Certainly, Shipley reports, the box office for *Holy Ghosts*, while satisfactory, was not as good as for the Alan Ayckbourn play that preceded it. Indeed, like the Crescent in Birmingham and the Questors in London, the BLT is far more likely to consign all its classical drama, including Ibsen and Chekhov, to the smaller space instead of the main stage. What hasn't been done yet, though, is soundproof one theatre against the other, so that if the main house (163 seats, end stage) has a show, the Forge (sixty seats arranged on three sides of a square acting area) is dark and the same vice versa. Each space is served by the same sound and lighting consoles housed in a hutch above the partition wall.

The bar is welcoming and lively, the dressing rooms better than adequate, the audience far more mixed than I was expecting on the night I went to see David Lindsay-Abaire's *Rabbit Hole*, a superbly taut and engrossing 2005 Pulitzer prize-winning drama later filmed with Nicole Kidman in the role of a mother whose young son has been killed in a car accident. The BLT production fully understood that the play is really more about grief than loss, and that the less mawkish the playing, the more powerful the drama.

The play turns the emotional screws when the seventeen-year-old boy who was driving the car that hit the child calls by the bereaved family home. When the play was produced at Hampstead Theatre in 2016 with Claire Skinner and Tom Goodman-Hill as the parents, this boy, Jason, was played by a splendid newcomer, freshly graduated from RADA, Sean Delaney. In Bolton, the role was taken with a comparable, and comparably effective, stillness and frankness by a theatre student, Jude Slides, making his BLT debut. Who is to say he will not be the next Ian McKellen?

. . . and a CAST of thousands in Donny

I once went to Oldham – I hadn't done anything, as Ken Dodd used to say of going to Halifax, but I went there anyway. I knew nothing about the place beyond the fact that the actor playing Macduff in a 1947 production of *Macbeth* at the Oldham Coliseum accidentally stabbed the actor playing Macbeth, and killed him; and that its football team occupies the highest, coldest plateau in the country, Boundary Park.

The play I saw there in 1980 was the first night of folk singer Mike Harding's hilarious, wonderfully vulgar *Fur Coat and No Knickers*, involving a stag night, a wedding, a drunk priest and a blow-up rubber doll. It has become a staple of amateur theatres either side of the Pennines these past forty years, not least at the populist Doncaster Little Theatre which tagged its 2017 visiting production with a health warning: 'not for the easily offended'.

The Doncaster Little Theatre, like the BLT, is a focus for other local amateur companies, as well as a producing company itself, inhabiting a cosily unassuming L-shaped building, not dissimilar to the BLT, which was a home for various small businesses, including a tile warehouse, until commandeered in 1995 by a carpentry teacher and other folk from the Methodist church which, in the 1930s, had formed there an amateur dramatic group called the Doncaster Literary Society.

Until 1995, the amateurs played in the old Civic Theatre – now an abandoned patch of grass – while bolstering their activities with play readings, theatre trips, quiz nights and parties. The members dug out the derelict warehouse with their bare hands, carefully removing all the syringes and condoms that had piled up over the previous ten years. When they opened with a production of Rattigan's *The Deep Blue Sea*, the cement mixer and bags of cement were still in the hall, stashed away behind the seating they'd rescued from a bingo hall.

It's a sad truth that theatre is no longer ingrained into every aspect of community life in the way it once was – except, perhaps, in exemplary outposts like the Doncaster Little. For since the DLT opened in this new home – with more young people now coming through its doors than was the case five, or even ten, years ago and two local playwrights, Will Tuller and Will Templeton, regularly putting on their own work – the place feels as necessary to Donny, as Doncaster dubs itself, as the Bush Theatre in London is to Acton or White City. A youth company puts on their own plays, too, and a group from the deprived, former coalfield area of Bentley – a staunch working-class enclave – clocks in to the theatre in King Street every Saturday morning.

'We are a facilitator for a lot of local projects,' says Keith Mears, the DLT chairman who used to work in the power industry, but went into teaching when the government chose to privatise it. He doesn't seem to mind that 50 per cent of his season is hired out to other amateur companies, allowing him to concentrate on home-grown stuff such as thrillers, cabaret nights and *The Railway Children*, with improvisation, the locally written new plays and musicals slipped in with perhaps surprising regularity.

Mears, who has ninety-nine blue seats to fill in his modest, single-raked auditorium, has no qualms about booking a second pantomime for the Easter holidays, especially as it comes from the little company run by local lad Thomas Howes, who played the second footman in *Downton Abbey* on television. Mears's predecessor as chairman secured a lottery grant of £400,000 spread over five years for community engagement. There was a slight hiccup when the campaign was derailed by some poor accounting. But that's sorted and Mears is back on track and talking of the theatre's fast approaching centenary. Before then, he wants to expand the building into a second storey for storage and rehearsal space, and for that he needs £1 million.

This might be a problem because the overall arts scene, indeed the whole tone of the city, has been transformed by the opening of CAST in 2013. This is a spanking new £22 million theatre and arts centre at the heart of a proposed new cultural quarter in a £300 million development that is, no question, a

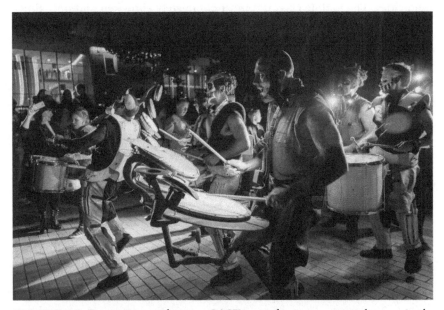

FIGURE 10 *Drumming outdoors at CAST, one of many year-round events in the community presented in the public square. (Photo: James Mulkeen.)*

resounding statement of aspiration and ambition. But I could find nobody at either CAST or the Little to say that this would undermine the original amateur impulse. On the contrary, the feeling is that the two enterprises will continue to complement each other, especially as CAST, which does cater, to a limited extent, for a few select amateur companies in its small studio, is a fully fledged professional outfit and its hire charges much higher than at the Little. Theoretically at least, CAST, whose patron, opera singer Lesley Garrett – a proud local girl – has been an active and generously committed fundraiser, is intended as a sort of replacement for the old Civic.

Its arrival has probably undermined the still vigorous campaign to save the Grand Theatre near the station, an 1899 Grade II-listed building, with Frank Matcham features, now owned by the shopping centre next door to it. Once a big touring date for big musicals, the Grand became a bingo hall in 1963, but was abandoned by Mecca in 1995 and has fallen into a state of serious disrepair. The campaign has at least saved it from the bulldozers, but it's hard to see how the local council (Doncaster Metropolitan Borough), or indeed the Arts Council, would be persuaded to pour in more funds while both parties concentrate on what the French call 'le grand projet'.

I'm told that when the spectacular glass walls of CAST were going up, folk used to press their noses against the pane: 'Bit good for Donny, ain't it?' The expectations of the citizens are being challenged in the spirit of cultural regeneration, perhaps similar to what has happened in Hull. The Donny demographic is a bit different, though: the population is mostly white working-class, with a very tiny proportion (2.5 per cent) of Asian and other ethnicities. The middle class is almost completely shrunken and only 9 per cent of the population have a university degree.

Still, the city has a thriving race track, a significant railway heritage, a magnificent minster and a fair amount of Georgian and Regency architecture. All the same, whether or not Doncaster can manage a Hull-style cultural transformation is a moot point, but they won't fail for want of trying. Ever since Princess Diana opened the huge Doncaster Dome in 1989, focal point of concerts and other big leisure activities, the die has been cast. And the name of CAST is deliberately chosen to reference not just the city itself, DonCASTer, but also its mining heritage and, of course, the collection of actors needed for a play.

CAST has an annual turnover of £2 million, of which 70 per cent is earned through the Box Office and hires and 30 per cent from the council. In front of the building is a big open square which hosts popular outdoor events in the summer. Inside the light-filled glass foyer, there's a coffee shop and bar, open all hours, before you enter a handsome horse-shoe auditorium with 620 seats (the big touring musicals skip Donny altogether, sparkling straight on to the Sheffield Lyceum), a gently curving circle and seven hanging clusters of modern lights, their colour variable, their effect one of warming welcome.

The studio has retractable seating, and can accommodate 160 people. There is a sound-proofed dance studio/rehearsal space, which is also licensed for performances, but more often given over to artists' development and workshops (CAST has five associate companies dealing in dance, digital, 'Urban Conceptz', puppetry and work with refugees and asylum seekers). Students from Doncaster College, which issues a performing arts degree validated by Hull University, have tuition here. The director, currently Deborah Rees, sits un-hierarchically at one end of an open-plan office, full of big windows and daylight. There's a play-reading group for the over-fifties in the circle bar; a youth theatre (who perform on the main stage); visiting comedy, and even dementia-friendly party mornings offering song, dance and a slice of cake.

In fact, if you study carefully the programmes and policies of even the most revered and established professional repertory theatres – the Bristol Old Vic, say, the Nottingham Playhouse or even the RSC – they are rapidly accelerating towards this conceptual community arts centre notion, with added ingredients of diversity and ethnic quota casting that are inapplicable in Doncaster. A recent CAST theatre project, *The Last Seam*, had a script entirely compiled from interviews with forty former miners in the nearby Hatfield Colliery which closed, after a colourful history of shut-down, new ownership, job losses and landslip, due to lack of demand for coal products, allegedly, in 2015.

And, in early 2018, the pick of local amateur talent presented a three-play season in the CAST studio: John Steinbeck's *Of Mice and Men*; a physical theatre take on the Pocahontas story called *The New World*; and Thomas Middleton's *A Mad World My Masters*, a Jacobean comedy that might well be one of the filthiest plays ever written in the English language – and a masterpiece of farcical, narrative plotting to boot. That season came from JKL Productions (the directors are Jan, Kevin and Les) which actually does define itself as 'an amateur community company' and is established at CAST as the only amateur group in the building.

One of the trio, Kevin Spence, is not only a trustee of CAST, and a key agitator for its construction and evolution, he's also a founder member of the Little in King Street, where he was involved in management, acting and directing for twenty years. And he's a prominent associate, nationally, in the Little Theatre Guild. If Doncaster may be said to have a theatrical Mr Big, Spence is that fellow. At the Little, Spence has played Vanya, Prospero, Macbeth and Leontes – roles he says he could never have hoped to play had he been a professional. So he knows exactly where he stands and has made the theatre his life anyway.

As a schoolboy in Mansfield he was bewitched by Tyrone Guthrie's production of *Cymbeline* at the old Nottingham Playhouse, Michael Crawford in *The Importance of Being Earnest* and John Neville as Oedipus.

His first practical experience, after graduating from Bristol, then Nottingham, University was with the amateur Caxton Players in Grimsby (whose patron is Patricia Hodge). Spence exudes the sort of can-do mentality of many leading amateurs and it's clear that the seriousness with which he goes about things places him firmly in the 'unpaid professional' category. The distinction becomes even more blurred however when you learn that one wing of JKL Productions is an academy of youth theatre. Spence is particularly devoted to his work with young people, having been a teacher of modern languages and drama throughout his other life in amdram. And he becomes positively evangelical about the role of the Little Theatre Guild in looking 'beyond our own parapets' to see the bigger picture with regard to training, permeation in the community and general encouragement and recruitment of youngsters.

One of his more adventurous undertakings at the DLT was a stage version of Kenneth Branagh's 1995 movie *In the Bleak Midwinter*, whose release coincided exactly with the opening of the Little: a group of actors getting together, unpaid, to put on *Hamlet* in a country church in order to save it from the property developers and convince the local council of the need for culture in the community. Although the movie veers off into a sometimes very funny study of thespian dedication, not to say, affectation, it also captures something of the very spirit of the LTG: the doing up of old premises in Bolton, Birmingham or Doncaster with a view to making a mark among your fellow, perhaps initially indifferent, human beings. And it expresses something, too, perhaps, of why Branagh himself was pleased and flattered to be invited to succeed Ian McKellen as the LTG's patron.

For, like the Geoffrey Whitworth – and as much as the Bolton Little and the Crescent in Birmingham – the theatres in Doncaster are clearly enmeshed in the overall texture of the professional theatre in the UK. Everything they do relates to the educational and culturally evangelical instincts that date from the turn of the last century and bloomed in the campaign for the National Theatre, the great flowering of regional and repertory theatres either side of the First World War and indeed the modern re-birth of the amateur theatre itself between the two wars.

On the whole, the phenomenon that is the amateur theatre in this country potters along unheralded in the media. But when British Telecom announced a sponsorship of £100,000 in 1991 for something called the BT Biennial in conjunction with the Little Theatre Guild, *The Times* proclaimed, 'The first mass marketing exercise in the history of amateur dramatics'. A play called *Happy Families* by John Godber was simultaneously premiered by forty-nine LTG member theatres, charting the frictions arising in a northern working-class family when the leading character (not unrelated to Godber himself) became socially and culturally mobile. It was, in effect, a wryly affectionate memory play and one that seemed to evolve from the nature of the commission itself.

The second BT play in 1993, *Shakespeare Country* by Peter Whelan, performed by forty LTG companies, also benefited from the relaxed, 'anything goes' atmosphere surrounding a project involving so many people in so many places. Loosely based on *A Midsummer Night's Dream*, there was a *Kiss Me, Kate*-style of aggressive stand-off between Oberon and Titania on the verge of getting married in Stratford-upon-Avon, interrupted by the arrival of a Country and Western singer from Texas claiming to be the son of William Shakespeare.

And the third BT play, Debbie Isitt's *Nasty Neighbours* in 1995, performed by no less than 100 LTG theatres, was a rancorous, frenziedly funny fall-out between a curtain-twitching busybody crushed under the expectations of his wife and the brash and vulgar new arrivals next door. This was the most Mike Leigh-like of Isitt's plays, many of which are frequently done by amateur companies, and she herself directed it as a feature film in 2000 starring Ricky Tomlinson (perfecting his couch potato slob act), the ever-electric Phil Daniels, Rachel Fielding and Hywell Bennett.

BT then moved on to sponsor the National Theatre Connections programme, which involved schools all over the country performing plays written by leading dramatists. This was a variation on the BT Biennial initiative which in many ways was a dry run for the NT's project. It certainly energised theatre in schools just as BT Biennial gave some valuable creative jolts to the LTG theatres and almost certainly made them reconsider their repertory choices in the years that followed.

It was always an imperative in the foundation of the first Little Theatres in the 1920s and 1930s that there should be a network of such theatres, creating a theatre culture shared across the nation. That powerful impulse lives on today – not only in the work of the LTG – but in the theatre as a whole. There is an increased emphasis in the regional theatre on co-productions (not always a good idea, but one driven by economic necessity, rather than political or social expediency), the thriving large-scale community theatre initiated in Devon and Dorset in the 1980s by Ann Jellicoe, the RSC's outreach and Open Stage policies, and the new plans at the National itself to work more closely, and more intensely, with the amateur stage.

8

Interlude: Amdram at the Movies, in Novels – and Novel Hamlets

As the amateur theatre became ingrained in the culture, it effloresced in movies and literature, especially movies, and especially as a creative source of jokes and send-ups. One of our not-too-guilty pleasures in life is laughing at, rather than with, the business of amdram. It's a different ballgame altogether when we contemplate supposedly serious, or professional, theatre on celluloid.

One of the greatest of such movies is Marcel Carné's *Les Enfants du Paradis* (1945), which relates a compelling love story while evoking the entanglement and heartbeat of Parisian theatre and vaudeville in the mid-nineteenth century. Simon Callow's brave attempt to return that film to the stage it immortalises (at the RSC in 1996) didn't succeed because, paradoxically, it is precisely the cinematic beauty of the theatrical feast – as well as the luminescent screen performances of Jean-Louis Barrault as the dreaming pierrot, Maria Casarès as the theatre owner's daughter and Pierre Brasseur as the legendary actor Frederick Lemaître – that makes for a transcendent, and rare, fusion of theatre and cinema.

Whereas most films touching on amateur theatre highlight the downside of the genre – the coarse theatre aspects – the best American theatrical movies are either high-class satires – the very best being Joseph L. Mankiewicz's *All About Eve* (1950) – or epic narratives such as Charles Kaufman's extraordinary *Synechdoche New York* (2008) starring Philip Seymour Hoffman as a crazed theatre director and Alejandro[i] González Iñárritu's *Birdman* (2014), the tale of a fading star, played by Michael Keaton, re-launching himself on the stage while channelling his former cinematic eminence as Batman.

While *Synechdoche* pullulates with a sort of Orson Wellesian cock-eyed grandeur, *Birdman* is shot on New York locations in and around the St James Theatre on 44th Street and features Edward Norton as a Method actor from hell and Lindsay Duncan as an ingratiating, self-regarding critic subjected to a glorious tirade of abuse from the wounded Birdman. Without the intensity of feeling unleashed by Keaton, that scene in a bar right next to the theatre might have seemed 'stagier' and perhaps even more amateur than it does, for Duncan's critic is far less plausible and insidious a figure than George Sanders's poisonous Addison DeWitt in *All About Eve*.

Four years before he made *Synechdoche*, Seymour Hoffman went for amdram broke in John Hamburg's *Along Came Polly* (2004) as a failed film actor returning to his theatre roots in a 'community' (amateur) production of *Jesus Christ Superstar*. Quite apart from the too poignant joy of seeing Hoffman grossing out with twinkly dance moves as the slobby wingman of Ben Stiller's romantic schmuck (ten years before Hoffman died of a drug overdose), he nonetheless nails that mixture of tragic self-assertion and smell of failure that occasionally attaches to an amateur actor who believes he's slumming after some kind of professional experience.

Hoffman's character is remembered, if at all, for appearing in a teen movie called 'Crocodile Tears', and therefore feels entitled to dismiss his fellow thesps as 'a freaking bunch of amateurs'. He announces on mic before curtain up on opening night that 'in addition to playing Judas at tonight's performance, I'll be playing Jesus as well' – which results in an almighty fracas in the wings spilling over into an onstage brawl. The nice irony is that Hoffman's overweening thesp later stands in for Stiller's fraught risk assessor at a crucial meeting and, in a performance of hilarious, semi-intentional rhetoric, wins Stiller's client an insurance deal of $50 million.

Even more peripheral to the main plot, but significant nonetheless, are the opening scenes of Sam Mendes's *Revolutionary Road* (2008) in which, by way of reprising their romantic triumph in *Titanic*, Kate Winslet and Leonardo DiCaprio act out the stifling tragedy of a suburban marriage in Connecticut with a mirage of escape from the 'hopeless emptiness' of the white picket fence idyll and the New York rat race in the colour and spur to self-expression (they think) of emigrating to Paris. This never happens, and the water closes over their heads once more, with terrible consequences.

But the writing is on the wall from the start when, shortly after their first meeting, DiCaprio as Frank Wheeler attends April's (Winslet) performance as an amateur actress – 'you trained, for Christ's sake' – and, again, decries 'a bunch of amateurs'. Her confidence is shattered and their violent row sets a pattern for the rest of the movie. Mendes says that the film is about the fact that we all have one chance in life. April's was the theatre and she was bullied out of it. In the end, she is the one who makes compromises, at first disguised as a programme of acceptance and appeasement involving a third pregnancy, but she pays a heavy price. Her main chance was lost, and she lived with that.

No such grim lifestyle compromise marks Christopher Guest playing Corky St Clair in the treasurable movie *Waiting for Guffman* (1996). Holed up in Blaine, Missouri, Corky is desperate to get back to Broadway after ten years of failure off-Broadway. Meanwhile, he is teaching drama at the local high school and directing the Blaine Community Players in the town's 150th anniversary show, 'Red, White and Blaine'. Renowned for the manufacture of foot stools, Blaine is celebrated as 'the home of stools' in a sung tribute, a camp-fire reminiscence and a pioneering Davy Crocket song delivered by a cross-eyed dentist, followed by a barn dance.

Corky, whom Guest presents as a fluffy, pouting pan-sexual with a glossy toupée and an invisible wife, has to step into the first night breach when the local garage mechanic can't take any more and stomps out of the show – but not before manufacturing his own hissy fit when he goes home to bite on his pillow and soak in a bubble bath after the town council refuses his demand of a few more bucks for the scenery. Still, he forces himself into the garage hunk's (far too large) costume and draws the admiration of a star-struck councillor: 'Corky can do everything there is, and there's only one other person who can do that – Barbra Streisand!' And all of this with the confident hope of a Broadway transfer: Corky has pulled in a favour from his past and secured the attendance at the pageant of Mr Guffman of the Oppenheimer producing organisation in Manhattan.

Needless to say, Guffman, like Godot, never turns up. But Corky returns to New York anyway, signing up for auditions and opening a memorabilia shop selling *Remains of the Day* lunch boxes and *My Dinner with André* action figures. This should be sadder than it is. It isn't, for the simple reason that, bizarre though it may sound, anyone I've ever known operating in a low status of participation in the business of show – at box office or stage door, in ticket agency or souvenir shop, like Corky – finds a way of making that work for them and feeling comfortable with it. The occupation of theatre is a joined-up business across the land, including amateurs, I'd suggest, all operating at different levels, but believing, in a curiously amorphous way, that they are all part of the same project. That belief may be misplaced, but it keeps you going. It's like organised religion: if it works for you then it must be true or, at least, valuable.

Waiting for Guffman is presented as a kind of mockumentary with to-camera interviews and labelling sub-titles and does for 'community' theatre, said the *New York Daily News*, what *This Is Spinal Tap* (1984) – also co-written by Guest – did for heavy metal rock bands. The edge, bordering on cruel satire, of the movie is explained by this connection and also by the fact that Guest – aka the fifth Baron Haden-Guest, a British aristocrat and brother of the writer and socialite Anthony Haden-Guest – was a regular on the top US TV satire show *Saturday Night Live*. He went on to make such other hilarious mockumentaries as *Best in Show* about dogs (and their owners) primped up on parade and *A Mighty Wind* about the commemorative reunion of three sad sack 1960s folk groups in New York Town Hall.

Guest uses the same roster of very funny actors in each film, and they explore the absurdity in the yawning gaps between achievement and aspiration, credibility and self-deception and, yes, professional and amateur. Drilling down into these fissures in the British theatre was a factor in Alan Ayckbourn's *A Chorus of Disapproval*, which became a Michael Winner movie in 1989, Anthony Hopkins following his NT confrères Michael Gambon and Colin Blakely into the role of the crazed, bullying Welsh director Dafydd Ap Llewellyn.

Dafydd, in the unspecified past, has done a lot of professional acting – he's now a solicitor – but where? 'Oh, all over, all over – mainly in Minehead'. Jeremy Irons plays the bereaved but soon socially in-demand new businessman in the town, Guy Jones. Guy gets cast first as Crook-fingered Jack, then Filch and finally Macheath in the *The Beggar's Opera*, his promotion reflected in his rising stock with the ladies and the crucial fact that his company owns some valuable, much-coveted land next to the office, which he might be in a position to make available to their menfolk.

Neither Hopkins nor Irons were big screen stars at this point in their careers, but Hopkins in particular is outstanding – blockish, ferocious, masking his vulnerability in a carapace of shouting. When he reduces Richard Briers in rehearsal to tears, he explodes: 'That's amateurs for you – when the crunch comes they can't take the bloody pressure'. And he throws the script on the floor and spits on it.

Ayckbourn did not like the film and found himself wondering why Winner wanted to make it, as its sphere of effectiveness was undoubtedly the theatre; you might equally ask, why then did Ayckbourn sell him the rights? He felt, according to his archivist, Stephen Murgatroyd, that Winner had obliterated how English people use amateur dramatics for their own ends, and that all his points about company, power, sex and escapism had become a bit blurred. But I'm not sure he's right about that. The lineaments of the play and its amateur dramatic dynamo seem pretty intact to me, even though the text is not so much re-written as re-moulded and heavily cut.

On the plus side, Winner filmed entirely in Ayckbourn's home town of Scarborough, where the play, like all his plays, had been premiered. This makes for an enjoyable tour of the locality and coast-line. And several scenes where the world of amdram and the characters' interior lives lock together are well realised: Hopkins, left eye squinting badly, confidentially pouring out his heart to Irons only to be told that the tannoy has been on and everyone backstage in the dressing rooms has heard him. And, even better, Irons and Prunella Scales as Dafydd's wife, Hannah, who has sought emotional relief with Guy, standing on stage and separating, finally, in whispers at the end of their furtive affair while Dafydd plots the lighting cues around them, barking instructions from the back of the stalls. That scene, an invention of genius, could only have been conceived by a complete *homme du théâtre* and one sensitive and privy to the workings of amateur theatre, too. Winner's version does it full justice.

The play, one of Ayckbourn's finest, runs at 140 minutes, even without an interval, whereas the film is done and dusted in ninety-nine, which gives an idea of the carnage. Initially, Ayckbourn had hoped to write a play about amateurs putting on *The Vagabond King*, and that, for the stage premiere at the Stephen Joseph Theatre, there would be dozens of real amateurs dotted around the audience standing up with a sung linking commentary on the Rudolf Friml operetta. But the Friml estate refused the rights and the Scarborough Operatic Society, who had been approached to take part, wanted their members to take only leading roles. Equity ruled that including amateurs in this way was, anyway, unacceptable (that stricture probably would not apply today). So the ever pragmatic playwright turned his attention to an amateur company played by professionals putting on John Gay's folk opera. It proved an inspired move.

The Scarborough premiere of the film *A Chorus of Disapproval* was given in the town's now demolished Royal Opera House, the night after its royal premiere in London (which Ayckbourn refused to attend). The theatre had been one of the locations during filming and 500 locals had queued to be extras in the *The Beggar's Opera* opening night scene. The extras, sat in their seats, filmed with the pros for six hours – one of them, Mrs Joyce Anthony, who had 'extra-ed' elsewhere on the shoot, told the *Evening News* that 'Mr Winner was marvellous to work for; he said that if he'd had me thirty years ago, he could have made me a star!' – and they were joined on the day by the Labour MP for Hull East, John Prescott, soon to become deputy prime minister to Tony Blair, whom Winner had befriended on a train journey south.

Each of the extras was handed a bingo card as they arrived with a chance to win a single prize of £500 – there was no other payment – when the numbers were called between takes, until the prize was won. The numbers were called by Prescott and Winner, a move which in itself, when they got to hear about it, attracted a chorus of disapproval from the Broadcasting and Entertainment Trades Alliance which represents the nation's bingo-callers. Winner was not only making his film with cheap labour; he and Prescott were denying work to the fully trained 'Sixty-six, clickety click' professionals.

The much derided 'bunch of amateurs' finally won their own movie title in Andy Cadiff's *A Bunch of Amateurs* (2008), a fairly low-level affair featuring an almost totally inert Burt Reynolds as Jefferson Steel, an over-the-hill Hollywood action hero who reluctantly accepts the challenge of playing the lead in *King Lear* in the UK in order to re-boot his career. His sloppy agent misleadingly tells him the production is in Shakespeare's Stratford.

But the Avon, and the RSC, are miles away from his actual destination of Stratford St John, a sleepy backwater in Suffolk where the amdram group, the Stratford Players – who include Imelda Staunton as Goneril (and Burt's smitten landlady), Samantha Bond as the Fool (and the tartly tongued director) and Derek Jacobi as a resentful Kent – are hoping to save their

FIGURE 11 *Burt Reynolds rehearses Shakespeare for the Stratford Players in* A Bunch of Amateurs *(2008), seated between the amateur thesps of a keen Imelda Staunton and an aghast Derek Jacobi. (Everett Collection / Mary Evans.)*

community theatre in the manner of Kenneth Branagh and co putting on *Hamlet* in their bid to save a church in *In the Bleak Midwinter*.

There's a *Lear*-like reconciliation theme in the arrival of Burt's daughter, an off-Broadway actress whose avant-garde efforts he derides – she takes her top off in *Pride and Prejudice* – to save the day when Cordelia is taken ill. His own mini-crisis of quitting the show in a mighty huff is resolved when he drives the village's mobile library (serving as his trailer) into the countryside during a storm, shouting for 'a town, a city, a Four Seasons', and launching into 'Blow wind, and crack your cheeks' after crashing the trailer and crawling around in thunder and lightning. Samantha Bond has followed him out to the blasted heath and talks him down. The Players raise money by selling fabricated stories of Burt's sexual prowess to the national Press and Burt rallies the troops: 'Let's go out and show them what a bunch of amateurs can do'. The reviews are raves and the show transfers to what looks suspiciously like a West End theatre.

The sub-text is that lazy Hollywood stars don't know what they are doing (Burt's Steel arrives having not even read the play) and that amateurs, in this instance at least, are the true professionals. This gives Jacobi the chance to pontificate *de haut en bas* – 'I should be Lear, it's every actor's dream', he says (indeed he was, two years later at the Donmar Warehouse in London); 'The Suffolk Herald hailed my Malvolio as definitive'; and, the *coup de grace*, 'he [Jefferson Steel] is an utter disgrace to the noble traditions of the amateur stage'.

In a publicity interview for the film, Burt said that he had made a friend for life in Sir Derek. The opposite was the case, according to Jacobi in his 2016 *Sardines* magazine interview:

> One day . . . Burt screamed at us. We didn't pay too much attention to it because we [the company of British actors] had been giving him *everything*. The man was a zombie . . . he was on pills, anti-depressants, anti-pain. He had gained over forty injuries during his career. He had a corset and it took them half an hour to get his costume on. He was almost a dead man walking. So we'd love him up and then he suddenly and spitefully turned on us because we were being a bit naughty. It was a shame.

Even so, as satirical writing about amdram, the script of Ian Hislop and Nick Newman, fellow writers on the irresistibly scurrilous and satirical *Private Eye* magazine, which Hislop edits, with additions from two Hollywood screenwriters, can't hold a candle to Guest's on *Waiting for Guffman*, either in quality or witty perception. But Hislop and Newman have been lately developing a partnership with the little Watermill Theatre in Newbury, Berkshire, where, in 2014, they launched a professional stage version of *A Bunch of Amateurs* which Newman, in a programme note, averred was probably more powerful and appropriate – as a piece about the redemptive power of theatre – on the stage than on the screen.

The reviews were strong, noting a more emphatic farcical element in the mix-up of tantrums and sexual imbroglios. And now, to complete the circle, and reverse the stage-to-screen progress of *A Chorus of Disapproval*, the play has been released to amateurs by Samuel French and productions have proliferated in village halls from Chipping Ongar to Aylesbury, Bucks, and Kingsley, Cheshire – all venues very similar to the one at the centre of the Stratford Players' campaign.

While *King Lear* is the context for *A Bunch of Amateurs* – though far less effectively so than in Ronald Harwood's *The Dresser*, another much-loved staple of the amateur repertoire – *Macbeth* and *Hamlet* of the great tragedies occur more frequently in film or fiction settings, with an atmospherically realised performance of *Othello* coming to the rescue of the plot complications in *Les Enfants du Paradis*. Terence Rattigan used a chaotic rep production of *Romeo and Juliet* to reveal emotional and domestic fall-out in *Harlequinade* (1948) – another amateur repertoire favourite – and the same tragedy is literally massacred in an amateur performance half-way through Edgar Wright's *Hot Fuzz* (2007), a genre-blending mash-up of horror, murder mystery, action and buddy movies starring Simon Pegg and Nick Frost.

These two are very funny as a pair of policemen in a quiet country village where nothing much happens – except in the last reel or so, when *Midsomer Murders*-style tranquillity is disrupted by a wave of grisly attacks. Wholesale arson, stabbings, eviscerations, falling church masonry at the village fête, decapitations – all are perpetrated by a gang of druidical hoodlums who turn out to be the villagers themselves. 'Heads will roll' can be their only possible verdict on a home-grown *Romeo and Juliet* in which David Threlfall's narcissistic Romeo and Lucy Punch's giggling Juliet murder Shakespeare's verse; and the star-crossed lovers' heads do indeed roll, right across the country lane, severed from their torsos inside an open-top sports car. The amateur *Romeo and Juliet* is targeted because, in a similar set-up to the local scramble for prime land ownership in *A Chorus of Disapproval*, Romeo is a solicitor and Juliet a council worker who have fallen foul of an all-powerful supermarket manager (blithely played with a Ronald Colman moustache by Timothy Dalton) with his eye on expansion.

The final scene in the mausoleum is all we see of the play, discharged with stilted awfulness by both actors and greeted with a mixture of disbelief and dismay by an audience who are, in fact, sitting in a real-life amateur theatre – the Barn at Welwyn Garden City in Hertfordshire. The film company paid the Barn £3,500 for complete use over six days, including four days of actual filming. They painted the bar red, re-hung doors to create access for the cameras, changed the Green Room to a dressing room set with mirrors and lights and filled the car park with trucks for generators and catering. This all happened between seasons, causing minimal disruption to the Barn's routine.

The presentation of amateur theatre bound up in the devious commercial aspirations of a close-knit community in both the Ayckbourn play and *Hot Fuzz* is light years, as opposed to a mere 200 years, away from the country house film and fiction of the eighteenth and nineteenth centuries. Or is it?

There is something unpleasant, vaguely amoral and 'alien' about both troupes of amateur players, just as amateur theatricals in Jane Austen's *Mansfield Park* (1814) – the theatrical 'germ' is brought to the house by Mr Yates, a foolish visitor from the world of 'fashion and expense' – no less than in Théophile Gautier's *Mademoiselle de Maupin* (1836), are threats to stability in society, forces of subversion. In the Gautier novel, especially, a milieu is created where social identity and emotional impulse are refracted through performance. Gautier's use of *As You Like It* as both an expression and a metaphor of sexual confusion at the heart of the novel is truly inspired.

The complexity of manners and social upheaval is stamped through two more works driven by home theatricals, both created in the shadow of imminent war. Jean Renoir's *La Règle du jeu* (1939) – 'Rules of the Game' – is an attack on French high society in decline, registering three interwoven romantic triangles and directly derived from a comedy by Alfred de Musset, with shades of two other French dramatists – Marivaux for sexual role-playing and Feydeau for bedchamber mishap and crossed wires. Virginia Woolf's last novel, *Between the Acts* (1941), captures an ominously pre-war mood of a country house pageant in June 1939, at the same time ineffably sad and vivid, as the director, Miss La Trobe, paces to and fro beneath the leaning birch trees with first night foreboding:

> Wet would it be, or fine? Out came the sun; and, shading her eyes in the attitude proper to an Admiral on his quarter-deck, she decided to risk the engagement out of doors. Doubts were over. All stage properties, she commanded, must be moved from the Barn to the bushes. It was done. And the actors, while she paced, taking all responsibility and plumping for fine, not wet, dressed among the brambles. Hence the laughter.

Between the acts of writing the novel and having it published, Woolf killed herself, which casts another shadow across the country house lawn. Just a few years earlier, Michael Innes had updated the private theatricals genre in the second of his long series of Inspector John Appleby mysteries, *Hamlet, Revenge!* (1937). During a performance of the play attended by politicians and Shakespearean academics and critics, the Lord Chancellor as Polonius is shot dead behind the arras by, as it turns out, an accomplice of Hamlet, who is played by the one professional actor in a cast of amateurs.

The play itself reflects the world of the audience at the fictional Duke of Horton's seat at Scamnum Court, which is one of high-level politics, espionage, affairs of state, misprised love and revenge. One of the visiting academics, Giles Gott, notes that the days of theatricals 'when the noble family of Bridgewater moved through the stately dance and rhetoric of Milton's *Comus* at Ludlow Castle' are over and that 'the basic attitude of a scurrying contemporary society to them was that expressed by Sir Thomas Bertram when he put a stop to such nonsense in *Mansfield Park*. Leisure had gone'. The abler people in the audience at Scamnum were governing England, it is noted, the others 'not so much leisured as laboriously idle'.

The Hamlet himself, Melville Clay, who also directs what turns out to be a first-rate production on a reconstructed Elizabethan stage – with minimal business, movement and clear verse-speaking – is full of wise saws and instances on the subject of amateur theatre, suggesting that acting is difficult for amateurs because it's all technique. And 'if acting is 100 per cent technique, technique is about 75 per cent timing'. Like the Shakespeare of Nugent Monck at the Maddermarket, Clay's production is conceived in order to depend on the rapidity and the continuity of the action.

While *Hamlet, Revenge!* instigated a persistent vogue for donnish detective fiction – Michael Innes was the *nom de plume* of the renowned Scottish critic and academic J. I. M. Stewart – the *Hamlet* and amateur theatre novel of Alan Isler, *The Prince of West End Avenue* (1996) sits more easily in a Jewish tradition of ironic fiction. Isler emigrated from Yorkshire to New York at the age of eighteen in 1952, serving in the US Army and teaching Renaissance Literature at Queen's College in the city. His poet hero, Otto Korner, who hung around the Cabaret Voltaire in Zurich in 1915 at the same time as Lenin, Joyce and Tristan Tzara – rather like Tom Stoppard's hapless diplomatic consul in *Travesties* – is directing *Hamlet* in the Emma Lazarus retirement home on West End Avenue, Manhattan, with a cast of 'semi-ambulants'.

He loses his Hamlet, just as he lost his girlfriend in Munich, and ends up having to play Hamlet himself, after some parallel real-life upheavals of jealousy, politics, sex and revenge centred around Goldstein's delicatessen in the neighbourhood and a grimly related story of the family's paintings and books travelling from Nuremberg to Central Park West and now the Emma Lazarus. As Otto finally takes to the stage, his Ophelia pinches his cheek: 'You should break a leg'; 'What kind of talk is that?'; 'Theatrical talk. It's a way of saying *mazel tov* without exciting the evil eye'.

Isler's *Hamlet* novel is smart and clever, nearly as clever as Ian McEwan's *Hamlet* novel, *Nutshell* (2016), which reduces the moody Dane to a prophetic embryo in his mother's womb. Shakespeare's Hamlet says, 'I could be bounded in a nutshell, and count myself a king of infinite space, were it not that I have bad dreams', whereas McEwan's unnamed embryo, the book's narrator, is more loosely expressive while floating around in his mother's amniotic fluid: 'To be bound in a nutshell, see the world in two inches of ivory, in a grain of sand. Why not, when all of literature, all of art, of human endeavour, is just a spectre in the universe of possible things.'

There is no direct correlation with amateur theatre, but the scenario of the play is re-cast from the embryo's perspective in the contemporary world, one where his poet father's brother has literally wormed his way in between his family and his hopes and he, the unborn, dreads the bouts of foreplay with his mother, Trudy, while lodged in the front stalls, awkwardly seated upside down. He contemplates suicide: 'To be stillborn – a tranquil term purged of tragedy – has a simple allure'. It's an ironic reminder, this brilliant book, that *Hamlet* is as much a spur to thought as to action and that the reactive appropriation of Shakespeare's most famous play in our culture, and in our theatrics, both professional and amateur, is one of the signal phenomena of our civilisation, and one we share worldwide.

9

The Magic of the Minack

The Minack Theatre, carved on a cliff side in Cornwall, is a story of romance and survival unlike any other in the British theatre, amateur or professional. A theatre on the edge of a cliff: whose idea was that? The question is asked sarcastically in Nicola Upson's 2009 novel *Angel with Two Faces*, and answered by a butch character called Ronnie Motley, one of two sisters, both theatre designers, closely associated with the book's amateur sleuth, the crime writer Josephine Tey: 'A woman called Rowena Cade. She's barking mad, of course – well, you have to be to carve a theatre out of a rock, don't you – but in the best possible way. She started it about three years ago [the novel is set in 1935], and we got roped into helping with the costumes for the show that our lot put on there. We've done it ever since – it's really rather magical as long as the weather holds.'

The background of Upson's novel is the real-life third production, in the third season, at the Minack. Motley was the collective name of a trio of famous theatre designers – two of them sisters – who had worked with the future pseudonymous novelist Josephine Tey (real name Elizabeth MacKintosh) on her 1933 play *Richard of Bordeaux* starring John Gielgud; for her work as a playwright, the elusive Tey called herself Gordon Daviot. The Motley crew never worked at the Minack, but the romance of the place is everywhere in the novel.

For this cat's cradle of reference and identity is rooted in reality: although the 'mad' Rowena Cade, not the Motley sisters, really did design the costumes for the show referred to in the novel, *The Jackdaw of Rheims*, she also really did make her one and only appearance in that show on the stage she had created, as a heavily cowled and cloaked pilgrim, one of a bunch of shadowy extras which included the murderer in Upson's fiction.

Mad or not, it's one thing to build a theatre in your own back garden; quite another to do so if that garden runs down to the edge of a cliff, which you then decide would make an even more perfect setting with the limitless vistas of the Atlantic ocean as a free-of-charge, not-for-profit backdrop. All such enterprise is heroic, regardless of who's paying for it, and thrives in the true spirit of amateur theatre in its pure form of home-made entertainment.

FIGURE 12 *The opening night of the Minack in August 1932, audience watching* The Tempest *at the bottom of Rowena Cade's garden. (Photo: Minack Theatre Trust.)*

Two more examples of this pukka British artistic enterprise: the Christie family – not Agatha's – after initiating a series of amateur opera evenings in their organ room at Glyndebourne, in Sussex, built an opera house as an annexe to that room in 1934 and developed an ever expanding worldwide reputation as a professional producing company; and the late Bernard Miles, film actor and cultural contrarian, launched his 1959 Mermaid Theatre, home of new musicals, Lionel Bart and both Restoration and Jonsonian comedy, with operatic performances in a barn at his north London villa in 1951. Acorns and trees.

And in the winter of 1931, Rowena Cade, aided by her gardener and a local builder, literally hacked, with her own fair hands, a semi-circular Cornish theatre out of granite blocks glued together with sanded cement – the sand Rowena carried in sacks on her back up ninety steps of her own making from Porthcurno beach below – on the Minack headland, just four kilometres from Land's End, our island's western extremity, and six kilometres going south and west from Penzance on the same peninsula.

The project was so unlikely and so bizarre – so much the hobby of a rich spinster who, for once, didn't just pay for a theatre, but actually built it herself without any heavy machinery beyond a rudimentary cement mixer – that the making of the Minack ('meynack' is Cornish for 'rocky place') is unique in our theatre history. The discreet use of explosives came into play during the construction as a way of dealing with the intransigent rocks and granite. Cade also improvised stone pillars through the little amphitheatre by using a flexible former into which she poured the cement. Removing the former at, hopefully, the right moment, she then carved hieroglyphs, Celtic runes and other decorations into the wet stone with a screwdriver.

Over subsequent years, the place has become a money-making Mecca for the amateur theatre throughout the country. A week's visit, with good weather and good audiences, can make a visiting company as much as £50,000, which amount covers some of their costs, but not those of the actors. Most of them regard the jaunt as a holiday, happy enough to be invited and camp out or stay with friends. The site at the bottom of Rowena's garden (she died, aged eighty-nine, in 1983) has grown by stealth and established itself as a year-round day-time tourist attraction, with performances from May to October, every production running for a week to a potential capacity audience each night of 800.

In all, 250,000 people visit the place each year. There is a coffee shop, exhibition centre, decent toilet facilities, amazingly well-appointed dressing rooms (since an upgrade in 2011) where actors, like their audiences, can catch regular glimpses of dolphins and basking sharks and a glorious sub-tropical garden snaking round the cafe and working its way into the back of the auditorium. Here, you find echiums, lapranthus and irises in a riot of colour, green and spiky foliage complementing the aloes, silver trees and birds of paradise in the coastal garden, an acre all told.

The one constant (or, rather, inconstant) factor is the weather, which can be vile, moody and changeable, but also (and quite often) hot and dry for anything up to six months. But British audiences like nothing more than braving the elements with a picnic and those at the Minack are no exception. In the old days, as the rain lashed down, the cry went up: 'You play, we stay, you play, we stay.' Once you've managed to find your way to the Minack, you may as well stay anyway after all the trouble it's taken you to get there, whatever the weather.

And this is one of the reasons I love the place so much, not unrelated to the fact that Rowena Cade herself acted the role of a pilgrim. The best theatre happens when the audience is as proactive as the performers. You earn the right to participation, not just by paying the cost of ticket, but also by the physical effort of attendance, or the idea of joining a pilgrimage or festive ritual. In the open air, this takes on the extra dimension of our elemental presence in the cosmos at large, as all the world truly does become the stage.

In this, the Minack, open to the skies and the ocean, is both the most Greek and the most Elizabethan public arena we have, and it is also, because of its topographical remoteness, fixed in permanent kinship with some of the great outdoor events in far-flung fields and beaches by the likes of Welfare State, Kneehigh (regular visitors to the Minack), the National

Theatres of Wales and Scotland, not to mention the modern post-Glyndebourne mania for country house opera and the metropolitan charms of the Open Air, Regent's Park and Shakespeare's Globe. The arena is much as it was when it opened in August 1932 with a production of *The Tempest*, with modifications and improvements I can later recount when detailing my own visits there down the years. On each visit, I have been touched by the magic and adventure of the place and each time marvelled at the strengthening of its spirit and structure.

There has been a steady evolution of the Minack legend over the past eighty years, as the once sole annual, or biennial, production of Shakespeare or a medieval morality has widened into a broader repertory of musicals, modern classics and opera, with up to twenty shows a season and visits of small professional companies, too, including Kneehigh. The latter's *Tristan & Yseult*, described by the critic Lyn Gardner at an earlier indoors performance as 'a great gulp of refreshing sea air', tapped into the venue's proud obsession with the Cornish myth from its earliest years.

The theatre is run as a charitable trust set up by Rowena Cade in 1976. Her family still owns Minack House, with three relatives serving on the five-strong board of trustees. Over fifty local people are employed during the summer season. The winter months are spent on repairing, re-wiring, re-turfing the stone seats, and general restoration while, as well as welcoming the tourists, work continues with local schools on educational programmes.

This all started when Rowena Cade came to Cornwall with her mother after the First World War. She was born in 1893, grew up in middle-class comfort in Derbyshire, the second of four children, and moved first to Cheltenham where, in 1914, she trained war horses for the front. Her father died in 1917. One of her brothers was discharged from the army with shell shock and spent the rest of his life in an asylum, which is what happened in those pre-post-stress-disorder days (the same thing happened to my paternal grandfather). Another brother joined the Indian Civil Service.

Rowena and her mother sold up in Cheltenham and went travelling for a couple of years, finally drawn to Cornwall where they settled at Lamorna, on the Penwith peninsula that spreads outwards from Penzance and includes the Minack headland, which they bought for £200. They commissioned a local architect to build them a house. When they learned, in 1922, that Rowena's younger sister, the feminist novelist Kay (Katharine) Burdekin, was returning from Australia without her husband, but with two young children, the plans were redrawn to accommodate them.

Amateur theatre was already flourishing in this part of west Cornwall, not least because of the presence in Porthcurno – still in evidence, in a superb and discreetly located museum – of the Cable and Wireless company, many of whose employees formed the backbone of the several groups of amateur players in the villages and countryside around. Rowena made costumes for them in 1929 for a production of *A Midsummer Night's Dream*, repeated the following summer, in the open air at Crean, a mile inland from the Minack.

The loose association of local players decided on *The Tempest* for their next production and Rowena volunteered the use of her garden at Minack House. But there was nowhere suitable for the audience to sit. Nothing daunted, Rowena, together with a local builder, Charles Thomas Angrove, and her steadfast gardener, Billy Rawlings, who had worked in the construction industry for many years, prospected a site beyond the garden, overlooking a steep gully below and the Logan Rock beyond, perched on the cliffs across the bay.

The three of them built a terrace at the bottom of the gully – the stage – next to Rowena's cliff garden, embracing the granite outcrops on either side as stage wings. The dogged trio worked through the winter months of 1931/2. A mass of moor stone in the middle of the slope, on a level with what is now the front row of seats, was cleared, and the slope tiered – with dry-stone walling and turf laid along the top of each row – to seat the audience. At stage level, initially, there was a front row of two dozen bentwood chairs, with a dozen or so deck chairs ranged just behind, while the stage area itself was a newly laid greensward.

The weather was perfect on opening night, 16 August 1932. The audience, wearing summer suits and dresses, cloche and panama hats, ties and bandannas, clambered down gorse-lined paths to several rows of terraced seating. More people lolled and picnicked in small groups at the top of the now grassy bank. To a passing seagull, it must have looked as though an organically composed giant human barnacle, or burr, had blown in from the ocean and stuck there.

Programmes for *The Tempest* were designed by Rowena's close friend and Minack mainstay of many years, the local artist Hilda Quick, and these were dispensed along with the tickets at a trestle table in the garden. Stage lighting was provided by an obliging moon, car headlamps and electricity carried along cables from the house. *The Times* carried an encouraging review and the general feeling, and certainly Rowena's, was that the adventure should continue beyond this auspicious opening.

And so it did, with *Twelfth Night* in 1933 (the local players were augmented by two young professionals from the Liverpool Rep and the Old Vic); an adventurous triple bill in 1935; *Antony and Cleopatra* in 1937 – production photos suggest glamorous Hollywood costumes and ostrich feather fans manipulated on tall thin canes; and, in the long hot summer of 1939, John Masefield's *Tristan and Isolt* and *The Count of Monte Cristo*, both performed by a professional company under the aegis of an ageing Violet Vanbrugh, famous in her own right, but less famous than her younger sister Dame Irene.

The theatre shut down for ten years on the outbreak of war. That early repertoire dictated how Rowena and her builders developed the stage, adding a balustrade, large shrubbery, sets of pillars, a dais and a throne that became, as it were, part of the Minack furniture, nearly as immovable as the stone table, known as the fish slab, onto which the bodies of Tristan and Isolt were habitually laid down the years.

In Nicola Upson's novel, the play at the Minack was part of a festival week also featuring a cricket match and a fair on the beach, but her story, starring Josephine Tey – which is one of incestuous love, misdirected passion, murder, arson and dynastic dysfunction – starts with a fatal accident on a horse in the Loe, the freshwater lake which is part of the Penrose Estate now run by the National Trust. In Arthurian mythology, it was here that the sword Excalibur was cast when the king died. And the first major upshot of the accident is that the Minack becomes a crime scene during that 1935 performance of *The Jackdaw at Rheims*, one of the Ingoldsby legends written by Richard Harris Barham in 1837. In the poem, a jackdaw steals a cardinal's ring, has a curse put upon him, later repents, and becomes a saint. Mid-performance, in Upson, a body disappears into the 'zawn' – or rift in the cliffs – where, at high tide, eighty feet below, the narrow inlet is filled with an angry, churning sea. A fictional simulacrum of Billy Rawlings bustles onstage laden with torches, climbing gloves and heavy tarpaulin (to serve as a stretcher if necessary) as the police arrive at cliff-top level.

The other two short pieces on that 1935 bill don't impinge on *Angel With Two Faces* – which, incidentally, contains a neat Josephine Tey sideswipe at Daphne du Maurier, 'the Fowey woman', who has switched publishers and is writing a new novel 'full of smugglers and adventure, apparently', i.e. *Jamaica Inn*. They do though sound intriguing in their own right – eccentric and unusual choices. *Gringoire* was the fictionalised story of the sixteenth century French poet and playwright Pierre Gringoire, model for Esmeralda's alternative lover in *The Hunchback of Notre Dame*; and *The Play of the Weather* (1534) was a morality play by the interesting Tudor musician and playwright John Heywood, whose part in mingling the so-called medieval interludes with comedy, replacing abstract characters with real people, earns him a small foot-note in the history of English drama.

The premise in Heywood's morality was that Jupiter, after chairing a debate among the gods about the climate down below, descends himself – as represented in the knock-about go-between character of Merry Report – to ask the earth-dwellers what they really want. The Gentleman wants temperate weather for his hunting, the Merchant gusty winds for his ships at sea, a Miller more rain for his water-mill, a Laundress hot sun for clothes-drying, a Young Boy wintry temperatures for trapping birds and snowball fights. In the end, Jupiter decides that everyone has a good argument and that the weather, therefore, should stay as exactly unpredictable as it is.

One wonders for how long the Minack might have sustained this original and exciting repertoire through the 1940s but for the war. For after it, survival became immediately more difficult. The second miracle of the second launch in 1949 was that it happened at all, really. And of course it did so because Rowena Cade decreed that it should, despite the severity of the interruption. Porthcurno was an enemy target because of the Cable and Wireless relaying telegraph messages between London and the rest of the world. But, with the Nazis invading France and the Low Countries, the coast-line itself needed protection. Huge defences were thrown up across Porthcurno beach and barbed wire entanglements and gun positions littered across the cliff tops. Rowena still managed to crawl under the barbed wire with a mower to keep the grass on the stage under control. She was busy, too, as a billeting officer for Porthcurno, arranging homes for children evacuated from the big cities threatened with air-raids.

The Minack as a theatre became part of the war effort when Gainsborough Pictures arrived to film a few scenes for Leslie Arliss's *Love Story* (1944) in which Margaret Lockwood, as a dying concert pianist in flight to Cornwall from London, tussles for the affections of Stewart Granger's former RAF pilot, who is losing his sight, with the vivacious Patricia Roc who's preparing to produce and appear in *The Tempest* at the Minack (or the 'Port Merryn Theatre'). Roc claims to have discovered 'a former Roman amphitheatre' and enlists the financial backing of a Yorkshire mining tycoon.

On the night of the performance, Roc is indisposed, unable to go on – as what, though, is not exactly clear, unless she's planning to astonish the audience as a curiously exotic, over-bejewelled and over-aged Miranda – while Granger is in London having an operation to save his sight. Lockwood plays a lushly emotional Cornish piano concerto in her stead, full of seagulls and sea wash. She collapses on stage, but she's saved the day. The romantic melodrama was hugely popular with war-time audiences and it retains some curiosity value in Rodney Ackland's dialogue and the pop-in appearances of such popular actors of the day as Walter Hudd, A. E. Matthews, Moira Lister and George Merritt.

The location filming was scuppered when a storm destroyed the set. So, although there are the occasional exterior glimpses of the headland, and long shots of romance and rehearsals – Granger and Lockwood (or their doubles) diving into the sea very near the zawn; Ariel (Joan Rees) skimming across the greensward into the rockery – and the audience filling up, the scenes in close-up are enacted on a not very good, and only vaguely approximate, papier-mâché replica of the Minack created back in the London studios. This makes for some deeply, well, amateurish interleaving of location and studio shots. And nothing in these corny Cornish scenes matches the terrific face-slapping show-down between Lockwood and Roc in competition for the attentions of the brawny Granger.

When the war ended, the theatre was in a bad state of disrepair and, to add insult to injury, the Italian prisoners-of-war who dismantled the cliff top defences threw the Cleopatra throne into the sea. Rowena and Billy Rawlings set about building more steps and balustrades, another large throne, and replenishing the broken pillars. But the finances were becoming a strain. Rowena's mother died in 1948. Rowena moved into the small wing she had created for her sister – who had long departed into her novel-writing and lifetime Sapphic relationship (identity never revealed) – and rented out Minack House to holidaymakers.

The Minack re-opened in July 1949 with Gilbert Murray's translation of Euripides' *The Trojan Women* performed by the girls of Penzance County Grammar School in long white Greek dresses, their hair pinned back in buns. A seventeen-year-old Andromache was the future stage and television star Avril Elgar. Rowena persuaded the Cornwall branch of the National Council for Social Services to take over the management of the theatre while she continued the development. But the theatre made losses during their three-year tenure. An attempt to involve the National Trust came to nothing, so she carried on funding the place herself, as she had done from the beginning and would continue to do until the trust was formed.

What put the Minack firmly on the national map as both a destination and a signal of post-war recovery was the Festival of Britain in 1951. For this nationwide celebration, the Minack premiered a play of its own for the first time, Nora Ratcliff's *Tristan of Cornwall*, re-booting the local amateur players into what would emerge as the West Cornwall Theatre group, regular mummers at the Minack. This production provided the fish slab, aka the Tristan table, still in use today. From that year onwards, the annual season would continue unbroken into this century, the programme expanding into three or four productions in 1956, then seven (including a ballet) in 1960 and ten in 1962, when the students of the Guildhall School in London produced Milton's masque *Comus* and other student groups from Oxford, Nottingham and Cambridge provided seriously engaging fare with John Whiting's *A Penny for a Song*, Shaw's *Saint Joan* and *As You Like It*.

1966: A family holiday, the little old lady and a *Tiger at the Gates*

In this momentous year, England won the World Cup, Billy Rawlings died, and I was starting a year's work, travel and reading before going to university. And so I agreed, I think somewhat sulkily, to go on my last ever family holiday to Cornwall. It rained a lot. I cheered up when Dad announced that the weather would soon clear and that, tomorrow, we'd visit the Minack Theatre at Porthcurno. Not knowing what to expect, you can imagine how surprised we were when we got there. We parked up and went on a tour of the theatre where we found Rowena Cade herself pottering about with a trowel. With her shock of white hair, ruddy features, bright, twinkling eyes, posh accent and ready manner she did indeed resemble 'the overgrown cabin boy' as Billy Rawlings always described her, togged out in a Fair Isle jumper, knee breeches and sensible shoes.

The day was glorious, and she chatted away about nothing much, mostly to my father, while my brother, sister and I scampered up and down the terraces. I do remember her being impressed that we had bought tickets for the evening performance of Jean Giraudoux's *Tiger at the Gates*, as most tourists at the Minack, like most day-trippers in Stratford-upon-Avon, don't bother with the play. We must have taken a picnic of sorts, but I don't remember when, or exactly where, we ate it. There was no coffee shop, ice-cream van or pasty stall to hand, as there is today.

By 1966, though out of view to the left of the auditorium, the first dressing rooms had long been installed, with a handsome stone loggia running along the top, decorated with Rowena's trademark twiddles. Billy had built 200 yards of 'Cornish hedge' (as he called the dry-stone walling) to mark off the theatre from the road – it's still there. Rowena had started etching the names of all the plays – and of Billy Rawlings – on the stone seat backs with the tip of her trusty screwdriver. And the first lighting box had been installed half-way down the theatre in 1960.

Since the war, the pill box, or concrete guard post, left by the military, was adopted as a rather brutal box office, and continued as such until 1997, when the shop and café were built. None of this we noticed, or knew about at the time, but we did clock the stage surface which was no longer a greensward but a flat, smooth area of different-sized hexagonal tiles arranged in a diamond formation at right angles to the audience to soften any severity in appearance. The cement was – and still is – heavily mixed with sand, creating a variegated reddish glow on this floor, too.

The rake had been levelled by at least four inches and the last wooden seats replaced by more comfortable stalls. The grass on the stage had, over the years, proved impractical and was finally removed at the end of a 1964 performance of *Much Ado About Nothing* by the Penzance Playgoers, which finished with an over-ambitious dance raising so much dust that the actors disappeared inside a great cloud of it and the first three rows of the audience half choked to death.

We loved *Tiger at the Gates*, which was costumed à la grèque – togas, sandals, flowing robes – in the production by the Interluders of Hertfordshire, who obviously understood horses for courses. In the previous season they had presented Ibsen's *Peer Gynt*, surely the best sort of heroic poetic play for this theatre, alongside *King Lear*. Giraudoux's play – in French, *La Guerre de Troie n'aura pas lieu* – is a witty, glittering and subtle discourse on the pros and cons of warfare as the Trojan leader, Hector, inside the city gates, attempts to defer the war with Greece. It sparkles, rather than soars, but, punched out with vigour and intelligence, as here, it proved highly entertaining. When first performed in London in 1955 in the same Christopher Fry translation adopted by the Interluders, Kenneth Tynan acclaimed 'a masterpiece . . . the final comment on the superfluity of war . . . the highest peak in the mountain range of modern French theatre'. Many years later I found a fine review of the Minack production written by the poet James Brockway in *The Cornishman*. Commending the bold choice of play, he observed that Giraudoux's voice was one of reason and intelligence in the 1930s, ridiculing war just as Hitler was already on the move, the Italians were winning glory by enslaving the Abyssinians and the Japanese were busy raping China. Insanity would triumph and war surely come, as it does in the play. But times, said Brockway, had changed, and war was no longer a mere tiger – no longer, as Hecuba puts it in the play, a baboon up a tree seen from below. War had come to mean the possible total annihilation of life on earth.

The Interluders returned to the Minack in Marlowe's *Doctor Faustus* and Shakespeare's *Richard III* before re-grouping as the Hertfordshire Players in 1972, since when they have been regular biennial visitors to the Minack, one of the staunchest stanchions in the programme policy, and always in a prime August seven-day slot. The company is a conglomerate of actors in the district who belong to amateur companies in Hertford, Ware and Welwyn Garden City. Flora Robson, disheartened after winning a bronze medal at RADA but not finding any work, gave up the stage and took a job in the Shredded Wheat factory in Welwyn, where she started a group called the Barnstormers in 1923, one of several amateur companies which flourished in the new town. Shortly afterwards she was cast by Tyrone Guthrie for a season at the new Festival Theatre, Cambridge, and by 1933 she was the leading lady at the Old Vic.

One of the other Welwyn companies, the Barn Theatre Club, hosts of *Romeo and Juliet* in *Hot Fuzz*, started life in a converted cow shed in 1932 and, in 1964, was a prime player in the move to create a company, the Interluders, with a specific brief to perform at the Minack. (The critic and playwright Jeremy Kingston once divulged that his delight in the theatre was first aroused when he was taken, as a six-year-old, to see *Toad of Toad Hall* at the Barn: 'I have never forgotten the moment when what I had assumed to be a tussock of grass jumped up and became a rabbit.')

Twenty visits over the years have included work of a remarkable range and, often, an epic scale: Friedrich Dürrenmatt's *The Visit*; Brecht's re-write of Farquhar's *The Recruiting Officer*, *Trumpets and Drums*; Jeff Wayne's *The War of the Worlds*; and (twice) the first part of David Edgar's RSC stage version of *Nicholas Nickleby*. One notable member of the Barn, and frequently a director at the Minack, is Steve Thompson, the professional playwright and television screen writer (*Doctor Who*, *Sherlock*) whose West End hits include *Whipping It Up* (2006), a very funny political satire set in the whips' office at Westminster, which starred Richard Wilson, Helen Schlesinger and Robert Bathurst.

To this day, the Barn continues to make a major contribution to the Hertfordshire Players, whose summer season is always regarded as a special occasion. The rehearsals are held in the garden of a private house in Hertford where Cromwell once addressed his troops; the owners are life-long members of the Hertfordshire Players. Then the week-long 'holiday' on the cliffs. Several generations of many families are involved, life-long friendships made and maintained. First-timers in the company are led like sheep into the Minack, their eyes covered, until they are allowed to take a first look from the back of the auditorium. Gasps of delight are not unmixed with sentiments of fear and foreboding.

1999: Ken Kesey's Merry Pranksters arrive for the total (sort of) eclipse

'Not one of my best ideas', admits the Minack's manager, Phil Jackson, who has been in post since 1990, having first started there as a car park attendant in the 1970s. Phil was born and raised on the farm at Crean where Rowena had made the costumes for that prophetic *A Midsummer Night's Dream* in 1929. He is in the sixth generation of a family of farmers and fishermen in a radius of three miles around the Minack headland. So it's a fair bet that the Swinging Sixties and the druggy counter-culture more or less passed him by.

Still, his regretted wheeze could have been a really wizard idea if a) spaced-out superstar Ken Kesey (author of *One Flew Over the Cuckoo's Nest*) and his forty Merry Pranksters had turned up with a show worth watching as, at 11am on 11 August 1999, the moon passed between the earth and the sun completing a total black-out of the sun, a phenomenon not visible in the UK since June 1917; and b) cloud cover had not ruined the whole thing anyway.

Not everywhere in Cornwall was left in the not-so-dark. The clouds parted just in time for the total eclipse to be visible at Goonhilly on the Lizard Peninsula. The first landfall of the shadow was due across the western end of Cornwall and I, like Ken Kesey, and indeed most of the BBC outside broadcast unit, banked on that being the case. So, I'd volunteered for the trip at the *Daily Mail*, where I was then working, and set off happily by train the day before to Penzance. That evening I moseyed on over to the Minack to catch *The Itch*, a loose, nay disembowelled, version of *The Changeling* by Middleton and Rowley performed by Kneehigh. Things could only get better. The sky looked clear and expectant. People were gathering all around in the fields. In the morning, the mood and the weather had turned greyish, but still we had a couple of hours for the mists to burn off or evaporate.

Kesey's original Magic Bus, as immortalised in Tom Wolfe's *Electric Kool-Aid Acid Test*, had made its definitive LSD-fuelled trip across America in 1964. The new bus, covered in swirls of paint, animals and super-heroes, magic mushrooms and fake diamonds, led a convoy of mini-vans to Cornwall, stopping off en route at Stonehenge. Kesey had last been there in the 1970s with some Hell's Angels and arch hippie Jerry Garcia of the Grateful Dead. He was disconsolate to discover the new, cordoned-off Stonehenge, now run by English Heritage and officiously resistant to the sort of madcap, libidinous incursions he'd rabble-roused among the ancient stones forty years earlier. There was no chance, naturally, that Kesey would take this stern, stone rebuff to his stoned in-the-buff carry-on as a hint that the hallucinogenic hippie day-dream was over. But it was. His time had gone. Both Garcia and the guru psychologist Timothy ('Tune in, turn on, drop out') Leary were dead.

Kesey's trip to the UK – he himself died two years later – was part-financed by Channel 4 and designed to show signs of the counter-culture defying the march of history. But even Kesey had no illusions about *The Quest for Merlin*, the musical passion play intended to summon the spirit of the Arthurian sorcerer who was, according to legend, due to reappear on English soil before the end of the millennium (he didn't): 'None of us can really act or even remember our lines.' And so it proved.

This was one of those shows guaranteed to get amateur theatre a bad name – a well-intentioned, unstructured heap of hocus pocus with the ever benign and twinkling Kesey, ruddy of complexion, snowy white-haired in the tufty, springy style of the filmmaker Ken Russell, and indeed of Rowena Cade herself, charming the audience with addled-brained nonsense and druggy doggerel until even they, who had entered upon the morning matinée with high expectations of fun and frolics, were battered into submission, then mutinous incredulity, by the sheer stark reality of the idiotic non-event unfolding before us.

So it came to pass that one of my most uncomfortable professional experiences as a critic was filing copy about the not-so-total eclipse I had been detailed to cover which had indeed happened but not as far as I was concerned. As I rambled apologetically on to the copy-takers at lunchtime about the excitement the eclipse had generated in this part of the world, and how little we'd seen of it due to the cloudy conditions, the breathing at the end of the line got progressively heavier with each leaden, literally unilluminating sentence. This atmosphere of indifference turned to one of outright hostility when I ventured a descriptive resumé of *The Quest for Merlin*. Time-honoured copy-takers' phrases – 'Is there much more of this?'; 'Are you sure this is what you want to say?' – started coming back at me down the line.

I had not endured so awkward, and finally humiliating, a copy filing experience since attempting a wittily destructive notice of the worst ever musical in the annals of the RSC, *Carrie*, in Stratford-upon-Avon, while the poor deluded fools of the company and their putative Broadway producers caroused on the banks of the Avon to the accompaniment of the loudest, and least warranted, fireworks display I'd ever been deafened by. I couldn't hear myself thinking, let alone writing. At the Minack, I could hear myself crying.

2017: On the bus to Land's End for
The Third Policeman

How about hitting the road to Porthcurno, on the bus to Land's End, and staying overnight in a village B&B in order to take the tourists' tour of the theatre on the next morning in the company of local storyteller Mark Harandon disguised as Billy Rawlings in flat cap, woolly cardigan and building boots? The idea struck me as a no-brainer at the end of June 2017, though the weather was not promising. Once again I took the long train journey from Paddington to Penzance, mooched around Penzance in the pouring rain and then boarded the Land's End bus as the sky began to clear. It really does feel like a journey into the unknown as you career along narrow country lanes, sometimes backing up to half a mile or more when encountering a farm vehicle or oncoming bus.

The show that night was laid on by the Miracle Theatre of Redruth, Cornwall, one of many small West Country professional companies that visit regularly. After I'd got my bearings, walked down a brambly path to the beach and then climbed back up Rowena's ninety granite steps to the theatre, the evening was on the brink of becoming, against all the odds, rather lovely. An audience of 500 (the capacity today is limited to 700, though the premises are licensed for 800) was assembling with pac-a-macs, sou'westers and picnics for Miracle's production of Flann O'Brien's *The Third Policeman*.

Phil Jackson, running around, like the rest of his staff, in a clearly discernible trademark yellow windcheater-style jumper, whisked me round the backstage area, the dressing rooms and the theatre itself, reminding me that although Rowena pottered on in the theatre to within several years of her passing, the last 'structure' she built herself was the Juliet balcony in 1974. It floats like a special 'box' to the left hand side of the auditorium, and couples do indeed sit there when Juliet herself is not wondering wherefore art thou Romeo. The last Shakespeare play title was etched into a stone seat at around the same time, and one of the slabs simply proclaims: 'Rowena Cade built this theatre.'

Phil is in no two minds about the commercial viability of the Minack: it's subsidised by the tourists, and that's that. But there's a hard-core local audience, too. One section of them turn up every single Friday night of the season, whatever's playing. And there they are, this Friday night, sitting together with their pasties and picnics in an excited huddle as if they were making their first ever visit. Chances are they won't have seen something as strange and surreal as *The Third Policeman* before.

Flann O'Brien himself thought that his 1940 novel might provide material for 'a crazy play', and he eventually found his first interpreter in Ken Campbell, who produced a 'Ken Dodd' tribute version (everyone in the cast wore a set of protruding dentures and an electrified shock wig) at the ICA in London in 1980. Miracle's treatment is less bizarre, distinctly small-scale (four actors, two of each sex) but high-spirited and joyously goonish, as O'Brien's feckless, nameless hero (one of the actresses) reports the theft of his/her father's gold watch, connives in the murder of an old man – the body, done in with pick and spade, was unceremoniously dumped overboard into the zawn below, accompanied by a satisfyingly loud 'splosh' sound effect – and is translated to an underworld of garrulous coppers, sympathetic unipeds and the atomic theory of bicyclosis.

No-one's very sure what exactly this is, but there's a rousingly climactic scene where the hero(ine) finds ecstasy on his/her wheels and does nothing so much as remind you of W. H. Auden's heartfelt couplet: 'I've often thought that I should like/ To be the saddle on a bike.' One of the plods, pleasingly, sports a curly-wurly handlebar moustache, which almost compensates for being spared the sight, as deliciously described in the book, of fourteen one-legged desperadoes bearing down on the country police station to rescue one of their own.

The company is adept, agile and likeable and use the space well, cutting silhouettes on the square rocks, and not too handicapped by a token piece of standing set doubling as the police station and the pub. And then comes in the magic, as the mackerel sky turns early summer blue then roseate before nightfall, allowing you to enjoy the natural scenery simultaneously with the play, which it seems to enfold in its limitless embrace. The ocean is still and glassy like a lake, the view flecked with a lone dolphin, gannets, seagulls and cormorants. Time stands still in the ultimate backdrop.

Next morning in the B&B, a table of hikers are stoking up before resuming their coastal walks in either direction, though one or two are joining me at the Billy Rawlings tour, which is called *Moving Heaven and Earth* and plays continuously every Saturday in the season between 10am and 2pm, fluctuating around whoever's tramping through the site. The landlord of the B&B, who is very particular about where exactly each of us sits at his long table, tells me that he once dated Billy Rawlings's granddaughter, 'A six-foot beauty who worked as an air stewardess with El Al'. The Billy actor, Mark Harandon, dubs himself a story-teller and relates how he paid a visit to Billy's ninety-year-old daughter, the air stewardess's mum, no doubt, but we glean no more dynastic info beyond that.

Harandon as Billy decorates his narration in Billy's marked St Levan accent (he assures us), recounting how he would drive a horse and trap for the ten miles to Penzance (a huge distance, it seemed) when he wasn't levering up stones with an iron bar, or splitting them with a shorter bar, a 4lb hammer and a stick of dynamite. The fence behind the stage area has created a safe crossover area for the actors between scenes while guarding against any mishap. These fears over the zawn are, according to Billy, a nuisance: 'Without the fence, there would be no interference with the laws of natural selection, as only an idiot would fall in. The stupid people are still here!'

As Billy talks and the Japanese tourists take photographs, the Miracle company are striking their set, running up the auditorium steps with bits and pieces and the police station while the opera company responsible for next week's *La Traviata*, in the shape of a bevy of bruisers in black sweatshirts, are lugging down their speakers and lighting equipment. Phil Jackson and co have already erected the stage left canvas-covered orchestra pit and the activity will continue, right through Sunday, with rehearsals and a full technical run in readiness for another opening on Monday night.

The rest of the season is completely sold out: twelve productions, one a week, including Jessica Swale's *Nell Gwynn* – now a staple of the amateur repertoire – *Treasure Island*, *Twelfth Night*, *Gypsy* and *Cyrano de Bergerac*. It is a lovely Minack coincidental touch that Margaret Lockwood's next film after *Love Story*, *The Wicked Lady*, is playing, too, in Bryony Lavery's 2009 scripted update that, by all accounts, turns the melodramatic story of the eighteenth century aristocrat-cum-highway-woman into an entertaining study of the choices available to ladies in society and the bedroom.

The company presenting *The Wicked Lady* is Shattered Windscreen, a lively fringe outfit that has associations with the Barn in Welwyn and the Hertfordshire Players. The buccaneering spirit of another wicked lady, Rowena Cade, lives on in the performances of generations who never knew her personally but know, respect and love what she started at the bottom of her garden nearly ninety years ago.

And because of its special character, there is a palpable sense, always, of a continuum in time, space and theatre across nine decades, even as the management adjusts to the changing world beyond this magical environment. In the Minack facilities, they use local produce, obviously, but also low energy bulbs and hairdryers and renewable sources for all their print materials. The garden waste is composted on site and Phil Jackson and his team work assiduously with the parish council and local residents' association to address all the local issues. Time may indeed stand still but the theatre welcomes all-comers, old friends, newcomers and visitors from Tokyo to Texas to join its crepuscular community as light fades across the ocean vista. This will never change. The elemental Minack marches on.

10

Off-Piste, and Unknown Territory in Lincolnshire, Bangor, Anglesey and Dumfries

The Minack is certainly off the beaten track, but is paradoxically high profile because of its history, scenic setting, its reputation as a Mecca for amateur companies all over the country and vast commercial success as a tourist attraction. Big city amateur theatres, and even small town urban amateur theatres, as we have seen, have to withstand competition in an ever expanding leisure market. But there are some smaller theatres that operate well beneath the radar and, partly because of that, perhaps, embody something deep-rooted and significant in not just the amateur theatre movement itself, but also in the social and political history of the country.

One such tiny phenomenon is the Broadbent Theatre in Wickenby, rural Lincolnshire, about twelve miles from Lincoln, six from Market Rasen, a converted 1878 Methodist chapel standing in open country. It is named for the father of the actor Jim Broadbent, Roy Broadbent, an artist and pacifist who drew up the architectural plan for the cosy little 100-seater theatre but died shortly before it opened in 1972.

Roy and his wife Dee, Jim's mother, were members of the Holton Players, an amateur group launched by them, and another pacifist couple, Jim and Millie Harper, in the neighbouring villages of Legsby and Holton cum Beckering in the West Lindsey district of Lincolnshire during the last two years of the war. The Harpers, too, were conscientious objectors, joining a pacifist community who had renounced the war, renounced urban life and, in 1940, had rented a farm as an educational commune where like-minded young idealists could learn about farming and agriculture.

Roy and Dee Broadbent met at Leeds Art School. Roy had been educated at Bryanston, a brand new progressive public school when he went there in 1928. His mother was heavily involved in amateur theatre in their home town of Huddersfield, his family a traditional Yorkshire engineering one with no connection whatsoever with farming. Dee's family, from Leeds, was similarly teeming with architects and engineers, and she went on from the art college to train as a sculptor at the Royal Academy while Roy also went to London and continued his studies and training at the Courtauld Institute and the Architectural Association.

The feeling of 'no more war' after the end of the 'war to end all wars' in 1918 was much stronger than we now remember, right through the 1920s and into the 1930s when Roy made friends with Dick Cornwallis at the Peace Pledge Union in London, an organisation of religious pacifists. Broadbent was a man of independent means, Cornwallis an ornithologist and farmer who was an accountant with Price Waterhouse. His father had been the British ambassador in Iraq.

Together, they hatched a plan with a Lincolnshire farmer, John Brocklesby, who agreed to lease them one of his rundown farms, Collow Abbey. They believed that their training school and the agrarian life would go hand in hand with a practical sense of a higher morality, a transforming standard of civilisation in a spirit of communal cooperation and liberty. No wonder their household god was George Bernard Shaw. Their first full-length production was Shaw's 1894 anti-war comedy and one of his first commercial successes, *Arms and the Man*.

Jim Harper's credentials for helping establish the Holton Beckering Land and Training Centre for Conscientious Objectors, as the project was called, were impeccable. He was a member of the ultra-socialist Independent Labour Party, secretary in his local branch of the Peace Pledge Union and, what's more, his family were Fen country people with farming to the fore. When the Holton Players started their play-readings in the last two years of the war, Harper made sure they joined the British Drama League to get the play-texts they needed. The great irony of this gang of middle-class bohemian artists and pacifists setting up shop in Holton was that the mobilised forces of the RAF were using nearby Wickenby Aerodrome to zoom off on their bombing raids.

And, although the Holton Players were immediately successful in their local community, there was always an element of doorstep disdain for these incursive 'conchies', a bunch of 'pretend' farmers with London money 'signalling to their mates in the Luftwaffe'. These comments were reported in a rudimentary, but informative, docudrama, *Remembrance*, by Ian Sharp, one of the present-day resident company, the Lindsey Rural Players, successors to the Holton Players, and presented at the Broadbent in December 2017.

The Jim Broadbent connection no doubt helped, but it was perhaps significant that one of *Remembrance*'s only two performances was attended by the artistic director of the National Theatre, Rufus Norris. One could easily imagine him responding with his own version of Ian Sharp's fascinating slice of war-time social history. Another hook to the show for Norris might have come from Blur and Gorillaz front-man Damon Albarn. Norris and Albarn have produced an opera, *Doctor Dee* (2011), and a musical, *wonder. land* (2015), both more than interesting.

Damon's father, the artist Keith Albarn, married Hazel Dring, sister of John Dring, a farmer closely involved with the Lindsey Rural Players in the late 1970s. Keith's father, Edward, a conscientious objector and peace activist, like his son, had moved to Holton cum Beckering in the 1960s, at Roy Broadbent's suggestion, and had taken a job at Lincoln art school. Keith and Hazel met at Nottingham School of Art and married in 1963. Damon himself helped out on the lighting at the Broadbent for Peter Whelan's *The Accrington Pals* in 1986 and appeared in a pantomime. (Coincidentally, one of Keith Albarn's childhood sweethearts, Tina Packer, now a theatre director and distinguished Shakespearean, taught Jim Broadbent at LAMDA.)

So, I wouldn't rule out the possibility, one day, of a 'conchie' war-time farming musical by Albarn and, say, a playwright such as Richard Bean, who knows about the Broadbent, directed by Norris. In that same audience at *Remembrance* sat 98-year-old Don Sutherland, the community's sole survivor, who had joined up after reading Aldous Huxley's *Ends and Means*,

FIGURE 13 *A special performance of Ian Sharp's* Remembrance, *celebrating the early days of the Holton Players (later at the Broadbent Theatre) at the end of the last war, was given in June 2019 to mark the 100th birthday of the agrarian commune's last surviving member, Don Sutherland, seen here, centre, to the right of the author, with cast and crew and visiting sons of the communards, Damon Albarn and Jim Broadbent, on the left. (Photo: Clare Lynch.)*

abandoning a steady job in insurance – security came second to 'taking a stand', as he recalls. All the communards received the same amount of money as family allowances, shortly before the government introduced the child benefits act in 1945. Mostly, they were 'townies' arriving on their bikes, but they soon buckled down to farm work.

Many of them stayed on in the area after the war, working as farmers, artists and teachers, and many of their families live in the area still, and join in at the Broadbent. One of the first communards was Francis Cammaert, who worked as a shepherd for a while before leaving to become a celebrated figure in the French Resistance. His nephew is the writer Michael Morpurgo, author – inconveniently, in this context – of *War Horse*. They were joined by a niece of Sybil Thorndike – Phyllis Walshaw, née Ewbank – who had trained at RADA and moved to Lincolnshire when she married a farmer. Phyllis became one of the group's star actors – she was very beautiful and scored a great success, Jim Broadbent recalls, in Shaw's *The Millionairess* – and one of its chief theatre directors. Her son, a retired farmer, remains one of Jim's best friends to this day.

The play-reading group gave its first public performance, an extract from Shaw's *Pygmalion*, in 1942. There followed various one-act plays culminating in that *Arms and the Man* in Holton Hall in 1947. Subsequent plays, each with three months of rehearsal and performed in halls and schools in the area, included canonical works by Chekhov, J. B. Priestley, Oliver Goldsmith, Tennessee Williams and Shakespeare. *Twelfth Night* in 1949 played a long run of fifteen performances in villages and market towns.

Market Rasen had a drama society full of people, as one of the Holton regulars said, semi-contemptuously, 'keen to tread the boards'. But the group wanted to make an impact fuelled by some of the idealism behind the agrarian project, something different. Jim Broadbent himself remembers, as a young lad, the play-readings downstairs in the house and the cigarette smoke wafting up. He joined in, aged six, in 1955, playing one of Nora's children in Ibsen's *A Doll's House*.

Eventually, they found a permanent theatre in Holton village, a long, half-cylindrical Nissen hut on farmland that had originally served as a Women's Auxiliary Air Force dining quarters during the war, before the place was used as a cinema for German prisoners, who considerately left behind them a perfectly practicable raised stage. Thus the newly christened Country Theatre, home of the Holton Players, opened in 1951 with *Spring at Marino*, an adaptation by Constance Cox of Turgenev's beautiful novel *Fathers and Sons*. The company was self-supporting with fifteen active members, productions running for a week, and seating for 150 customers. Roy Broadbent is remembered (though not by Jim) as something of a purist. No-one was allowed front-of-house in costume and anyone he didn't like the look of couldn't come in.

Unfortunately, in 1960, with rehearsals underway for the nineteenth-century melodrama *Maria Marten*, the theatre was destroyed by fire. This catastrophe eclipsed the play's gruesome murder in the red barn – Roy Broadbent was playing the murderous William Corder, the role made notorious by Tod Slaughter in the 1935 film melodrama – so the show went on in the jovially despised theatrical hotbed of Market Rasen. There followed a few years of perfunctory touring once more in schools and halls. It seemed as though the Holton Players were drifting towards oblivion.

Then, suddenly, a new dynamic presence in their midst – Malcolm Bates, an adopted boy and mad keen theatre lover, remembered affectionately as 'the only gay in the village' – stirred a recovery. Bates was a morning verger in Lincoln Cathedral, an artist in residence at a local college and an unofficial town-crier. He had helped to stage a Holton Players production of Lionel Bart's *Oliver!* – in which Roy Broadbent played Fagin and Don Sutherland, Mr Brownlow – and was determined to keep the youngsters engaged beyond this one-off performance. The insurance banked from the fire at the Country Theatre was £800 and Bates was certain that they could raise further funds needed to convert a disused Methodist chapel at Wickenby that had come up for sale. Bates enthused Broadbent and together they persuaded five others to invest what capital they had in the purchase and conversion of the chapel.

In this interim period, at the end of the 1960s, Jim Broadbent, when he'd completed his schooling at Leighton Park (a Quaker school in Reading, Berkshire) got a job as a student assistant stage manager with the Liverpool Playhouse, through his father's contact with director Kay Gardner. She had moved on from the Theatre Royal, Lincoln (where Roy served as a board member) to run the Liverpool theatre. Jim stayed there for five months before going to art college in Hammersmith, London, with a view to combining his two interests of acting and theatre design, but on completing the foundation course, he realised he only wanted to act.

This impulse was confirmed over a dinner with Roy at the Ark restaurant in Notting Hill, where they found themselves sitting next to some 'quite loud' drama students. Roy said, 'Why don't you go to drama school?' And Jim replied that he was already thinking of it. So he applied to LAMDA. On completing the course, and just as he was starting out in his first professional job in 1972, Roy died, suddenly, aged fifty-seven. He had completed work on the new theatre, which was promptly named in his memory when it opened later that year. The Holton Players re-grouped for the occasion as the Lindsey Rural Players and so they remain to this day.

Jim is proud of his father, but says he still can't work him out. 'He was a powerful presence, fairly tall, obviously charismatic and inspiring . . . By the time I knew him at all he was still anarchic but pretty much apolitical, school of 'a curse on all their houses' sort of thing. He was a bit of a star and always made sure he had a big part in any play.' He remembers him playing Shotover in Shaw's apocalyptic, Chekhovian masterpiece *Heartbreak House*: 'Very good make-up'.

Dee Broadbent lived until 1994 and always attended dress rehearsals, along with others of the old Holton Players. In a BBC radio programme about the Broadbent, broadcast in June 2017, Jim said that he found it heartening that the enterprise had kept going in a well-equipped venue, offering four productions a year from the Lindsey Rural Players as well as their very active youth company and other visiting amateur and professional groups, too.

As honorary president of the LRP, Jim is supportive rather than heavily involved, writing the odd cheque if they need to do something in the car park or with the sound system. In 2007 there was a minor crisis when a new sewage system was urgently needed at a cost of £50,000. Jim helped raise £13,000 towards that sum by making his debut on his dad's stage with a reading of Alfred Lord Tennyson's 1864 narrative poem *Enoch Arden*. Tennyson, son of a country clergyman, was born in Somersby in the East Lindsey district of Lincolnshire. His imposing statue (with dog) stands on the cathedral green in Lincoln. It was therefore an appropriate choice, this gripping verse melodrama of a merchant sailor who travels abroad to support his family, including a poorly child, and who is then ship-wrecked. He returns home ten years later to find the sick child dead and his wife, his childhood sweetheart, married to his best friend. The three-month sewage system closure allowed for a chance also to renovate the heating, seating, lighting and decoration in the auditorium.

Most of us share the odd qualm over the standards of amateur theatre if you place it next to professionals, though Jim suggests the unevenness is mainly to do with the relative ability of directors. On the whole, he reckons you are as likely to see a very good actor in amdram as you are on the professional stage. 'There's certainly, at least, always a possibility of that in my experience.' And not just for the obvious reasons, he found Ian Sharp's *Remembrance* an amazing production, 'A very complex and interesting piece of theatre'.

The spirit of the Holton Players lives on, even in the slightly chaotic pantomime I saw there, *Babes in the Wood*, eccentrically presented at the end of January after all the other local panto competition had evaporated. Finding the theatre at all had proved a challenge to my cab driver from Lincoln, but there it stood, isolated in the gathering darkness, coloured lights proclaiming its identity, an eager audience crowding into the virtually non-existent foyer, where a display of signed tiles pays discreet tribute to the founding fathers and leading lights. There's no bar, but a pop-up service of drinks and ice-cream pre-show and in the interval. The bar staff all know the audience and vice versa, and there's a hugger mugger sense of conspiracy and homeliness that is warming, cosy and peculiar to amdram. And this applies here particularly, where the roots of the operation really do go back so far and almost everyone in the audience, and on stage, has some connection with Roy Broadbent and his pacifist comrades.

I spend some time with the LRP's archivist, David Broughton, a retired architect who specialised in designing and constructing sets for the Broadbent and his wife, Charlotte Broughton, a retired tutor for the disabled in

Mansfield, who is the theatre's house manager and who played the role of Dee Broadbent in *Remembrance*. The theatre, for them, is a statement of belonging and, in their case, of commitment and ideology. David and Charlotte met in Hull, where they were both members of CND, the Campaign for Nuclear Disarmament.

Back in the centre of Lincoln, I reflect on this vitality and sense of deeper purpose as I take a look round the Theatre Royal, a beautiful, intimate Victorian jewel of a theatre, designed in 1893 by Bertie Crewe and WGR Sprague, once a powerhouse in the old weekly rep days (between 1954 and 1976) and, subsequently, through various owners, and such successful producers as the West End and panto impresario Paul Elliott, a staging post for some well-cast commercial spin-offs. Today, the place is owned by a local property mogul whose wife programmes a diet of dance bills, tribute shows (Abba, the Eagles, Rod Stewart and Motown) and live cinema screenings.

For anything approaching serious, or surprising, theatre, the good people of Lincoln and outlying areas are going to have to rely increasingly on the several amateur theatre companies in the city and the dogged, spirited little Broadbent Theatre and its resident company whose efforts are imbued with a famous history. Jim Broadbent recalls auditioning on the Theatre Royal's stage at the very start of his career. How perfect it would have been to launch his professional career in his home town local rep. He was turned down.

Bangor, Northern Ireland

Admittedly, I travelled out from Belfast to Bangor, County Down, on a lugubrious October morning, but it did seem a little like visiting the place that time forgot or the Isle of Wight. The train curls right round the south side of the Belfast Lough and you eventually start looking into some quite nice back gardens as the coastal vista opens up beyond the stop for the George Best airport.

The town was once a monastic settlement and launching pad for missionary work across Europe. It served a less evangelical purpose as a popular holiday resort and day-trippers' destination in the first half of the twentieth century, but that purpose is in abeyance, although the marina looks prosperous enough. Churches everywhere: at least five on and around the street in the centre of town where the new 100-seater theatre of the Bangor Drama Club (BDC) opened in April 2017.

I'd been told about BDC staging amateur theatre in the town since 1935 and I knew they had a reputation for regularly winning the Association of Ulster Drama Festivals and being fiercely, and proudly, independent. So independent-minded are they, in fact, that they have seceded from the Little Theatre Guild on the grounds that they didn't see the point of it as they were not exactly benefiting from their membership. I liked the sound of this cussedness – and the fact that they prefer to think of themselves as 'unpaid' rather than 'amateur' – and was also drawn by the fact that two of Northern Ireland's finest actors in the modern era – Doreen Hepburn (Scottish by birth) and Colin Blakely – are alumni of the BDC.

They appeared together in Bangor in 1956 in Colin Morris's *Reluctant Heroes*, the first of the Whitehall farces. In the same year, having played with the BDC for the previous decade, Hepburn turned professional with the Ulster Group Players at the start of a career that took her to the Arts in Belfast, the Abbey in Dublin and the RSC in Stratford-upon-Avon. The ebullient Blakely followed her into the Ulster Group Players in 1957 after appearing like a comet at the BDC, his home town theatre, over just two or three seasons in *Hobson's Choice*; James Bridie's 'Burke and Hare' play, *The Anatomist*; and the Broadway comedy *My Three Angels* by the married writing team of Sam and Bella Spewack, librettists of *Kiss Me Kate*. He soon became a leading player at the Royal Court and in Olivier's new National Theatre at the Old Vic in London. The BDC sponsors an annual Colin Blakely memorial award, dating from the year of the actor's premature death, aged 56, in 1987.

The first recipient of the award was Michael Ievers, an education lecturer, who joined the BDC in 1981 when there were 400 members and a waiting list of five years to direct a play. The story of the company since then has been one of dogged survival, near collapse when they occupied the virtually dilapidated Little Theatre halfway down an alley and, over the past few years, recovery and consolidation at the new address on Hamilton Road. This new place is a conversion, sponsored by the housing charity Ulster Garden Villages and others, to a modest total of £300,000, of an 1873 hall once owned by the Independent Order of Good Templars. The new theatre is known as Studio 1A and the BDC is a registered charity with twelve directors and a well-established structure of committees. Like many amateur companies, it now shares its facilities on a hire basis with other organisations, evening events and youth work, producing perhaps five or six of its own shows each year.

And, more than most, it is a family affair: the Ievers family has been a driving force through several generations and Michael's work as both actor and director is complemented by the contributions of his first wife, his second wife, his adult daughters and a younger son. The current chairman, Sean Greer, is handy with lights and sound, as well as being a good actor, while his wife, Clare, a civil servant, has followed her aunt and her father, who built sets and stage-managed for the BDC, onto the boards as both actor and director.

The theatre is known as a 'festival theatre' and here Michael Ievers points to the defining characteristic of the amateur world in Northern Ireland in its history of drama festivals, local and national, adjudicated by professional actors or directors. These festivals, he claims, and the spirit of competition, have encouraged a much higher quality of amateur work leading to the emergence of – not only Hepburn and Blakely – but also, more recently, actors such as John Lynch, Liam Neeson and Jamie Dornan – who shot to fame first in *The Fall* on television with Gillian Anderson, and then again in the movie of *Fifty Shades of Grey*.

Forty years ago, after the war, many of these festival companies in and around Belfast were created within a church community, such as the unequivocally titled Christian Brothers Past Pupils. Another, the Belvoir Players, who supplied one of the RSC's Bottoms in the Play for the Nation production (see Chapter 1), was founded in response to the perceived need for some sort of cultural outlet on a new housing estate in Belvoir Park, and is still going strong, with new facilities and an expanding youth academy. Beyond Greater Belfast, the festival companies had a more secular basis – in Holywood, Larne, Ballymoney, Bangor and elsewhere. Only a few of these companies remain and the average age of the membership has risen. Adjustments and new strategies are required all round. There is an acceptance in the BDC – as in so many amateur groups throughout Britain – of the necessity of finding a business model that does not depend on a single income stream. In addition, not just the core activity of putting on plays, but a consideration of how the arts interests in other local communities might evolve, is at the centre of their thinking.

Most of the contemporary Irish plays the BDC undertakes are by writers in the Republic. I was astonished at the accuracy of Dublin accent, lilt and cultural idiom in their performance of Geraldine Aron's *Same Old Moon* ('Oh yeh, we do the accents, no problem at all', says Clare Greer). Even more surprising, perhaps, is that their repertoire in the early days, and to a large extent today, is indistinguishable from other British amateur companies.

Having started out in 1935 as a play-reading group in a Main Street hotel, their first public performance in 1937 was of pukka farceur Vernon Sylvaine's once popular, one-act *The Road of Poplars*, and their first full-length production, in the following year, Dodie Smith's *Call It A Day*, a jaunty comedy, which had recently been a hit in London and New York and featured one female character trumpeting the pleasures of shopping in the Harrods sales with the line, 'Oh to be naked with a cheque book!' This set the pattern for the following two decades at least, with West End hits by A. A. Milne – the author of *Winnie The Pooh* was, in his day, as successful a West End playwright as Dodie Smith and Noël Coward – Emlyn Williams and J. B. Priestley.

The company won a prize at the 1958 Ballymoney Festival, adjudicated sternly by the great director Tyrone Guthrie, with John Patrick's *Teahouse of the August Moon*, an American comedy that satirised the US occupation of Okinawa after the war and starred Marlon Brando in the film version. This was an adventurous choice, as indeed was a twenty-fifth anniversary

production of Oliver Goldsmith's *She Stoops to Conquer* at the Festival
Finals in Belfast three years later. But Guthrie was even harsher in his
judgement on this latter occasion, lambasting the actors' lack of breath
control, the lighting ('bad'), the décor ('dull, chilly and bleak'), the costumes
('in poor taste') and the vocal delivery: 'Is it Irish, or English? Someone
mentioned Kildare, some of the characters spoke with Southern Irish accents,
some with Northern Irish, but most of them seemed to come from Croydon.'

Obviously an attempt to give a contemporary Irish slant on the old
comedy had backfired badly, as far as Guthrie was concerned at least, and
himself a virtuoso master at animating large-cast period classics and
Shakespeare. But he flattered the BDC and the other amateur companies by
giving it to them straight and not patronising them by suggesting the public
should be 'too indulgent' towards them. In this, he highlighted the perennial
problem of amateur theatre being handled in kid gloves by the – often equally
amateur – reviewers in the name of encouragement, quite apart from the
drab marks-out-of-ten assessments they are (or at least were) routinely
lumbered with. The best kind of encouragement is always the fiercest
criticism, and Guthrie surely must have whipped up a storm of renewed
endeavour. Two years later, in 1963, the adjudication at the finals by Michael
MacOwan, another distinguished director and teacher, was equally trenchant.
There's a definite sense of these competitions not only producing better
actors, but raising standards overall.

One stage career nipped in the bud was that of a nineteen-year-old David
Trimble, the future leader of the Ulster Unionist Party and First Minister of
Northern Ireland, who, in 1964, on his way from Bangor Grammar School
to Queen's University in Belfast, appeared in *Celebration*, a two-part comedy
about a wedding and a funeral, by Keith Waterhouse and Willis Hall. Young
Trimble 'probably made the best of the material', said a local reviewer,
'though he was a little disjointed'. Trimble proved a lot smoother on the
political stage. I happened to meet him at a social function celebrating Oscar
Wilde's birthday fifty years later and raised the matter of his foreshortened
stage career. He blushed charmingly and changed the subject by the simple
expedient of walking smartly away in the other direction.

Trimble's acting career was born and buried on the stage of the British
Legion Hall further along Hamilton Road, a venue used occasionally during
the 1960s along with the Little Theatre, the rackety venue halfway down a
dark alley, which they shared with the Bangor Operatic Society. Thirty years
later, an even younger hopeful than Trimble blossomed in Bangor. Fifteen-
year-old Christopher Logan appeared as a cherub in an *Old Tyme Evening*
and went on to become a regular around all the amateur groups in the area,
including the Bangor Operatic Society, before going to RADA alongside the
likes of Ben Whishaw and Sinead Matthews. He soon established himself as
a whip-smart comic actor and a brilliant impersonator of the outrageous
Kenneth Williams in a touring stage version of the 1960s BBC radio sketch
comedy show *Round the Horne*.

The company's club and rehearsal rooms were, from 1947, a former Home Guard station, which in turn was converted into the 76-seater Studio Theatre in 1994 when the Little was demolished. When *that* became difficult, verging on unviable, as a working theatre, the campaign that ended in the conversion of the Good Templar Hall got seriously under way. Opening with Brian Friel's *Lovers* (the ribbon-cutting honours were done by Sylvia Hermon, the North Down constituency MP who sits as an Independent), it has made for a comfortable cube of a theatre, designed with ten rows of ten seats, a foyer nearly as rudimentary as at the Broadbent, no permanent bar, a poky but serviceable technical nook for sound and lights, no wing space to speak of, and no facility for flying. Instead of the Broadbent's tile display, there's a wall of donors' bricks, each bought for £150.

The mysterious presence of a doll in a pram in the foyer is explained as a stage prop for that night show's (*Same Old Moon*) second act, which is being played out against a predominant design of black drapes, though box sets, I'm told, are possible. Another one-act play by the same author provided Northern Ireland with only their sixth triumph (in sixty-four years) in the British Final of One-Act Plays festival in Southport in 1990. On the other hand, the BDC is the only amateur club in the province to have twice won the title.

Same Old Moon is a full-length, two-act, rites of passage play for an aspiring writer, Brenda Barnes, as she grows up in Dublin, moves to Galway to live with her granny, arrives in London in Coronation Year (1953) and has the facts of life explained to her by a nun pushing a boudoir biscuit into a donut. She discovers her writer's voice, marries a Rhodesian Jew, moves to Africa and returns, without her husband, to seek emotional closure with her abusive, alcoholic father beyond the grave. It is a semi-autobiographical portrait of the artist as a young woman and as such sits slap-bang in the post-James Joyce modern tradition of ambiguous nostalgia and confessional rawness, something that simply had not struck me when I saw the West End premiere in 1991 – the play came across then as a short-winded scrapbook of snippets and suffered from the fact that Brian Friel's *Dancing at Lughnasa* (or 'Dancing at Lasagna' as it's commonly known to the Italian community in New York) was running concurrently in the original, glorious production.

Same Old Moon had first been presented by the Galway-based Druid company in 1984. I had gone north to see the play in Bangor after visiting the Dublin Theatre Festival, where Druid were re-visiting another play of theirs, Eugene McCabe's *King of the Castle*, in which an all-powerful land-owning farmer pays a labourer to impregnate his young wife, thereby undermining his authority with the society he both dominates and employs. It is a fierce and stark drama, an acknowledged modern classic that meditates on the eternal Irish questions of identity, place, borders and nationality.

In a general sense, all of modern Irish drama is about these things, and the tonally much lighter plays of Geraldine Aron no less so than those of McCabe, Friel, Tom Murphy, Frank McGuinness, Conor McPherson and others in the contemporary pantheon. The last sixty years of new Irish drama have constituted one of its golden ages and the Bangor Drama Club has played its part in maintaining that repertoire. It is strangely moving to see it honoured in the North, adding another layer of distant piquancy and perception.

Theatre Royal, Dumfries

The theatre of Robert Burns and J. M. Barrie, the oldest operating theatre in Scotland, was saved by the local amateurs in 1959 when the handsome building on Shakespeare Street – which had stood, in one form or another, since 1792 – was threatened in the town centre development and the wholesale demolition of ancient, crumbling buildings.

The Guild of Players, the amateur company formed in 1913 to provide 'an improvement in the public attitude towards, and taste for, the drama, by means of plays of outstanding merit, by lectures and readings', had been virtually homeless until 1943, when they took a lease on a property in Shakespeare Street and named it, predictably enough, the Little Theatre. In the development scheme, it was discovered that the back wall was unsoundly constructed on earth, so that was doomed, too. On the verge of buying an old wash house in Burns Street, the Guild heard that the Theatre Royal, closed as a cinema since 1954, might be for sale. They scraped together the requisite £1,700 and then a further £1,500 for the urgent restoration work needed on the roof and the walls.

This was a pivotal moment in Scottish theatre. Local businessmen chipped in to buy a set of 160 seats from an old cinema elsewhere in the town and, in October 1960, Sir Compton Mackenzie, author of *Whisky Galore*, cut the ribbon and the curtain rose on the first live show seen on the stage since 1910, a Guild of Players performance of J. M. Barrie's *What Every Woman Knows*. The Guild issued bonds and applied for grants. Educational institutions including the Dumfries Academy and High School signed up as corporate members. In 1963, the Performing Rights Society issued a licence allowing the sale of tickets to the public, so now the members' theatre could be leased out to other organisations, as well as touring companies. Very soon, these included the Glasgow Citizens, the Dundee Rep and the Scottish Chamber Orchestra. The theatrical pride of Dumfries and Galloway was well and truly restored, and another chapter in an extraordinary history completed.

Although the interior of the theatre is drastically altered since both the original and the Victorian re-modelling by the prominent theatrical architect C. J. Phipps in 1876, the exterior frontage is almost the same. The old entrance, though, is blocked off, replaced in the new spectacular modern extension next door, part of the acquisition, over a number of years, of properties on Shakespeare Street itself and along Queen Street on the stage

FIGURE 14 *Theatre Royal, Dumfries, much loved theatre of Robert Burns and J. M. Barrie, saved by the local amateur group The Guild of Players in 1959. (Credit: GE Photography.)*

door flank of the building. There is a bust of Burns in the auditorium – one of only four in existence that faces 'left', in this case towards the stage.

The accumulation of history is everywhere in Dumfries. The central area still echoes the medieval street plan, notably in and around the Greyfriars Church square, with its white marble statue of Burns, who spent the last seven years of his life (1791–96) in the town, having given up the farm he ran for a few years six miles to the north. The narrow Friars Vennel, main thoroughfare for pilgrims, Irish immigrants and invading English armies, still runs, as it always ran, down to the fifteenth-century arched sandstone bridge. You cross that bridge to visit the Burns Centre and the Dumfries Museum, which holds four of the silver tokens issued to anyone subscribing more than ten guineas to the building of the New Theatre, as the Royal was first known, when it opened in September 1792. The token was a season ticket in perpetuity.

The town, keen to provide entertainment for visitors, notably the Caledonian Hunt, had responded enthusiastically to a theatre-building campaign led by an actor-manager, George Sutherland, who ran a company of actors at the George Hotel. The audience capacity of the New was 600, divided between the wooden benches in the Pit, the dress circle of boxes arranged in a horse-shoe above the Pit, and a gallery. As well as the hunting aristocrats, the audience comprised wealthy families coming into town from their country estates and the soldiers quartered there who had been raised to fight the French.

Although he was a Republican, Burns was never a narrow nationalist – he worked as a tax collector for the government Excise at this time and was a British dragoon – but he caused a furore when he attended a gala performance of *As You Like It* in October 1792, one month after the opening. He was alleged to have sat through the national anthem and joined others in calling for a chorus of 'Ça ira', the song of the French Revolution. Burns loved the theatre, but wrote little for it. In 1785 he had produced a spirited, colourful cantata, with a cast of highway vagabonds, *The Jolly Beggars*, in response to John Gay's *The Beggar's Opera*, the first British hit musical. Burns had also written a New Year's prologue for Sutherland's acting troupe at the George which the manager 'spouted to his audience with great applause' in the first wee hours of 1790. After the 'revolutionary' incident in the Pit, Burns was summoned to the Excise to explain himself, hotly denied the allegation and kept his job.

One month later, in November 1792, he wrote a feminist 'occasional' address, 'The Rights of Woman', partly as a mirror to fellow Excise man Tom Paine's recently published *Rights of Man*, but mostly for the benefit night of the visiting London actress Louisa Fontenelle, who spoke it from the stage (she later married the manager of the theatre and emigrated with him to America where she died of yellow fever):

While Europe's eye is fix'd on mighty things,
The fate of Empires and the fall of Kings;
While quacks of State must each produce his plan,
And even children lisp the Rights of Man;
Amid this mighty fuss just let me mention,
The Rights of Woman merit some attention.

Without a royal patent, theatres at that time could only perform comedies, melodramas and musical frippery, but that changed when the theatre received a letter of patent in 1811 and was consequently re-christened the Theatre Royal. The re-modelled theatre of Phipps in 1876 catered for an enlarged audience of 1,000 people. The Pit now had sixteen rows of seats with backs on them and there were eight iron columns installed round the horse-shoe to support the dress circle, with another eight supporting the gallery. The portico at the front was covered with a new façade, which approximates to the appearance of the frontage today.

This was the theatre visited by J. M. Barrie as a student at the Dumfries Academy. Enchanted by Phipps's new theatre, the future author of *Peter Pan* liked to sit in the front row of the Pit, as far to the side as possible, so that he could both watch the action and peek backstage behind the scenes. As the twentieth century dawned, the live acts of conjurors, acrobats and unicyclists were increasingly interspersed with five-minute reels of Charlie Chaplin and Felix the Cat. When sold to a firm of auctioneers in 1909, the variety of usage included roller-skating for which a maple floor was installed, still there today, though covered up. By the 1920s, the theatre was a cinema and Phipps's plasterwork ripped out. Re-named the Electric Theatre, it continued as a cinema until 1954, when the doors closed for good. The Guild picked up the story five years later.

The modern Theatre Royal can be said to date from 1964 when the Guild bought an adjoining property along Queen Street and the storage warehouse behind a shop on Shakespeare Street. But its survival has been perilous, negotiated through fearsomely choppy waters of funding and development crises, hedged around with fears of closure. There was a total redecoration in 1968 when the warehouse was converted into a rehearsal space, or studio, a bar and scenery dock.

In the early 1990s there were discussions with the district council about the development on the site of 'a vibrant theatre and arts centre as a focus for the area' while a feasibility study recommended that the space should be further extended. This led to the purchase of another property – conveniently run-down – next to the first one on Queen Street. At this point, in 1997, it became apparent that the desperately sought Holy Grail of Lottery funding could only be achieved if a Trust was formed. The Guild agreed to this but only on condition that the bid for the funding was successful. Not surprisingly, the bid was defeated, after a period of protracted wrangling, in 2000.

The ever resourceful Guild then dressed up an admission of this inevitable defeat in a turnaround call for change. And so the Dumfries Theatre Royal Trust was established, with four representatives from the Guild and nine from other interested parties. Another bid from the Trust in 2002 yielded, after an initial rejection and a scaled-down submission, a thumbs-up for a total rebuild, including a fly tower and further extension. About £6 million was raised, most of it European and Lottery money, architects drew up complete plans over a two-year period and had almost arrived at tendering when the local council suddenly withdrew support by voting down a commitment to support the running costs once the theatre was operational.

This may have been something to do with the council's building of their own DG1 sport and entertainment centre, which opened in 2007 and has been closed since 2014 following the discovery of major defects. Still, the set-back allowed the Guild to withdraw from the Trust and alone resume the search for funding a much modified re-build. Fears of closure escalated when the rendering on the outside became loose and dangerous, the heating system failed, visiting companies fell away and audiences dropped to levels of 50 per cent and under. The Guild now urged the district council to buy the theatre and, after the re-build, lease it back to them. But there were no funds.

The end was nearer than nigh when the Holywood Trust, a charity supporting young people in Dumfries and Galloway, offered a large sum towards the re-build in order to keep the Theatre Royal open, it said, as 'an important community resource which could be passed on to future generations'. An architect, a project manager and a fundraiser were appointed, and two adjacent properties on Shakespeare Street, in front of the already converted warehouse, purchased to provide a new entrance with an attractive glass atrium. In all, the cost was a reasonable-sounding £2.4 million. Well, there's no fly tower and still no wing space on the stage left side. Work began in 2014 and was completed by the end of 2015.

The attics of the two houses on Queen Street now constitute a long, low-ceilinged rehearsal studio used by schoolchildren and junior Guild members for rehearsals, improvisations and indeed putting on little shows. Around the auditorium there are now three dressing rooms, large enough to accommodate Scottish Ballet and other major ensembles, impressive props, wardrobe and scenery stores and workshops and an office for the five or six permanently employed staff that include a theatre director who does the programming, a business administrator and a marketing assistant. The more rumbustious auditoria of George Sutherland and Phipps is now a clean-lined and comfortable arena of 190 seats (with wheelchair access for five people) in a maroon colour scheme.

The audience is fresh and fairly lively, the bar a-buzz in the interval at one of the many feminist staple plays of the amateur circuit, Amanda Whittington's *Ladies' Day*, in which four female fish factory workers from Hull 'come by' tickets to Ladies' Day at Royal Ascot in the year the social calendar event relocated to York (2005). The production could have been more raucous and wasn't very rooted in any idiom or culture, but that might have been down to the classic amdram predicament of the director, who confessed in a programme note that this was the sixteenth play he had directed for the Guild – 'if you count all three times I've directed *Bazaar and Rummage*' (by *Adrian Mole* writer Sue Townsend) – and that the process had been 'rather fraught at times, as I was in hospital for two weeks'.

The point about the women in *Ladies' Day* is that they all in some way feel that they deserve better. And, in this, they join hands across the ages with the Scottish bard, whose verse for Louisa Fontenelle's benefit concludes with the provocative injunction:

When awful Beauty joins with all her charms,
Who is so rash as rise in rebel arms?

But truce with kings, and truce with constitutions,
With bloody armaments and revolutions;
Let Majesty your first attention summon
Ah! ça ira! THE MAJESTY OF WOMAN!

Theatr Fach, Llangefni, Anglesey

There is a great scene in Brian Friel's *Translations* when a British soldier who can't speak Gaelic is making poetic love to an Irish farm girl who can't speak English. A mutual act of emotional colonisation is a moving counterpart to the soldier's land-grab mission of imposing English place names on the girl's rural Irish district. So I was intrigued to learn, when visiting the Theatr Fach (Little Theatre) on the Pencraig estate in Llangefni – which is about 200 miles from Cardiff in the south and 90 miles from Liverpool to the east – that when the company there produced Arthur Miller's *The Crucible*, one of the most reverberating plays of the twentieth century, they played the village scenes in Welsh and the authoritarian courtroom drama in English. And, as in the Friel play, there were no sur-titles.

It is ironic, and perhaps surprising, that Anglesey, which is an island joined to the north Wales mainland by two bridges across the Menai Straits, voted resoundingly to leave the European Union in the cataclysmic referendum of June 2016, thereby (in the pro-Brexit vote) rendering their fierce nationalist independence seemingly more like isolationism. For, although the Welsh language is taught in schools, and 85 per cent of the population in a place like Llangefni are Welsh-speaking (though most, of course, are also bi-lingual), and there is a considerable Welsh literature and indeed Welsh theatre, no-one else speaks their language apart from a few thousand people in Patagonia, descendants of the settlers who went there in 1865 because they thought the Welsh language was under threat.

It is still under threat, but the amateur theatre in Wales has a robust history of defending its culture in language, most notably in the annual National Eisteddfod, a ceremony of druids, plays, poems and songs that takes place each year in the middle of a large field in changing locations around the country. Here, professionals and amateurs work alongside each other in a way that focuses on issues of national identity, language and independence in a far more intense fashion than at comparable international bean feasts in Edinburgh or Dublin.

And the theatre in Wales itself is not divided, exactly, but split down the middle and ranged behind the two recently created professional flagship companies – both funded by the Welsh Arts Council – of Theatr Genedlaethol Cymru (TGC), the Welsh-language national theatre formed in 2004 that none of the rest of us knows about, and the English-speaking National Theatre of Wales (NTW), founded in 2010, that performs in weird and wonderful locations all over the country. The latter is much like the National Theatre of Scotland, established in 2006 by the Scottish government, and similarly peripatetic, and paradoxically homeless, chiming resonantly in the critical zeitgeist of immersive and site-specific theatre.

In May 2011, Michael Sheen led an NTW community production of *The Passion* in his native Port Talbot (Sheen's Port Talbot compadres include Richard Burton and Anthony Hopkins) involving some professionals, but mostly a local amateur army of brass bands, choirs and street-dancing children who followed his Christ-like procession over seventy-two hours, from the wilderness of the dunes to the baptismal sea, the Last Supper in a social club and the agony in the garden of Gethsemane on a council estate. And then he was crucified – but not by the critics. One of them, Susannah

Clapp of the *Observer*, declared Sheen's *Passion* to be one of the outstanding
theatrical events of the decade that had just begun.

The Welsh-language TGC, on the other hand, is quietly raising political
issues in the context of what it sees as a rear-guard action to save the
language. And the story of Theatr Fach in Llangefni has long been part of
that campaign. It is possible to argue that the crossover between amateur
and professional in Wales is far more symbiotic than elsewhere in the UK.
That is because, until the 1960s and the advent of Welsh public funding for
the arts, all repertory theatre in the country was amateur, and in a state of
accumulative recovery after the decline of all Welsh drama at the end of the
nineteenth century due to the Methodist revival.

The turning point came when the Methodists calmed down a bit and
modified their objections, thanks to the first stage adaptation in 1909 of *Rhys
Lewis* (1885), a renowned Welsh-language novel by Daniel Owen recounting
the autobiography of a fictional preacher of Bethel. There followed forty-five
more performances in 1910 as small amateur groups proliferated and a total
of four hundred more performances before the outbreak of war. The sprouting
of amdram continued after the war with many more societies sponsored by
churches and chapels.

In Llangefni, a mathematics teacher in the local secondary school, George
Fisher, produced plays in English and Welsh in the school hall and then in
the Town Hall. In 1951, the town council bought the Pencraig estate for
£8,000 and Fisher saw the potential for a permanent theatre in the old
stables, which the council gave him for a peppercorn rent and a trial period
of two years. He and his colleagues in the drama society they had formed –
teachers, council workers, electricians – then bought the stables for £250
and, in the time-honoured tradition of all such societies, transformed it into
a theatre themselves.

In May 1955, they opened with a double bill of Pushkin's *Rusalka* in
Welsh and Philip Johnson's *It's Autumn Now* in English, thereby establishing
the artistic principle of alternating productions in the two languages.
Although today the stone clad Theatr Fach performs only in Welsh, for
many years the annual programme comprised three plays in Welsh, three in
English and the pantomime. A grant from the Gulbenkian Foundation
contributed to the installation of a fly tower, a new lighting desk and dressing
rooms in 1961. Further appeals and grants converted other spaces on the
site into a work and store room, a rehearsal room, foyer and bar. The
auditorium has seating for 110.

Meanwhile, the popular Welsh-language melodramas that followed *Rhys
Lewis* onto the stage were given a twist by Saunders Lewis, the poet and
politician who founded the National Party of Wales, which morphed into
Plaid Cymru (or, same thing, Party of Wales). Manon Wyn Williams, a young
playwright and professor at Bangor University, says that Lewis's historical
plays are the only true classics in the Welsh language. One of them, *Siwan: the
King's Daughter*, a medieval tale of love and adultery, was played live on

BBC Wales in 1960 by Siân Phillips and her then husband Peter O'Toole. Wyn Williams also suggests that the formation of the public service Welsh-language television station, S4C (Sianel Pedwar Cymru, meaning Channel 4 Wales), founded in 1982 simultaneously with Channel 4, further encouraged Welsh playwrights and brought many fine amateur actors into the professional ranks.

Theatr Fach in Llangefni was the beneficiary, too, of the renowned Teatr Y Gegin, Criccieth, an amateur drama workshop and powerhouse, formed in 1963 – along lines of nationalist idealism similar to those of the Pike Theatre in Dublin in the 1950s – which produced the plays of W. S. Jones, generally known as Wil Sam, in the 1960s as well as those of a young successor to the Welsh theatre cause, Meic Povey, who was able, through television work, to turn fully professional at the age of eighteen. Wil Sam, a motor mechanic and garage owner who spent his whole life in the local area of Eifionydd on the Lleyn Peninsula, did not turn fully professional until he was in his fifties.

Whereas the plays of Saunders Lewis (1893–1985) are written in a high literary style, Wil Sam (1920–2007) was a dialect specialist who often channelled his homespun humour through his alter ego, Ifas y Tryc (Evans the Truck), and had no qualms about mixing English phrases into a sort of Welsh pidgin, as when he complained of tax problems with the 'England Refeniw' or of pompous English visitors who proved that 'Britannia rwls ddy Wêls'. Critics applauded Wil Sam's penchant for combining elements of absurdism with village hall farce, while one of his obituarists, quoting a favourite Wil Sam aphorism, 'The Welsh language isn't a dish of trifle to be kept in a dark place', averred that, in his plays, the poetry of the language can be heard at its most rumbustious.

I certainly caught a tang of that when I saw a short Wil Sam play, *Dalar Deg*, at Theatr Fach. It struck me as fairly Irish in its farcical portrait of inbred social life on a remote 1960s farm where the farmer and his block-headed (to the point of being backward) young labourer hire a housekeeper because they can't boil an egg between them. The Llangefni performance of this vivid little rural, Ortonesque scenario skated over the dark implications and left me pondering what other untold secrets and murky activity might be swimming around in the unfished pool of Welsh-language drama. The piece was directed by Tony Jones who joined the company forty-odd years ago, along with his wife, Audrey, who was playing the doomed housekeeper.

Tony was offered a job, and £7 a week, in 1974 by the Welsh-language predecessor of the Theatr Genedlaethol Cymru. As he was earning £30 a week in business at the time, he demurred. Audrey, who says that Theatr Fach would never have got off the ground, or survived at all, without the keen participation of the English people in the area, worked for the Welsh Film Board. Theatre, for both of them, remains a hobby, something they have always fitted around other commitments such as business, family, breeding ponies and attending chapel.

Manon Wyn Williams, on the other hand, married and a mother, winner of two medals at the National Eisteddfod with plays premiered at Theatr Fach, is fully committed to the dual cause of Welsh nationalism and language. She has written a verbatim play, after an exhaustive interview process, on the power station on Anglesey, which the Japanese-owned company Horizon want to expand with consequences both negative and (to a lesser extent, probably, she concedes) positive, on people's livelihoods, their schools, their language and the tourist board. The play is based on the real-life story of a family who resisted Horizon's attempts to buy them out, and won.

The Welsh actor and director Daniel Evans, who has worked mostly in England, as an actor at the National Theatre and as artistic director of the Sheffield Crucible and the Chichester Festival Theatre, told the *Observer* in March 2018 how proud he was of his roots in the amateur theatre of the Rhondda Valley where he grew up. As a child, his grandmother used to take him to the Park and Dare Theatre in Treorchy, home to the famous male voice choir, which was founded in 1913 by mine workers in the Park and Dare collieries. He recently directed *Esther* by Saunders Lewis for the TGC. There seems not to be that much of a cultural divide between north and south Wales, but I blunder into trouble with several members of Theatr Fach when I mention the name of Dylan Thomas, who always wrote in English, never in Welsh. They have presented *Under Milk Wood*, but without much enthusiasm.

Thomas acted at Swansea Grammar School and mixed his work as a journalist on the *South Wales Evening Post* with a headlong enthusiasm for amateur dramatics in the newly founded (in 1929) Swansea Little Theatre where, between 1932 and 1934, his roles included Simon Bliss in Noël Coward's *Hay Fever* ('an artist with an excessive temper and untidy habits ... well done ... by D. M. Thomas', reported the *Mumbles Press*), Count Bellair in George Farquhar's *The Beaux' Stratagem* and Witwoud ('impressive and clever') in Congreve's *The Way of the World*.

This promising progress through the high peaks of English high comedy juddered to a halt when, cast as a Parisian journalist in *Martine* by Jean-Jacques Bernard, Thomas stayed in the pub – no doubt researching his role – and missed the performance. Soon afterwards, he left for London. The Swansea Little Theatre is still the foremost English-speaking amateur theatre in Wales. Their church hall in Mumbles, where Thomas acted, was replaced by permanent premises in a derelict former show room in the South Dock area of the city, where it was opened, with 150 seats, in 1983 by the singer and ex-Goon Harry Secombe – and named for Dylan Thomas.

A former chairman of Theatr Fach, Emyr Rhys-Jones, who hails from Denbighshire and is born and bred bi-lingual, states unequivocally that '*Under Milk Wood* is about southerners, not about us in the north', so perhaps there is a little bit of a divide after all. The only tribute season to a Welsh playwright he knows of was that mounted in 2002 by the professional Teatr Bara Caws in Caernafon, the oldest community and touring theatre company working in the Welsh language – and that was in celebration of Wil Sam.

Rhys-Jones opines that the keenest of actors in the amateur theatre are not often the best actors. Theatre for him and, you feel, Theatr Fach, is not about high standards, critical reputation or fitting in with the familiar repertoire of modern and classic plays you find in most British amateur companies. One factor they do have in common is the ageing of the audience and the slowing down of the rate of recruits to the company from its own youth theatre club. Otherwise, the purpose of an all-Welsh programme in Llangefni is clear: the protection and promulgation of the Welsh language in the work of contemporary writers and their distinguished forebears.

11

Riding the Wave towards a Brave New Dawn

In 2012, the Sky Arts television channel ran a championship-style knock out competition, *Nation's Best Am Dram*, to find the best amateur theatre company in the country, inviting entrants to submit a video sample of their work to be assessed by a panel of professional judges – the producer Bill Kenwright, who chaired the process, the actress Miriam Margolyes and the theatre critic and parliamentary sketch writer of the *Daily Mail*, Quentin Letts (Letts has since moved to the *Sunday Times*).

The entrants were whittled down to a shortlist of twenty companies and, from there, eight quarter finalists were selected to progress to a live performance on stage at the Theatre Royal and Derngate, Northampton. Those eight companies were the Heath Players from Essex, the Crossmichael Drama Club from Dumfries and Galloway in rural Scotland, the Fissiparous Theatre from the Wirral, the Tell Tale Theatre from Toxteth in Liverpool, the Little Theatre Bingley in Yorkshire, the Regent Rep from Christchurch in Dorset, the Strathclyde Theatre Group and the Edinburgh Grads, formerly a student group.

The programme was seen as a quiet move afoot to restore the reputation of amdram and related by some commentators to the Open Stages initiative at the RSC, the community arts spectacle of the Olympic and Paralympic ceremonies and even the intimate fringe theatre experiences created by a company such as You Me Bum Bum Train, in which a solo participatory spectator is subjected to a bizarre and random series of supporting scenarios populated entirely by unpaid volunteer actors.

The best community theatre in Britain usually has one foot planted firmly in the professional camp. *Nation's Best Am Dram* had no such connection, being unapologetically 'old school', drilling right down to the village hall and grassroots ambience of the amdram genre unsullied by professional expertise. This led to a lot of eye-rolling from visiting professional mentors such as television stars Martin Shaw and Richard Wilson, drafted in to oversee the odd rehearsal. The former was left cold by Tell Tale's 'mission to change the face of amdram' while Wilson shrivelled at Bingley's clumsily executed 'idea' of Macbeth and Banquo encountering the witches in a gay bar called The Blasted Heath. Harriet Walter, on the other hand, applauded Strathclyde: 'They are all actors, they know how to act.'

The final shoot out, staged at Bill Kenwright's Theatre Royal, Windsor, with a performance of their choice on Shaftesbury Avenue being the prize, was between Crossmichael and Regent, each having a go at Joe Orton's biliously funny one-acter *The Erpingham Camp*. It didn't look even marginally amusing in the extracts we saw, but it was clear that Regent were trying it on as an old-style seaside professional rep while the clearly much better actors of Crossmichael simply went about doing the play as it came to them, without self-consciously stretching to act it. They had heeded Kenwright's advice: 'Stop acting, trust the play, less is more, get the words across.'

As Regent blustered on, it suddenly dawned on me that I recognised one of their leading actors: the jolly man playing Erpingham as a Churchillian cigar-chomper was none other than David Gillard, forty years the opera critic of the *Daily Mail*, but apparently unrecognised – or at least unacknowledged – by his arts page confrère, Quentin Letts. The sugar glass bottle supposedly smashed on Gillard's bonce missed altogether and flew out into the audience, a classic amdram mishap that rather undermined the Regent's tetchy young drama teacher director who was hoping only for 'artistic recognition' and did not believe that anyone could possibly think that Crossmichael were better than his actors.

So it was that Crossmichael travelled from their tin hut in the middle of a field to the ornate, plush setting of the Lyric in the West End. An audience of 1,000 punters were treated to a production of Molière's *The Hypochondriac*, which refreshed a fine old tradition of Scots Molière north of the border. The actors convinced Kenwright and his colleagues that – despite a harlequin character tripping over the chaise longue and bumping into the other furniture – this company was 'a credit to every amateur theatre group in the land'.

The TV programme clarified for me an obvious distinction between professional and amateur theatre. When the latter consciously apes the manners and acting tropes of the former, and perhaps tackles the more difficult plays in the repertoire, they are putting themselves at serious risk of being on a hiding to nothing. There was nothing precious or self-regarding about the Crossmichael players and the lack of it shone through their acting, which was honest and unpretentious.

Communities create history and the future of amateur theatre

We have already glimpsed – as at the National Theatre of Wales, for instance – how incorporating amateur participation in big, professionally supervised productions away from conventional performance spaces can provide an exhilarating experience unlike any other theatrical event. There is nothing to compare with a really good crowd scene. I have twice seen semi-outdoor stagings of Thomas Hardy's *The Dynasts*, once in Exeter in the 1970s and once in Chichester in 1989, with James Bolam as a newly crowned Bony riding a horse from the cathedral coronation through the Sussex streets towards the battlefields of the Festival Theatre. In both instances, a seething mass of humanity defined the character, tone and purpose of the performance.

Indoors, when John Gielgud played Caesar at the National in John Schlesinger's 1977 production of *Julius Caesar*, the *Daily Express* critic Herbert Kretzmer bemoaned the lack of a convincing crowd of plebs: 'Inside the first minutes, a bit player wearing a Costa del Sol souvenir straw hat took to the stage carrying a cardboard poster with the name "Caesar" on it. He was joined by some rhubarbing mates to suggest the Roman mob. They stood around like extras on a TV commercial for Martini ...' Gielgud himself remarked acidly that, in his youth, any self-respecting production of the play, and he was thinking Max Reinhardt, would create a seething mass of humanity of anything up to 250 extras.

These would have been amateurs. Not even the foundation of Actors' Equity in 1929 banished unpaid supernumeraries from big classical shows. In more recent times, we have seen two *Julius Caesars* which became truly exciting in the deployment of a huge crowd: Peter Stein's at the Edinburgh Festival in 1992 (200 amateurs) and Deborah Warner's at the Barbican in 2005 (100 extras, bursting at barriers during moments of political crisis, said Paul Taylor of *The Independent*, 'like a cross between a red carpet crowd at a Leicester Square movie premiere and spectators at the London Marathon'). Such a primarily *scenic* use of amateurs, however admirable, still begs the question: what if the amateurs were *endemic* to the show, part of its conception – both the Stein and Warner versions were international co-productions with a different mob in each participating European theatre – and indeed its subject matter?

The only way this can happen in a practical sense is if the project is based in the community of amateur actors itself, as it was, to a certain extent, in those revivals of *The Dynasts*, and certainly was in the Welsh passion play starring Michael Sheen to which I alluded in Chapter 10. There are many such adventures pursued today and perhaps their best example was the work initiated by the Royal Court playwright Ann Jellicoe who, after writing two plays that are part of the legendary canon in Sloane Square, *The Sport of My Mad Mother* (1958) and *The Knack* (1962), and serving as the theatre's literary manager, decamped with her family to Dorset in the west country and began producing community plays there in 1979.

Jellicoe's Colway Theatre Trust produced over forty large-scale pieces with a south west of England historical connotation. Major playwrights – David Edgar, Howard Barker, Fay Weldon and Nick Darke among them – along with a handful of professional directors, designers and technicians, were the spring to mobilise a community. In 1985, Jellicoe passed the baton to Jon Oram, whose renamed Claque Theatre continues to evolve spectacular, living history community epics, not only in Devon and Dorset, but all over Britain.

This enterprise has certainly fed back into the professional theatre. In 1987, Edgar's play for Jellicoe in Dorset, *Entertaining Strangers*, a story of a titanic struggle between a pioneering woman brewer and a fundamentalist parson, was remounted at the National Theatre, with Judi Dench and Tim Pigott-Smith in the leads. A cast of 180 amateurs performing in a Dorchester church was succeeded in Peter Hall's promenade production in the NT's smallest auditorium, the Cottesloe (now the Dorfman), by a cast of sixty, which included Shirley Henderson, Sally Dexter, Michael Byrne, Hugh Bonneville and Steven Mackintosh. Michael Billington saw both productions and reported in the *Guardian* on the revival at the National: 'What you lose, inevitably, is the moving sense of a community coming to terms with its own past; what you gain is a greater sense of dramatic focus and the high definition skill of the professional actor. In Dorchester, I was moved to tears; at the Cottesloe I looked on with admiration.'

These plays in the community, and many others like them, have shown the professional theatre where they are missing out in not belonging to the people who come to see their shows. I must confess I had never thought of the Home Counties as a seedbed of community drama. Not, that is, until I heard about the pageants in Guildford, Surrey, devised and directed in Shalford Park, and along the town's streets, by David Clarke, a schoolmaster and amateur theatre director who also founded and ran the Cloister Players.

Clarke, who trained at Goldsmith's in London and Guildford School of Art, caught the outdoor performance bug when he participated in Guildford's pageant in Coronation Year (1953). After completing his national service and beginning his career as a teacher, he designed the Guildford pageant of 1957 celebrating the 700 years since Henry III granted the town its royal charter, and founded the Cloister Players in 1958, which specialised in large-scale, lavishly costumed productions in historic settings such as cathedrals, castles and country houses.

It was for Clarke's Cloister Players production of *Romeo and Juliet* in 1974 that Rowena Cade built her Juliet balcony in the Minack, a lasting legacy. Clarke flirted briefly with a film career, but remains celebrated for his directorship of the Guildford Festival of Arts and his pageants. These community spectacles – running for several days and with a cast of thousands – were not historically gritty or political (except in the wider, more important, sense of engaging with the community) in the manner of Ann Jellicoe's productions.

But, as Celia Imrie, locally born and bred – she appeared with the Cloister Players as a dancing fairy in *A Midsummer Night's Dream* staged in the beautiful Tudor manor house and grounds of nearby Loseley Park – attests, these events seeped into the lifeblood of the town, and Clarke became a renowned local personality. Imrie's early ambition to be a dancer was transformed into an acting impulse by Clarke's encouragement. While still a pupil at Guildford High School for Girls (where playwrights Ella Hickson and Lucy Prebble are also prominent in a later generation of alumnae), she played one of the daughters in Lorca's *The House of Bernarda Alba* in the town's civic hall, and Olivia in *Twelfth Night*, also in Loseley Park, both directed by Clarke for his Cloister Players.

Shortly after Imrie's involvement, Clarke returned to his Guildford pageants. In 1968, the Pageant of England involved 1,000 performers, 100 technicians, 6,000 costumes, 100 animals – and a participatory audience of 40,000 people over two weeks. The Silver Jubilee Pageant of 1977 was another royal celebration, which earned him the Queen's Jubilee Medal and a visit to one of the performances from Princess Anne. Clarke was in demand elsewhere, and when the York Mystery Plays first went inside the Minster, Clarke produced the populist spectacles of 1980 and 1984, complete with a live performing bear.

My point is that these events, from the re-awakened Mystery Plays, to the amateur pageants, outdoor theatre productions and community projects all over the country are probably the key-holders to the future of the amateur, and indeed professional, theatre in this country. An audience's sense of ownership in its own theatre is, on the whole, a thing of the past and would now be defined in 'stakeholder' terms if it existed at all. In the regions, a rep theatre once belonged to its town just as, in London, the RSC or the National, or indeed the Royal Court, once belonged to its specific constituency.

All those connections are dissolved and new methods of engagement must be pursued, which explains the vigorous expansion of youth, community and outreach work in professional theatres everywhere. Those same connections aren't yet dissolved in the amateur theatre for the simple reason that the audience springs directly from the community and indeed the perpetrators of the work itself. It's a social and cultural commitment, whatever the standards of the end result, understood by the participants on all sides of the operation. Looked at in this way, the amateur theatre, in its spirit and in its purpose, are clear signs of the cultural integration now yearned for, and indeed actively pursued, in the professional theatre all over the country and, significantly, at the RSC and the National.

Funding bodies and sponsors go along with these aspirations because they so clearly reflect the need – in an increasingly distracted culture, fractured by the galloping, indiscriminate phenomenon of the social media – to hang on to, expand and re-define the core theatre audience in this country. Like so many things, what happens next depends on what happens in the nation's schools. A unique research project, Time to Listen, funded by the Arts Council and involving schools working with the RSC and the Tate Gallery, has highlighted a growing concern over the impact that declining arts and cultural provision in schools will have on future generations.

Meanwhile, in 2017 the NT was awarded an additional grant of £1 million to help reach new audiences across the country. On this three-year Public Acts programme, inspired by the Public Works initiative in New York, the theatre is working with local partners in six areas of 'low arts engagement' – Doncaster, in partnership with CAST, hub for local amateur and training groups, as we have seen; Greater Manchester, with the Lowry in Salford; outer east London, with the Queen's, Hornchurch; Sunderland, with the Empire and Fire Station; Wakefield, with the Theatre Royal, an absolute little gem of a theatre, designed by Frank Matcham; and Wolverhampton, with the Grand.

The first major fruit of the Public Acts programme was a boisterous performance of *Pericles* on the Olivier stage in August 2018 which struck the *Times* critic as 'amateurism in the best sense of the word, not shoddy or second-rate, but something done with a collective, co-operative spirit and a sense of joy'. As in Jellicoe's community plays, the technical team were professionals at the NT and the professional actors – six of them led by a compelling Ashley Zhangazha in the title role and including Ayesha Darker, the RSC's Titania in *A Midsummer Night's Dream* with those amateur mechanicals – marked with an asterisk as Equity members in the programme.

The 200 amateurs let loose on the stage, gathered around the hub of NT partner theatre the Queen's in Hornchurch, included a ska band, a gospel choir and a rainbow coalition of races, ages and abilities (two of the cast

FIGURE 15 *A boisterous performance of Shakespeare's* Pericles *was the first fruit of the National Theatre's Public Acts programme. Ashley Zhangazha, centre, is all at sea in the title role with some of the cast of 200 community participants. (Photo: James Bellorini.)*

were in wheelchairs), no bad thing at all for the travelogue, peripatetic side of the play. As with the RSC's *A Midsummer Night's Dream*, by no stretch of goodwill could you claim this was a production of the play worthy of a National Theatre. You could justly say, however, this was an *occasion* worthy of a national theatre.

The *Times* concluded that the director, Emily Lim, 'deserved a medal for corralling 233 performers into a rolling, broiling show that thrummed with life. Whenever the whole cast entered the stage as one, it felt like a coup. This is our stage, it said.' And good luck to them. The sea poetry went rather by the board, and the narrative thread was sacrificed to crowd effects and general brouhaha. But for a play about a refugee hero taking flight and finding home, it could not have been better timed: 'A nation's worth is truly shown by how they treat a stranger, not their own!'

Increasingly, the National Theatre, and the rest of our national theatre, needs the amateurs all over again, not just to refresh and extend their agendas while reaching new audiences, but as a renewed expression of their own purpose and justification for the public investment of subsidy by the tax-payers. One of the earliest NT posters proclaimed that the National Theatre is yours. It is also ours.

In this context, it seems impossible for the Arts Council not to find a little more support at least for the amateur theatre, especially those members of the Little Theatre Guild who find it increasingly hard to maintain their venues, keep up with the regulations imposed on them (fire, safety, access, and so on) and meet the ever increasing costs of materials. We should acknowledge more generously the part amateur theatre plays in producing personnel – actors, writers, directors, designers, technicians – who form the core and nucleus of a professional theatre that remains the envy of the world.

Epilogue

Most important of all, though, is the survival and continued practical prosperity of the amateur theatre itself. Although there are areas of decline, as we have noted, it seems highly unlikely that the true spark of it will disappear. The impulse for performing plays in our spare time is more ingrained in our collective national psyche than in any other country. The scale of the operation of amateur theatre – even in partial decline – is still immense, over 2,500 groups, it is reckoned, putting on 35,000 productions a year. That's not a hobby. That's an obsession bordering on a disease of healthily epidemic proportions.

We started with tales of how the professional theatre has been invaded by the spirit of amateur theatre, sometimes deliberately, sometimes inadvertently. Something quite new has been happening in the last couple of years with professional shows setting out to analyse and take joy in their amateur counterparts in mime. One striking example was the National Theatre of

Scotland's *My (Left) Right Foot: The Musical* – in which an amateur theatre company prepares an adaptation of the movie starring Daniel Day-Lewis as Christy Brown, a touchstone portrayal of cerebral palsy. The play was written by a similarly disabled writer, Robert Softley Gale, as a way of both counter-acting and poking fun at the attitudes of non-disabled people.

It worked brilliantly and was touching and hysterically funny, the troupe having settled on *My Left Foot* after discarding as impractical both *Twelve Years a Slave* and Pinter's *The Dumb Waiter* (or possibly, they say, 'The Deaf and Dumb Waiter'). There was a refreshing double edge, too, in such clichaic sentiments as, 'We are all disabled inside', and of course it was absolutely the privilege of the show's leading actor, wheelchair-bound Christopher Imbrosciano, to resent the terms of his 'inclusion'. He'd only rolled up that morning to paint the radiators. And with a nod to *La Cage Aux Folles*, the show ended with a rousing chorus of 'I Am What I Am Dram'.

Also bubbling under is another celebratory rehearsal room epic, *Am Dram: A Musical Comedy* by Alex Parker and Katie Lam, which surfaced briefly in workshop format at Andrew Lloyd Webber's The Other Palace. It sounded all the familiar amdram notes of ludicrous aspiration and risible vanity. The company itself, the Great Osterford North Amateur Dramatic Society, GONADS for short, was stuck in a rut on its latest show and fretting over the next one, *Calamity Jane*, in only six and a half months of rehearsal time. Their director was a self-regarding poseur who had 'done' *Les Mis* in Romania and wore his purple beret on a slant. And their musical director was a fresh-faced cherub in a T-shirt more hardened in musical theatre lore and practice than a fictional amalgam of Craig Revel Horwood and Lionel Blair.

But, at its core, the show, billed as an affectionate send-up of amdram, had a serious point to make. One of the latest recruits to GONADS was a former professional actress who had lately moved into the area. She auditioned successfully for the lead role in *The Golden Empress* but, towards the end of rehearsals, out of the blue, was offered a 'proper' professional job in a small role in a new musical version of *The Importance of Being Earnest*. She leaves the GONADS in the mire.

The poor girl is humiliated in rehearsals for *The Importance*, and has her small role cut to ribbons before the unseen, disembodied director suggests she deliver her one remaining line from the wings. She returns to GONADS, tail between legs, to a surprise and welcoming chorus of 'We Are Family'. She is restored to her leading role, at last appreciating that amateur theatre is the place to be – for the good of her soul and a fulfilling sense of friendship, purpose and community.

BIBLIOGRAPHY

Eric Bentley, *The Brecht Memoir* (1985).

Paula Byrne, *The Genius of Jane Austen* (2017).

Simon Callow, *Charles Dickens and the Great Theatre of the World* (2012).

Humphrey Carpenter, *OUDS, A Centenary History of the Oxford University Dramatic Society* (1985).

Averil Demuth (Ed.), *The Minack Open-Air Theatre* (1968).

Michael Dobson, *Shakespeare and Amateur Performance* (2011).

Kate Dunn, *Exit Through the Fireplace* (1998).

Gwenan Evans (Ed.), *A Few Drops of Water* (1989).

Chris Goulding, *The Story of the People's* (1991).

Michael Green, *The Art of Coarse Acting* (1964).

Sara Hudston, *Victorian Theatricals* (2000).

Celia Imrie, *The Happy Hoofer* (2011).

Henry James, *The Scenic Art – Notes on Acting and the Drama 1872-1901* (Ed. Allan Wade, 1957).

Christopher Luscombe and Malcolm McKee, *The Shakespeare Revue* (1995).

Norman Marshall, *The Other Theatre* (1947).

Helen Nicholson, Nadine Holdsworth, Jane Milling, *The Ecologies of Amateur Theatre* (2018).

J. B. Priestley, *English Journey* (1934).

J. B. Priestley, *Theatre Outlook* (1947).

Sybil Rosenfeld, *Temples of Thespis* (1978).

Michael Simkins, *What's My Motivation?* (2003).

Michael Simkins, *The Rules of Acting* (2013).

Frank O. M. Smith, *This Insubstantial Pageant* (1982).

Norman Veitch, *The People's* (1950).

Geoffrey Whitworth, *The Theatre of My Heart* (1930).

Geoffrey Whitworth, *The Making of a National Theatre* (1951).

INDEX